Poetics of the Body

POETICS OF THE BODY

EDNA ST. VINCENT MILLAY, ELIZABETH BISHOP, MARILYN CHIN, AND MARILYN HACKER

Catherine Cucinella

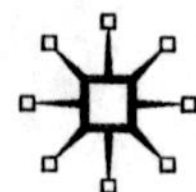

POETICS OF THE BODY
Copyright © Catherine Cucinella, 2010.

All rights reserved.

First published in 2010 by PALGRAVE MACMILLAN® in the United States—a division of St. Martin's Press LLC, 175 Fifth Avenue, New York, NY 10010

Where this book is distributed in the UK, Europe and the rest of the world, this is by Palgrave Macmillan, a division of Macmillan Publishers Limited, registered in England, company number 785998, of Houndmills, Basingstoke, Hampshire RG21 6XS.

Palgrave Macmillan is the global academic imprint of the above companies and has companies and representatives throughout the world.

Palgrave® and Macmillan® are registered trademarks in the United States, the United Kingdom, Europe and other countries.

ISBN: 978-0-230-62088-9

Library of Congress Cataloging-in-Publication Data

Cucinella, Catherine.
   Poetics of the body : Edna St. Vincent Millay, Elizabeth Bishop, Marilyn Chin, and Marilyn Hacker / Catherine Cucinella.
      p. cm.
   Includes bibliographical references and index.
   ISBN 978-0-230-62088-9 (alk. paper)
   1. American poetry—Women authors—History and criticism. 2. American poetry—20th century—History and criticism. 3. Human body in literature 4. Women in literature. 5. Millay, Edna St. Vincent, 1892-1950—Criticism and interpretation. 6. Bishop, Elizabeth, 1911-1979—Criticism and interpretation. 7. Chin, Marilyn—Criticism and interpretation. 8. Hacker, Marilyn, 1942—Criticism and interpretation. I. Title.

PS151.C83 2010
811'.5099287—dc22   2009036126

A catalogue record of the book is available from the British Library.

Design by Scribe Inc.

First edition: April 2010

10 9 8 7 6 5 4 3 2 1

Printed in the United States of America.

To my daughters, Carrie Fiocco Chacon and Nicki Fiocco Mizer,
who teach me about the power of bodies and to my granddaughters,
Toni Marie Fiocco Mizer and Isabella Fione Chacon, who
teach me about the possibilities of bodies.

To Marcella LaGamma Williams (1922–2005), whose
body gave me life and who shared her dying with me.

Contents

Acknowledgments

The writing of this book has been an incredible journey, and many people have helped and inspired me along the way. I give my thanks to two incredible teachers and scholars, Renée Curry and Steven Gould Axelrod. Renée's mentorship and friendship helped me develop the skills and confidence necessary to undertake this project, and her strength and intellect offered a model that sustained me over the years. Steve's support provided me a solid base from which to launch all my endeavors, and his generosity and kindness strengthened my resolve to write this book. In addition, I offer sincere thanks to Anke Gleber for our hours of conversations about the female body and other things and our excursions to Extraordinary Desserts; to Dawn Formo for her willingness to talk theory and pedagogy and for her infectious laughter; to Kwakiutl Dreher for her insights regarding body, spirit, and place; to Marilyn Chin for the shared lunches and laughter and for her willingness to talk about her craft; and to Camille Roman for her careful reading of my manuscript and for her helpful suggestions.

Without the support of my sister, Leslie DeFrancesco, I could not have found the emotional space to complete this program. I thank her for the closeness we share. I also wish to acknowledge the importance of the unwavering belief of my nephews and nieces, Bill Burton, Patrick Burton, Betsy Burton, and Noel Hathaway—because they believed, so did I. My son-in-laws, Armando Chacon and Michael Mizer, along with my grandsons, Brandon Mizer and Austin Chacon, all kept me both sane and distracted when I needed both sanity and distraction. My cousins Karen Nowakowski and Christine Boczanowski have each contributed to this project in ways they will never know. I thank them for "always being there."

I cannot over estimate the value of friends; therefore, I thank two very special women, Barbara Bloodhart and Anita Nix. My life would be poor without each of them.

I offer my deepest appreciation to Brigitte Shull, editor, and Lee Norton, editorial assistant, at Palgrave. Brigitte's support and advice always came at just the right moment of panic and despair. Lee has been wonderful throughout this project, always listening to my concerns and offering solutions to problems that seemed to me irresolvable.

Finally, I owe more than I can ever express to Chris Ruiz-Velasco for his unwavering love and patience and for showing me the amazing resilience of the human body. He read every word of this book (many, many times). *Poetics of the Body* is much better because of his insights, comments, questions, and criticisms. I am forever grateful for his wit, intellect, and humor—he keeps me intellectually nimble.

Introduction

The poetry of Edna St. Vincent Millay, Elizabeth Bishop, Marilyn Chin, and Marilyn Hacker afford a crucial look at what it means to possess a body—particularly a female body. Creative and intellectual expressions do not occur separate from the body, and as Elizabeth Grosz states, "The writer would be unable to type, the musician unable to perform, without word processor or musical instrument becoming part of the body image" (*Volatile Bodies* 80). The body and body image become integral parts of creative acts, and this obvious observation carries with it important implications. As I discuss more fully in Chapter 1, linking embodiment and cultural production often devalues the product of that production and marginalizes the artist, especially in the case of women, men of color, and gays and lesbians. Millay, Bishop, Chin, and Hacker all seem to recognize this danger, and yet, each writes a poetics of the body. This poetics suggests the importance of the body in the creative process, and the poetic bodies that circulate in their work, to varying degrees, sustain *and* hinder creativity, uphold *and* humble intellectuality, bolster *and* betray masculinity, celebrate *and* disavow femininity, define *and* redefine sexuality, and reinforce *and* challenge disciplining regimes of gender. As Millay, Bishop, Chin, and Hacker depict the body in their poems, they offer one that defies the traditional rigid categorization of either immanent or transcendent; instead, the body often becomes the site where immanence and transcendence occur simultaneously, conditionally, and tangentially. Within their poetics of the body, the body itself remains intimately connected to all subject positions; however, this connection vacillates between foreground (most often in Millay and Hacker) and background (most often in Bishop and Chin). At times, the body resides somewhere between these two grounds pointing to its conscious and unconscious influence in the work of each woman.

When I talk about the body in these poems, I am speaking about representations of the body, and, in most cases, the body is the female one. These poets all celebrate this body in some sense, but individually, they also acknowledge the precarious position of the female body within American patriarchal culture—a culture still maintained by the normativity of whiteness, maleness, and heterosexuality. At times, a similarity emerges regarding the issues with which each poet deals, and at other times, the issues prove very different. For example, all investigate the body's relationship to gender and sexuality. Millay and Bishop write as white women, and the body they depict is most often white. Although Hacker too is white, the body that emerges in her poetry is not exclusively white. Hacker also writes as an Ashkenazi Jew, and because she gives voice to victims and survivors of the Holocaust, the markings on the body in her poetry carry an added significance. Because Chin writes as a Chinese American woman, the issue of race and cultural displacement complicates the issues of gender and sexuality in her poetry. Although Bishop and Hacker write as lesbians, they do not present the same body, nor do they offer the same sexualities and desires. Whereas the lesbian body along with its attendant sexualities emerges blatantly within Hacker's poetry, the lesbian body and lesbian desire manifest as coded in much of Bishop's work. All four women also demonstrate concern with adornment, costume, and masquerade but disguise functions differently in the poems of each poet. I do not find, nor do I look for, an essential female masquerade. In addition, none of the poets whom I discuss relies on a single representation of the female body; instead, they each offer multiple representations, so I do not argue for an essentialized or universalized female body. Rather, in *Poetics of the Body*, I look at its multiple presentations within the work of Millay, Bishop, Chin, and Hacker. The many bodies that these poets offer attest to the importance of deciphering the body at the intersections of the social, historical, and theoretical, and these poetic bodies help us to understand the body's place in the world.

In Chapter 1, I detail various discourses and theories of the body both of which make clear that to siphon off the corporeal from the intellectual, creative, or the spiritual denies the subject full access to any of these areas. On one hand, theorists of the body challenge the notions that posit the body as the *natural* site of gender and sexuality as they unhinge the body from both (Butler, Grosz). On the other hand, these theorists insist on the importance of the body in relation to both sexuality and gender. Theories of the body clarify the "constructedness" of the body itself, thus destabilizing its status as a natural or immanent object. Of course, this point proves crucial for feminist and racial-ethnic discourses. This unmooring of the body from the natural and the precultural frees those peoples usually confined to the body (women, men of color, gays, and lesbians). However, these various groups cannot leave the body behind (nor can white men, for that matter). By arguing for the body as a cultural construction, theorists provide a way to claim embodiment as one of many positions that constitute subjectivity.

As I discuss more fully in Chapter 1, the body has for a very long time served as counterpoint to the mind. Early Western metaphysics (read Plato) privileged mind over body and rationality over the sentient. Because the mind-body binary emerges as one of the structuring paradigms of Western thought, investigations into the body's position in that binary often challenge prevailing hierarchies (male over female, white over nonwhite, civilized over primitive). Representations of the body in the work of artists, writers, and poets comprise a crucial element in grounding the theoretical discourses about the body. Humans have long evidenced a fascination with the human form. "Getting the body" right has propelled artistic creation and innovation for centuries. Early Egyptian artists, following the mandate to represent everything from its most characteristic angle, strove to present everything in the human form they found important (hence the head in profile, a full-face eye in the side view of the face, front view of shoulders and chest, side view of arms and legs, and both feet seen from the inside). The Greek artists broke from confining mandates on how to depict the human form believing that through the position or movement of the body they could present the inner life. Even a cursory look at art from various historical eras reveals changes in the representation of the human form as perceptions of the body changed. Poetic renderings of the body further provide important glimpses into its fraught position within society. In the work of women writers and poets, we most clearly see the politics of the body as these women, writing within a system based on sexual differences that casts the woman as inferior other, struggle to "get the female body" right. Although philosophizing and theorizing the body and its relation to mind and spirit are important in understanding our material or lived existence, recognizing and analyzing the artistic or poetic renderings of the body prove just as important. Therefore, in *Poetics of the Body*, I move from a generalized discussion of theories of the body to in-depth analyses and close readings of Edna St. Vincent Millay (Chapter 2), Elizabeth Bishop (Chapter 3), Marilyn Chin (Chapter 4), and Marilyn Hacker (Chapter 5).

Millay commodifies and flaunts the body—both in her person and in her poetry and presents a body spectacularly rendered, one that invites censure by flaunting most conventions. Recent scholarship identifies this poet as "a modernist. . . , postmodernist, or self-conscious and successful alternative modern, or musical lyricist, ironic sentimentalist, female female impersonator, feminist, psychologist, cultural icon, and cultural critic" (Freedman xviii). These diverse identifications highlight the difficulty of "pinning" down Millay herself let alone the body in her poetry. She uses very traditional poetic forms that simultaneously work to constrain the body, its sexuality, desires, and excesses *and* to blatantly offer the body up to scrutiny, and in many of her poems, the body seems both subversive and compliant. In poems such as "I, being born a woman and distressed," Millay disregards patriarchal restraints on female desire and sexuality. I can point to "I, being born a woman and distressed" as a feminist poem, and I can argue that Millay's poetics of the body continually disrupts traditional gender ideologies. However, Millay's poetics and politics are seldom this straightforward. In poems such as "First Fig," "Second Fig," "The Witch-Wife," "Oh, oh you will be sorry for that word!" "The Plaid Dress," and several of sonnets in *Fatal Interview*, Millay's poetic bodies, with their attendant sexualities and desires, prove difficult to read. More often than not, her poetic representations of the body in these poems generate ambiguity, uncertainty, and unease. This ambiguity complicates any reading of Millay's poetics of the body; however, I argue that this ambiguity itself opens the space for transgression and resistance.

Indeed, Millay's early success with *Renascence* demonstrates the embodiment of her poetry by critics and reviewers. The scholarship seems to conflate Millay's work with both her physical person and her poetic personae. Her body, personality, sexuality, and lifestyle merge until her poetry seems an extension of her body. One critic writes, "Her poems were as well-turned as her own slim ankle" (qtd. in Thesing 97). Reviewer and scholar after scholar draw attention to Millay's coppery red hair, small stature, captivating green eyes, and brash exhibitionism. Mention of her gender and age mark these early responses: "brilliant child," "simple, little-girl language," "emotion of youth," "the young, girlish poet herself," and "wide-eyed naëf." Thus the bodies in Millay's poetry signified for her contemporaries her own body; however, I suggest that her poetic bodies also function to challenge the very paradigms of femininity for which critics praised Millay. The femininity that Millay enacts in her person and in her poetry oscillates between submissiveness and rebelliousness, and this oscillation unmoors gender from the body.

As feminists argue, embodiment often places women writers and poets in a dangerous literary position, and indeed Millay's fall from the literary canon exemplifies the danger of conflating the person with the work and the personae with the poet. Yet, I argue, Millay's poetry uses this conflation to taunt the disciplining systems of the 1920s, 1930s, and 1940s. The poet herself challenged gender stereotypes and blurred the lines of sexuality, and many of her poems evidence this same challenge. Although in my analysis, I attempt to keep open a gap between Millay the poet and Millay the poetic persona. Chapter 2, more than the others in *Poetics of the Body*, deals with the historical context in which Millay wrote, and I situate her poetry more directly within a biographical context. I make these moves because in order to understand the poetics and politics of the body in Millay's work, we need to understand her use of her own body. Many scholars deal with how and why Millay used her body as prop for her poetry. Most notably Cheryl Walker, in *Masks Outrageous and Austere: Culture, Psyche, and Persona in Modern Women Poets*, situates Millay's use of the body in a context of self-commodification. Thus Millay presents the body, literally and figuratively, as a vehicle of co-option within the intersecting ideologies of patriarchy and capitalism. We can, however, never be sure of what presentation is the *real* Millay.

Performance, masquerade, and the specular become important devices in Millay's poetry, and in this chapter, I investigate how the body performs to defy gender and sexual categorization. The early Millay seems so *intent* on wielding the body as the thing that exceeds all cultural (patriarchal) mandates, and yet, the body that proves more difficult to situate in relation to Millay's intentions is, I argue, the more dangerous body. Not knowing whether the poems bespeak compliance or advocate resistance to gender ideologies founded on sexual differences proves more unsettling to those ideologies. Millay's poetic bodies comply, but they comply with an attitude of either irony or excess and with just enough of either or both to put into question the earnestness of the compliance. The shakiness of the compliance and the uninterpretability of the resistance may be the most effective strategy *of resistance*.

Elizabeth Bishop offers many of the same challenges to disciplining regimes as Millay, and, like Millay, Bishop utilizes pastiche, performance, and masquerade. She also uses both metaphor and metonymy to complicate her representations of the body, and she carries into her poetry a white, alcoholic, asthmatic, lesbian body. Many critics suggest that Bishop's body somehow failed her and that this failure caused Bishop great anguish and, often, embarrassment. While recognizing Bishop's frustration with her illness (eczema as well as asthma) and the consequences of her alcoholism, I suggest that ultimately Bishop does not view her body as failure: she wrote the poetry she wrote precisely because of that body, and as Renée Curry adamantly reminds us, "Bishop's body was also white, and this fact has been unduly overlooked" (76). Bishop's constant awareness of her body's capability to "misbehave" underpins the ambivalence about the body that emerges in her poetry. Throughout her lifetime, Bishop's illnesses forced her into seclusion or even into erratic behaviors. In addition, in her own person, Bishop took on a ladylike and even diminutive manner that downplayed the body. In other words, her physical characteristics as well as how she presented those characteristics led many to view Bishop as reticent, prim, and proper. This observation begins to explain Bishop's fascination with masquerade and disguise both of which she utilizes in her poetry. On one level, Bishop writes a poetry of disavowal in regards to the body. She hides or masks the body, yet she cannot and does not deny it. In addition, she refuses to present a static body, one universalized as either male or female. Instead, this poet offers poetic bodies that inhabit liminal spaces, bodies that seem unreal and disembodied but are nonetheless material and immanent.

Bishop often draws on the trope of liminality in her poems in order to question what it means to be as well as to examine what it means to have an embodied existence. Whereas Millay offers an ambiguous body that invites various interpretations, Bishop's poetry suggests an ambiguity *about* the body itself. Bishop writes poems that seem always to work, on some level, within a framework of contrarieties as they point to the paradoxical aspects of the self. For example, in her house poems such as "The End of March" and "Song for the Rainy Season," Bishop uses the house metaphor to reveal the illusory aspects of a coherent and fixed subjectivity, and she reconfigures this metaphor to suggest instability rather than stability and illusion rather than actuality. In a poem such as "The End of March," Bishop locates being-ness in liminal spaces, and in her poems dealing directly or indirectly with the body, she positions the body at the limits of gender, reality, or physical borders.

Bishop seldom peoples her poetic houses—no *bodies* inhabit them. For example, in "Jerónimo's House" a litany of objects functions as the markers of its inhabitants: "left-over Christmas decorations," a blue woven wicker table, "two palm-leaf fans," uneaten food, "four pink tissue-paper roses," and "an old French horn" (34). In this poem, however, Bishop offers no descriptions of people, yet in both poems, a corporal presence hovers in the background as the poetic body teases with its nonpresence.

Similar to the conflict between Bishop's desire for a stable, coherent subjectivity and her realization of the fiction of that subjectivity (as well as her understanding of the dangers of the illusion), the desire for a stable, coherent body exists simultaneously with her recognition of the fictive nature of the body itself. Her poetry celebrates the body while warning of the dangers of exposing it too fully—of forgetting the masquerade. Specifically, Bishop's poems "In the Waiting Room," "The Gentleman of Shalott," "O Breath," "Exchanging Hats," and "Pink Dog" (all of which I discuss more fully in Chapter 3) represent, thematize, and theorize visible, invisible, clothed, unclothed, resisting, yielding, abject, grotesque, beautiful, male, female, white, dark, material, and transcendent bodies.

The body or bodies that circulate within Bishop's poems often seem to lack materiality, but these bodies never lack significance. Bishop's poetic bodies emerge through realizations of sameness and differences ("In the Waiting Room"), through images reflected in a mirror ("The Gentleman of Shalott"), through descriptions of bodily processes ("O Breath"), through the exchange of clothing ("Exchanging Hats"), and, finally, through the depiction of a naked dog ("Pink Dog"). However, the body in Bishop's poetry always refuses containment by rejecting a site of stasis in an either-or paradigm. Because Bishop positions them on thresholds and in-between spaces, her poetic bodies disrupt the culture-nature binary, a binary that relies upon a myriad of other binarisms: mind-body, reason-passion, sense-sensibility, reality-appearance, transcendence-immanence, and form-matter. The body within Bishop's poetry shifts from these traditional binarisms, thus becoming a reconfigured epistemological subject and object, the thing at the center of knowing as well as at the core of the knower, him or herself. The multiple representations of bodies that manifest in Bishop's poetry demand different methods of knowing precisely because these bodies reconfigure and redefine with and among the poems. We cannot read "one" body in Bishop's poetry any more than we can locate one subject. Consequently, ways of knowing the body also shift in these poems. This reconfigured epistemological subject-object and the way one knows that subject-object unhinge traditional understandings of the body's relation to sex, gender, language, and culture.

In Chapter 4, I discuss the work of Chinese American poet Marilyn Chin, focusing on "That Half Is Almost Gone," "Blues on Yellow," and "Where We Live Now," from *Rhapsody in Plain Yellow*; "A Chinaman's Chance" and "The Last Woman with Lotus Feet" from *Dwarf Bamboo*; and "How I Got That Name" and the Diana Toy poems from *The Phoenix Gone, The Terrace Empty*. A deep commitment to the poetry of activism propels most of her work, sometimes lending a blatant political overtone to a poem and at other times juxtaposing the political and the personal in startling ways—a juxtaposition that Chin blatantly presents in the title and subtitle of one of the last poems of Section 1, "The Parent Node," in *Dwarf Bamboo*: "After My Last Paycheck from the Factory, Two Thin Coupons, Four Tin Dollars, I Invited Old Liu for an Afternoon Meal: *for the Chinese Cultural Revolution and all that was wrong with my life*" (21–22; emphasis in original). "Tienanmen, the Aftermath," from *The Phoenix Gone, The Terrace Empty*, opens with a stark image of carnage, and then moves to the speaker in bed with her lover (88). Chin's poetry gives personal voice to the politics of immigration, exile, cultural displacement, oppression, and assimilation without reducing those issues only to the personal. However, assimilation proves her most overriding concern, and as her poetic voice unravels the complexity and consequences of this process, Chin interweaves various other concerns: loss, cultural history, silence, family relationships, sadness, sacrifice, and gender. All of these issues tie directly or indirectly to the body and to its movement, pain, visibility, and invisibility.

Rhapsody in Plain Yellow, Chin's most recent volume, is strikingly postmodern in the poet's experimentation with form, language, and content. With the skill of a *bricoleur*, Chin borrows from grand narratives to create new stories, mocking, adapting, and rewriting traditional forms. The poems whisper with allusions to Chinese folk songs, ancient Chinese poetry and myth, Maoist dance drama, Confucianism, and the poetry of Emily Dickinson and William Carlos Williams. In all her work, she insists on pushing the limits of poetic expressions by offering "hybrid forms" such as a mixture of epigrams and haiku, and she offers an eclectic style while sounding a voice tinged with irony, wit, brashness, accusation, grief, compassion, and love.

In *Rhapsody*, just as she does in her previous volumes (*Dwarf Bamboo* and *The Terrace Empty/The Phoenix Gone*), Chin uses the body as the site of convergence of both time and generations. The body becomes the place where familial and cultural histories collapse, often universalizing both the body and experience. However, the body that emerges in Chin's poetry *also* particularizes immigrant and gender experiences, and it refuses both homogenization and marginalization. This poet gives us the female immigrant body and the anorexic body (again, female and immigrant). However, the body in Chin's poetry seldom proves easy to decipher as her poetic bodies bespeak a biculturalism that intermingles Western and Eastern understandings of the corporeal.

In Chapter 4, my discussion of the body in the poem "How I Got That Name: An Essay on Assimilation" focuses on two seemingly unrelated issues: the body itself and time. Grosz, however, insists that we must indeed link the body to both time and space: "If bodies are to be reconceived, not only must their *matter and form* be rethought, but so too must their environment and *spatio-temporal location*" (*Space, Time* 84). Obviously, bodies are located in both time and space, and we experience and understand both through our bodies. For example, the long title poem from *Rhapsody in Plain Yellow* contains two stanzas in which Chin plays with notions of space and time as she questions the mind-body connection. The words in these stanzas appear free-floating on the page, and the body manifests as unanchored, occupying no space. As Chin explores being-ness, body, space, and time, she also gives us a grounded body, unmoving and lacking motion. This contradiction parallels the double bind of many people of color: invisible in white culture but limited by a nonwhite body.

Chin's poetry resonates with the movement of bodies from China to America, and in her poems, past bleeds into present. The body in many of these poems simultaneously inhabits multiple spatiotemporal locations, and this fluidity disrupts Chinese, Chinese American, and white American expectations. It is this fluidity rather than tokenism that influences my inclusion of Chin in this volume. Significantly, Chin not only presents sexed and gendered bodies, but she also presents bodies identifiably racialized as Other. The immigrant body in poems such as "A Chinaman's Chance" and "The Last Woman with Lotus Feet" (from *Dwarf Bamboo*) must operate in various and often–oppositional temporal and spatial contexts. As the immigrant body immigrates and migrates, locates and dislocates, and as it negotiates these oppositional contexts, it also gathers unto and into itself multiple stories thus becoming a palimpsest. Back-stories remain legible, and cultural, familial, and personal histories become visible. Chin makes clear that theorizing the body within a framework of immigration demands rethinking the importance of time and location.

However, unlike the blatant political aspect of Chin's poetry, the corporeal aspects seem muted and ephemeral. Indeed, in the eight-poem sequence that comprises the "Homage to Diana Toy" section of *The Phoenix Gone, The Terrace Empty*, the body literally disappears. These poems detail the progression of Toy's anorexia and her ultimate suicide. Although much Chinese American literature utilizes tropes of eating and consumption, most suggest filth and excess. Chin upends this trend by focusing on the disappearing body of a Chinese American woman. The body here becomes the thing to deny, the repository of disappointment and alienation. In "Homage to Diana Toy," Chin gives us a body disconnected from time and space and confined to a continual now (Toy is in a mental institution).

Chapter 5 addresses the work of Marilyn Hacker, lesbian, feminist, activist, and poet who writes almost exclusively in received forms such as the sonnet, the villanelle, the pantoum, and the sestina. Rather than constraining Hacker, these forms provide apt frameworks for the irony, brashness, playfulness, and sexuality that distinguish her poetry. The intensity of Hacker's voice and the sometimes subtle and sometimes blatant corporeality of the images strain against poetic form to produce poetry that engages us intellectually, emotionally, and physically. In "Cancer Winter," the sonnet cycle from *Winter Numbers*, Marilyn Hacker maps language onto the body as she writes about her breast cancer, surgery, survival, love, and lust. In Chapter 5, I argue for the importance of the body in articulating stories—one's own story as well as those of others'. Details of the body (how it looks, what it does, and what it wishes to do) fill Hacker's poetry. The body, in many ways, contains the story—it is the narrative. Hacker writes a poetry of desire, a desire articulated by body language, and she offers a body unrestrained by heterosexual normativity, and unlike Bishop, who wrote "coded" lesbian love poems, Hacker relishes in woman loving woman. Specifically, I look at "Against Elegies," "August Journal," and several sonnets from "Cancer Winter" from *Winter Numbers*, "Ghazal" from *Desesperanto*, "Scars on Paper" from *Squares and Courtyards*, "Sestina" and "Villanelle" both from *Selected Poems*, and various sonnets from *Love, Death, and the Changing of the Seasons*, and I evoke aspects of queer and narrative theory, as well as the philosophical work of Hannah Arndt and Adriana Cavarero regarding narrative, desire, and gender. Hacker, like Millay, flaunts the body, but unlike Millay, she defiantly and unambiguously flouts gender conventions—and Hacker's poetic bodies emerge as the story—the narrative of living and loving. Hacker gives us bodies that negotiate the mandates of heterosexuality by "un-writing" those mandates into a lesbian framework.

Mary Biggs rightly observes that Hacker's work "foregrounds women especially, and Jews and gays" and that in *Desesperanto*, Hacker journeys "*backward* into her childhood and the communal Jewish past" (11, 14). Biggs also points to *Winter Numbers* as the volume in which "Jews and the qualities of Jewishness become fully present, as theme and echo" (8). The poems in these two volumes deal directly with the Jewish experience and how the Holocaust constructs and influences that experience. Indeed, either directly or indirectly, Hacker's sense of what it means to be a Jew does implicate the body, and attention to this connection enriches *our* understanding of the significance of body to this poet. In the fourteen sonnets that comprise "Cancer Winter," Hacker twice identifies herself as "an unimportant Jew" (81, 83), and in three poems, she refers directly to the Holocaust and its victims. Her poetics of the body often depicts injustices against the body, all bodies.

Poetics of the Body ends with a conversation between Marilyn Chin and me. Chin opens the conversation by addressing the difficulty of finding time to write as a tenured professor at San Diego State University, and she shares her views on teaching, her move to long poems and "short, short" fiction in her work, her commitment to writing a poetry of activism, and the viability of poetry today. Candidly, Chin acknowledges the "anti-identity, antibiographical" impulses in contemporary poetry, and she unapologetically proclaims that her poems are identity poems—they always begin with her. Yet, she admits they always move beyond her. Chin, herself, says, "The personal concerns grow into larger concerns always." She also identifies second-wave feminism as an integral part of herself, and she pays tribute to "Adrienne Rich and her generation of feminist poets." Although, at times, bewildered and amused by today's young women, Chin sees "some very powerful young women out there." During our conversation, Chin and I also talked about the sense of place in her poetry, her negotiation with and use of Chinese traditions, and the East–West hybridity that marks her poetry. Chin also speaks about the significance of food and the body in the Diana Toy poems, a significance that she ties to excess and lack. She further explains the connection of these elements to the cycles of feast and famine in China. Through her poetry, Chin claims a voice for Chinese women. She says, "I'm a Chinese woman. How many Chinese women get a chance to speak?" Chin provides both an eloquent and strong voice for this rather silent or silenced population. By her own admission, she writes slowly, taking several years between books, yet Marilyn Chin is a major figure in Asian American poetry.

On some level, the work of each of the poets in this study proves problematic to critics—no one seems quite sure where to place each of them. While it proves tempting to locate each woman within recognizable literary movements, poetic categories, and theoretical frameworks, doing so undermines my view regarding the difficulty of "pinning down" a body as it circulates within Millay's, Bishop's, Chin's, and Hacker's poetry. Throughout this study I argue that these poetic renderings of the body reveal its continuous reconfiguration and renegotiation within a disciplining system, and I seek to demonstrate the intersection of mind and body with language. Millay, Bishop, Chin, and Hacker reveal the languages *of* the body and the languages *on* the body. In this sense, then, poetic language lifts the body from its place of immanence to a realm of transcendence without jettisoning the very materiality of the body. These poets, in various and diverse ways, hold the body with all its messiness up to scrutiny, and in so doing, they also present a poetics of the body that first reveals and then reconfigures cultural metaphors of and for the body.

THEORIZING THE BODY

Despite, or perhaps because of, disciplining agencies' insistence on the containment, restraint, and management of the body, the body emerges as a crucial element in the work of many women poets. Edna St. Vincent Millay, Elizabeth Bishop, Marilyn Chin, and Marilyn Hacker, each in their own way, refuse to idealize, sanitize, or contain the body. Instead, each of these poets writes about, on, or through the body, thus rendering it both a poetic subject and object. Millay's, Bishop's, Chin's, and Hacker's poetic bodies circulate in registers of desire, creativity, intellectuality, spirituality, and sexuality, and these poets give us female, male, whole, shattered, distorted, small, large, visible, invisible, desiring, desired, strong, weak, ailing, and dead bodies. These poetic bodies attest to the body's often contentious position in relation to gender, sexuality, race, and class. Even the seemingly decorous poetic body flaunts conventional boundaries as each woman utilizes the trope *of* the body or the body *as* trope to investigate constructions of self, knowledge, language, and poetry.

Without reducing the work of these women to the body, in this study I theorize the function and representation of the body in their poetry. As many feminist, postcolonial, and race theorists remind us, leaving the body out of our discourse widens the gap between theory and practice. Thus theorists of the body must keep the body in view—not the abstract theorized body, the one that becomes universalized and essentialized within all discourses; rather, we must keep before us particular and specific *bodies*. This move ensures that the epistemological object of various discourses becomes the subject of those discourses. Identifying the body as particular rather than universal, as constructed rather than essential, as specific rather than generic, acknowledges the particularized body (or bodies) as subjects rather than objects. In addition, acknowledging the particularity and specificity of bodies repositions them at the center of discussions regarding gender, sex, sexuality, race, nationality, and subjectivity both ontologically and epistemologically. Bodies become the *way* we know things and the *way* we are as well as constituting *what* we know and *who* we are. Bodies then circulate within epistemological and ontological realms without belonging exclusively to either.

Of course, this focus on the body runs the risk of reducing everything to biology or, more specifically, to a biological determinism. However, just as Gayatri Chakrovorty Spivak has argued for a strategic essentialism, those who theorize the importance of the body call for the strategic use of the body. More importantly, rethinking the body in relation to both ontology and epistemology opens a challenge to the mind-body split that underwrites much of Western philosophy. This split positions the body as the thing that burdens the mind or spirit, and the fundamental assumptions of this tradition rely upon understanding the body as the deceiver. Because we cannot trust it, we must find a way to transcend the body and its concomitant elements. Thus philosophy hands us the universalized and, in many ways, transcendent body—"unreal" and nonexistent except in the realm of philosophy and theory. The "body" of Western philosophy becomes one *unmarked* by gender, sexuality, or race while simultaneously understood as the male, heterosexual, white body. Implicit in this "unnaming" and "unmarking" of the body resides the notion of the transcendent quality of maleness and, by contrast, the immanent quality of femaleness.

This reification and the idea of transcendence imply a disdain and distrust of the body and all things associated with it. Susan Bordo's description of the body in relation to "that which is not-body" aptly defines perceptions of the *female* body as "the albatross, the heavy drag on self-realization" (5). This rendering of the body as the thing that impedes "self-realization" implicates the female body as well as nonwhite male and female bodies as that which destabilizes all certainties regarding the gendered, sexualized, racialized, and coherent self.

While not the only legacy of Western philosophy's distrust of the body, this transcendent-immanent binary proves crucial to feminist arguments regarding creativity and intellectuality, concerns that underwrite feminist debates regarding essentialism, or the "givenness" of a thing. Diana Fuss offers a concise definition: "Essentialism is classically defined as a belief in true essence—that which is most irreducible, unchanging, and therefore constitutive of a given person or thing" (2). For some feminists, this "givenness" proves problematic. On one hand, in order to enact social and political change for women, feminists must argue *as* women. Such a stance assumes a female essence, and as Fuss correctly and clearly articulates, it also assumes a shared oppression of women *as* women under a "totalizing symbolic system" that operates "throughout history and across cultures." In addition, essentialism makes possible a feminine language—with *écriture féminine* manifesting as the extreme and sophisticated example (2).

On the other hand, the assumption of an essential femaleness, a transhistorical and transcultural system of subjugation, and a "truly" feminine language elide differences *among* women, refuse the specificity *of* women, essentialize a system of oppression, and, on some level, marginalize creative and intellectual works by women. The feminist debate regarding essentialism also implicates the body. Again, I turn to Fuss: "For the essentialist, the body occupies a pure, pre-social, pre-discursive space. The body is 'real,' accessible, and transparent; it's always *there* and directly interpretable through the senses. For the constructionist, the body is never simply there, rather it is composed of a network of effects continually subject to sociopolitical determination" (5). The body *as* body (along with its gestures, postures, location, and adornments) is crucial to the maintenance of essentialism, but the body is also the thing that makes visible the many differences among women. The body, however, cannot, and does not, signify only as a cultural construction. It seems to me that all discourses and theories of the body fail to "pin down" the body as either an epistemological object or subject or to fix the body firmly within an ontological register. Therefore, I make no attempt to do either. In fact, I believe that this failure attests to the falseness of the mind-body binary and that it dislodges the body as a fixed term in that binary. I argue that the body with its attendant characteristics and the poetic representations (conscious and unconscious, overt and covert) of the body continually disrupt normative social constraints.

However, this disruption does not operate transhistorically or transculturally. The body, as rendered by Millay, does not behave or misbehave in the same fashion as Bishop's poetic body, nor that of Chin or Hacker. For example, Millay flaunts the body, keeping it in view and on display, whereas Bishop gives us the body through distortion, metaphor, or metonymy (the body is reflected, or like something, or emerges in a process or object). The body in Bishop's poetry emerges from *social conditions* vastly different from those under which Millay wrote; the body in Bishop's poetry arises from a *subject position*, again, vastly different from Millay's, and finally, Bishop's poetic body evidences a social, cultural, and personal *understanding* different from that of Millay, Chin, or Hacker. The body that Chin presents contains and speaks the narrative of cultural displacement and discomfort—often times a body fragmented by the convergence of ethnicity, time, gender, and sexuality. Like Bishop, Hacker experienced bodily illness, yet, unlike Bishop, Hacker renders this illness visible in and through her poetry. Hacker's poetry does more than flaunt the body; it flaunts the conventions that seek to restrain the body.

I do not see the body's disruptive potential as intrinsic (essential) to it, nor do I view this disruptiveness as exclusively imposed by culture. However, I do suggest that hierarchal and totalizing systems and the "isms" they spawn, such as sexism, heterosexism, and racism, generate from binary oppositions that depend on the body itself (male or female, desire for bodies sexed differently from one's own or same-sex desire, white or nonwhite). Therefore, I posit that the body in and of itself is not disorderly; rather, its position as the second or deprivileged term of the binary marks it as unruly in need of containment. The mind-body binary seeks to siphon off the body from the mind and all it encompasses, yet as I will demonstrate through my readings of the poets under discussion, the body intimately engages in the creative and intellectual work of the mind. Its mere presence in the work of Millay, Bishop, Chin, and Hacker attests to more than a binary disruption. In the poetry of these women, representations of and negotiations with the body reveal order, rationality, and coherent subjectivity as necessary illusions to disciplining regimes. I believe that in order to make sense of the body's place in the world, to comprehend its ontological and epistemological importance, and to theorize the cultural and artistic representations of the body, we must turn a critical eye to issues of race, especially "unmarked" or unremarked upon whiteness.

Because normative whiteness emerges as a pervasive ideology, critical whiteness becomes a crucial element in theorizing the body. As I discussed above, Western metaphysics presents a legacy of power, rationality, maleness, and whiteness in our understanding of the body. Joe Kincheloe and Shirley Steinberg assert that "a dominant impulse of *whiteness* took shape around the notion of rationality of the European Enlightenment, with its privileged construction of a transcendental white, male, rational subject who operated at the recesses of power while at the same time giving every indication that he escaped the confines of time and space" (5, emphasis added). This escape from "the confines of time and space" proves significant to theories of the body, as I will discuss. Significantly, by locating this "transcendental white, male, rational subject" within a matrix of power, Kincheloe and Steinberg make clear the importance of marking and naming the body—of making visible the invisible norms of maleness, rationality, and whiteness. Further, they identify "rationalistic modernist whiteness [as] shaped by its close association with science. As a scientific construct, whiteness privileges mind over body; intellectual over experiential ways of knowing; and mental abstractions over passion, bodily sensations, and tactile understandings" (5). Thus Western philosophy, rationality, and epistemology must banish the body, but they cannot escape the body, *nor* can whiteness do so. This realization becomes important in this study because recognizing the body as a crucial component of epistemology and ontology, as well as whiteness, repositions those traditionally associated with the body (women, men and women of color, gays and lesbians). If the body is *central* to the ways we know and to identity itself, then those typically marginalized, those perceived as too embodied, move to the center.

Although I understand the utopian element in my logic, I also assert that these disciplining regimes never entirely or successfully banish the body. It remains both a visible and invisible component in the construction of self, language, and knowledge, as the poetry of Millay, Bishop, Chin, and Hacker demonstrates. If I theorize the body as these women represent and use it without acknowledging that the term *body* carries with it the describer *white*, I keep in place the binaries that structure whiteness (mind-body, intellect-experience, reason-passion). Extending Renée Curry's reminder that "white women writers who write do so as white women, from within ideological, social, economical, political, and psychological frameworks of whiteness," I assert the body that these white women writers present more often than not is the white body (*White Women* 1). The poetic bodies that emerge within the work of Millay and Bishop often function as the repositories of privilege. In her poetry, Hacker, however, often presents the body as a racialized one, and she does not limit race to nonwhite. In several poems the speaker uses the descriptor *white* when describing people, and sometimes tacitly and sometimes ironically, Hacker acknowledges the privileges of whiteness. The unacknowledged, unmarked, and unexamined whiteness of the body underscores its ambiguous place in relation to and within social orders. The *white* female body possesses the potential to disrupt these orders while simultaneously by virtue of its *whiteness* sustain these orders. However, I do argue that these poets particularize the body, and in so doing, they reject Western metaphysics' universalizing, essentializing, and neutralizing of the body, and they challenge the mandates of Western systems of thought that casts the body and all things associated with it to the realm of the inferior other. Even today, despite the multitude of images of the body that surround us, having too much or too little body, too much sexuality, too much body consciousness or concern invites disgust, censure, and containment. This excess of body results in a diminishment of the value of an individual. Western metaphysical distrust of the body continues, on some level, to privilege mind (reason, rationality) over body.

Just as Platonic thought continues to influence contemporary understandings of knowledge and subjectivity, Platonic beliefs, combined with Aristotelian principles, inform notions of "the body." As Bordo rightly points out, "Plato imagines the body as an *epistemological* deceiver, its unreliable senses and volatile passions continually tricking us into mistaking the transient and illusory for the permanent and the real" (3). Within this paradigm, the body does more than mediate one's encounter with reality (Truth); it prevents both a recognition and an understanding of Truth. Bordo goes on to detail the historical shifts that occurred in theories regarding the body and its relationship to Knowledge, Truth, and Reality. She points to the sixteenth century where the body retains its image as an "epistemological deceiver" and where it also emerges as "the site of our *locatedness* in space and time" (4). This "locatedness," or grounding, impedes objectivity, thus constructing all thought as "persepectival." Accordingly, "the only way for the mind to comprehend things as 'they really are' is by attainment of a dis-embodied view from nowhere" (4). In other words, in order to have access to pure Knowledge, Truth, or Reality, one must somehow leave the body behind and must transcend the limitations that the body's "unreliable senses and volatile passions" impose. In addition, the imperative to leave the body behind helps construct, and certainly reinforces, the mind-body split that permeates Western metaphysics, and it reifies the first term of the binary, "mind."

Real danger emerges when the mind becomes the privileged entity. If body becomes the thing that disturbs and disrupts reason and rationality, then it also becomes the thing demanding discipline and punishment. As Michel Foucault makes clear in *Discipline and Punish* and *The History of Sexuality* volume 1, discipline and punishment result in subjection and objectification, and simultaneously, subjection and objectification initiate discipline and punishment. Throughout *Discipline and Punish*, Foucault links the two terms, as the following passage illustrates: "At the heart of the procedures of discipline, [the examination] manifests the subjection of those who are perceived as objects and the objectification of those who are subjected" (185). Although, as Béatrice Han in her study regarding the transcendental and historical in the works of Foucault points out, Foucault "progressively stress[es] subjection to the detriment of objectification" (117). Foucault insists that subjection depends on controlling and disciplining the body. In his history of punishment, Foucault finds that "it is always the body that is an issue—the body and its forces, their utility and their docility, their distribution and their submission" (25). Thus, the manifestations of the body such as physical desire, sexuality, gender, reproduction, skin color, and illness become the objects of discipline and restriction.

Besides these things, which overtly connect to the body, the cultural production of white women, men and women of color, as well as that of gay and lesbians also needs disciplining because hegemony reduces the writing (and all other art forms) of these people to an *embodied* creativity. Embodiment implies excess, and as such, it demands restraint. The mind-body split underwrites this view because hegemony places this embodied creativity in opposition to an intellectual one. Conversely, the marginalization of literary (artistic) work of nonwhite, nonmale, nonheterosexual people reinforces the mind-body binary. For example, early blues singers—almost exclusively black women—sang of the physical ache of sexual longings, the physical effects of abusive relationships, and the physical conditions of poverty. The blues continues, along with jazz, to imply art arising from lived experiences, and thus, these creative expressions seem less created or crafted and more instinctual than other musical genres. The same perceptions plague the literary works written by some white women, most men and women of color, as well as the works of many gay and lesbian writers. Because the aesthetic standard implies objectivity (both in relation to the creator and the viewer or listener), the valued aesthetic object becomes the one distanced from the artist's (viewer's or listener's) "locatedness in space and time," a "locatedness" that implies a body, and by extension, aesthetic standards demand that the artist and viewer or listener transcend the body. "True" art then arises deliberately from the creative mind; marginalized art generates instinctually from bodily experiences. Both views unfix the mind from the body, and both serve to justify inclusion and exclusion based on *aesthetic* principles. Whether "absent" or present, the body seems always implicated in cultural production as the thing to be elided, denied, or transcended. Therefore, the body, with its attendant characteristics, as "always" the issue, functions as a primary assumption in *Poetics of the Body*.

My goal in this book emerges as twofold: first, to argue that poetic representations of the body reveal the paradox of the body itself, its role in maintaining *and* disrupting disciplinary regimes; second, to suggest that reconfiguring how we view the body redefines how we understand the interdependence of mind and body. Subjectivity, creativity, or intellectuality does not depend on a collapse of the mind-body binary, nor do these things insist on a reversal of the terms; instead, subjectivity relies on being able to claim the particularized body and the cultural body, being able to disavow both, being able to move between a particular body and a universalized body, being able to experience transcendence through the body, and being able to encounter the sensations of the body through the body itself and through the mind's perceptions of the body. We cannot leave the body behind, but we are not tied to the body except when culture or society insists on universalizing and essentializing bodies.

Theorizing the body means rethinking how and why the body exists, knows, feels, resists, and complies. Individuals experience things on and through the body on at least two levels: first, *through* cultural expectations and mandates, and second, *outside* those same cultural expectations and mandates. Much of what we think of as "natural" to the body—sensations of pain, visual perceptions, reactions to smells or sounds—generate from culture. However, regardless of shared culture expectations, other factors intervene to disrupt these mandates. These disruptive elements (race, sex, gender, sexuality) all in some sense adhere to the body. The experiences of an individual then become natural to his or her particular body— not natural in the sense of universal, but natural in the sense of normal, and therefore, unexamined. Yet these experiences do prove essential to a particular gendered, sexed, or racialized body. However, even this observation, or argument, emerges fraught with contradictions because no matter how particular or specific we get, it becomes nearly impossible to untie the social from the individual.

How then do we think outside of social constructions? Does social constructionism then replace biological determinism? The answer is yes and no. Just as we cannot unfix the constructed from the "natural," we cannot unmoor the "natural" from the constructed. We can, however, expose the dangers of insisting on the *naturalness* of the natural-constructed binary itself, and we can, by attending to how the body circulates in our discourses, our theoretical frameworks, our politics, our art and literature, and our popular culture, retheorize the significance of the body in all these areas. In addition, I suggest that attention to how various writers and poets utilize metaphors *of* the body and metaphors *for* the body, as well as how they represent it, furthers our understanding of the connections between ideology and material existence. The body, I suggest, simultaneously stabilizes and destabilizes these connections.

This understanding proves significant because each of us inhabits the world as a material being negotiating a myriad of ideologies. Any analysis of poetry involves encounters with these ideologies within at least four specific contexts: (1) the specific ideologies prevalent at the time the poet wrote the poem and the time of its publication, (2) the emerging ideologies in the period in which the poet wrote and published, (3) the ideological influences of the critic him or herself, and (4) the ideological implications of the poem's form, content, and language. All these contexts reaffirm not only the link between ideology and material existence but also the connections between ideology and poetics. Each of the poets in this study—Millay, Bishop, Chin, and Hacker—write from within personal, social, and cultural ideological frameworks.

Millay published her first poem at age fourteen, and she wrote during both World War I and II as well as during the heyday of high modernism. She lived a bohemian lifestyle and claimed a place in the avant-garde alongside the leading artists, writers, and thinkers of the era. She espoused both political radicalism and feminism and wrote social protest poetry as well as war propaganda. Bishop's poetic voice emerged as modernism waned, yet she "has been called a modernist [as well as] a formalist, a postmodernist, a feminist, and even a confessional poet" (McCabe 133). Like Millay, war and the nation's discourse of war marked the political and social atmosphere in which Bishop wrote (World War II, the Korean and Vietnam wars), and significantly, as Camille Roman makes clear, "the nation's [World War II] narrative . . . pressed upon Bishop as she pursued her fledgling literary career and a private life of tumultuous romance" (28). After the war, Cold War politics and culture further influenced Bishop's poetic voice and her personal life (8–9). In addition, Bishop wrote as an expatriate living in Brazil with her lover, Lota de Macedo Soares, for eighteen years, and like Millay, she also wrote within a framework of whiteness. However, unlike Millay, Bishop belonged to the social elite, and this position also shaped her personal ideologies.

In an interview with Bryan Thao Worra for the *Asian American Press*, Chin offered the following answer when Worra asked about what themes she favored in her work: "I always write from my subject position: which is a Chinese American minority poet, born in the Chinese diaspora of Hong Kong . . . to a poor family . . . all roads and themes are built from my personal experience." This response points to the ideological contexts that influence Chin's poetics. Born in Hong Kong, Chin grew up in the northwestern region of the United States during the mid-1950s through the 1960s, and she attended college in the late 1970s and early 1980s, years of great political and social change. Chin makes clear her social and political activism in her poetry and interviews, a legacy of both the emerging sociopolitical ideologies of the 1970s and 1980s and the activist poetry that she read. Poems such as "Beijing Spring" and "Tienanmen, the Aftermath" illustrate Chin's commitment to writing poetry in response to political events. Chin's poetry emerges within an intersection of ideological perspectives: immigrant, bicultural, and feminist. Like Chin, Millay ascribed to a feminist politics, but she did not write overtly political-feminist poetics, and Bishop's feminist sensibility emerges more subtly than Chin's. Unlike the other poets in this study, Chin's poetry, feminism, and activism reflects her position as a minority, nonwhite woman.

Like Chin, Hacker "came of age" within the political and social changes of the 1960s and 1970s, and like Chin, Hacker claims the position of activist. Her poems often manifest her commitment to the politics of living lesbian in the late twentieth early twenty-first centuries. Whereas Chin grew up as Chinese American on the West Coast of the United States, Hacker, the daughter of Jewish immigrant parents, lived on the East Coast. Like Bishop, Hacker often writes as an expatriate living in Paris, yet the ideological contexts that shape Hacker's poetry are very different from those that influenced Bishop's. Hacker's poems, published in the 1990s, directly address issues regarding the body, cancer, and AIDS, and they reflect the prevailing ideologies that have at times marginalized those diseases. Hacker does not limit her concerns to illness; rather, she writes an expansive poetry that challenges the ideologies that propel bigotry, that exposes the atrocities of the Holocaust, that lays bare the consequences of repressing desire, and that consistently presents the body as the crucial element in the tellings.

As a feminist poet writing in the 1970s, Hacker continued to write in received forms when other feminist poets moved toward free verse and open forms. In a much quoted 1996 interview with Annie Finch, Hacker discussed her reactions to Adrienne Rich's rejection of traditional poetic forms and of Rich's explanation that her feminist convictions regarding woman's relationship with the language mandated a move away from male dominated traditions: "My own self-examination, as much visceral as rational, did not produce the same recoiling. Perhaps because of a literary generation's distance, I would have felt more constrained, as the writer and reader that I am, by assuming an extra-literary obligation to wrench poems away from my own conception of them because of my politics or my gender" (24). Hacker's decision evidences the emerging ideology of feminism that challenged male forms of discourse, and her choice illuminates her personal ideological perspective regarding language, poetry, and the self. In an earlier interview (1979, published in 1980), Hacker reminded us that "the language that [women] use was as much created and invented by women as by men," and she points to a tradition of female poets using traditional forms (Hammond 22). Hacker's feminist activism clearly emerges as she urges women to rediscover this tradition and to recognize women's "considerable contributions, innovations, and inventions . . . We've got to reclaim the language, demand acknowledgement of our part in it, and proceed from there." Whether they write in the mid to late part of the twentieth century or in the early years of the twenty-first century, ideology underpins the poetry of these women.

Although the scope of this book does not include an in-depth examination of ideology per se or theories of ideology, ideology remains ever present throughout these pages. Therefore, I find it necessary to discuss the concept of ideology and to identify the various assumptions that underpin my understanding of the term. For the most part, today we derive our understanding of ideology and its function from Marxism and New Historicism. In his study on language as the "critical fetish of modernity," Geoffrey Harpham provides a generally accepted principle regarding ideology: "As Marx and Engles were the first to recognize, ideologies work incessantly to obscure or efface history by bestowing on certain ideas or attitudes the powerful appearance of truth" (72). With this aspect of ideology's function in mind, through the poetry of Millay, Bishop, Chin, and Hacker, I point out how "universal truth" has obscured or effaced the history of the body within the cultural, political, and social discourses specific to each poet.

"Ideology," according to Louis Althusser, "represents the imaginary relationship of individuals to their real conditions of existence," and rather paradoxically, "ideology [also] has a material existence" (162–65). These seemingly contradictory aspects of ideology undergird my use of the term in this book. I argue that each of the poets in this study, either consciously or unconsciously, recognizes that the body concretizes material existence and renders visible the imaginary relationship about which Althusser writes. Furthermore, the body's potential to "denaturalize" the natural (i.e., workers' conditions under capitalism, women's circumstances under patriarchy, and nonwhites' situations under racism) threatens ideology's totalizing agenda. Finally, according to Harpham, "Marx and Engles call 'ideology' all those thoughts that naturalize and universalize sectoral conflicts within society, sowing concord, in places where 'objectively,' there should be discord" (80). Thus ideology continually works to obfuscate conflict and contradictions at the very sites from where both *should* arise: workers because their basic bodily needs often go unmet, should revolt; women, because their bodies often endure abuse, should rebel; blacks, because their bodies often mark them as inferior, should protest. However, ideology and the narratives it produces convince us that oppressive conditions arise naturally—they simply are—and because these conditions exist naturally, protest proves futile. In addition, these narratives convince us of their validity, *despite* our own knowledge, knowledge generated from evidence of our own particular body. This tendency to disregard the body's "truth" (hunger, pain, illness, and physical desires) exemplifies Platonic notions—after all the body *is* the ultimate deceiver keeping us from Knowledge, Reality and Truth.

Yet, and again paradoxically, the body and our understanding of it function as a model through which we understand the concrete and abstract dimensions of our world. The body as metaphor proliferates in popular culture, in literature, and in political rhetoric, and as cognitive linguistics makes clear, in our daily encounters with complex abstractions such as anger, desire, thought, ideas, nation, politics, and the mind, to name a few. For example, we often equate body heat to anger, desire to hunger, and we talk about *heads* of states, *digesting* ideas, the *ills* of the nation, an *ailing* economy. Zoltán Kövecses, in *Metaphor: A Practical Introduction*, tells us that Gregory Nagy in *Figurative Idioms* lists over two thousand idioms that relate to the human body. According to Kövecses, "This remarkable finding shows that a large portion of metaphorical meaning derives from our experience of our own body. The 'embodiment' of meaning is perhaps *the* central idea of the cognitive linguistic view of metaphor and indeed of the cognitive linguistic view of meaning" (16). I find Kövecses's arguments extremely significant as they point to the glaring paradox in the philosophical positioning of the mind and body in relation to each other and each in relation to subjectivity. The body emerges as the problem in all equations, yet as Kövecses suggests, the body becomes the touchstone (the vehicle in the metaphor) for what and how we know.

Perhaps the use of the body as metaphor for the political most clearly demonstrates the contradiction of evoking the body as the more concrete term or conceptual domain in metaphor. The use of the *body politic* has a rich history. Adriana Cavarero tells us that "for thousands of years the political order has been figured precisely through the metaphor of the body" (*Stately Bodies* vii). The paradox of utilizing the body to represent the political order, a paradox that Cavarero thoroughly explores and that Millay, Bishop, Chin, and Hacker seem to appreciate, arises from two distinct sources: first, the fraught position of the body in Western thought, and second, the mortality of the body itself. Cavarero explains, "Something very strange indeed seems to characterize the history of the West: while politics rejects the body from the specific on which it founds itself, it also retrieves the body as the shaping metaphor of political order . . . A good example is the expression *body politic*, which although technically relevant to the Middle Ages, still operates today in political language, both as an explicit term and as an allusion to bodily organs and functions carried out in the state by its various parts" (vii–viii). Beginning with Plato, Western philosophy, history, and politics relegate the body to the realm of the "alogical." The very foundation of Western thought (history) pits the body against the logos, clearly privileging the latter. Yet, as Cavarero points out, politics embraces the body as an ordering metaphor.

The trope of the body, then, brings with it into political discourse the potential for disorder, disruption, and decay. The body *as body* sickens, ages, and dies.

In her discussion of the body politic, Moira Gatens suggests that "the metaphor of the body is an obvious way of describing political life," and she rightly points out that "discourses which employ the image of the unified political body assume that the metaphor of the human body is a coherent one, and of course it's not" (83–84). Each of the poets in this study utilizes this notion of the body politic in order to reveal the instability of the political ideology under which each writes, and each woman renders poetic bodies that continually disrupt normative social mandates as well as cultural understandings of the body and its relationship to the mind and to the self.

TEXTUAL AND CORPOREAL CONVERGENCE

EDNA ST. VINCENT MILLAY

EACH OF THE WOMEN WHO COMPRISE *POETICS OF THE BODY* deals with a lived-in, physical body, and each woman's experience with her body proves unique to her. Elizabeth Bishop's bodily reality often involved illness and addiction; Marilyn Chin's body, by her own admission, remains a constant reminder of her "otherness," and, at times, Marilyn Hacker, like Bishop, confronts the body's betrayal through disease. Edna St. Vincent Millay, also, like Bishop, experienced her body through the mediation of illness and addiction. Unlike the other poets, however, Millay deliberately, consciously, and effectively used her body to promote her poetry and herself as poet, and the body that Millay put on display is an overtly, hyperfeminized one.[1] Just as each of these women experiences her body differently from the other, each poet "handles" the body differently in her poetry. Millay and Hacker write openly about the body and its attendant needs and desires; Bishop writes a poetics of the body that positions it in spaces of liminality—somewhere between celebration and abjection. Chin's poetic bodies manifest as constant reminders of the body's location in space and time. Despite these differences, the body is significant, intentionally and unintentionally, in the work of Millay, Bishop, Chin, and Hacker.

Although Hacker's poetics of the body often echo her own personal experiences with disease, aging, sex, and sexuality, her poetry and her body maintain a separation, as does Chin's body and the immigrant body that often marks her poetry. This separation proves crucial to perceptions of artistic and literary merit. Historically, when the gap between the woman poet and her poetry narrows or disappears, the "literariness" of the work often becomes questionable. I am speaking specifically about when the poem and poetry, or both, are *perceived* as extensions of the bodily person of the poet, an extension that occurred in the case of Millay, as my earlier reference to a reviewer's observation that Millay's "poems were as well-turned as her own slim ankle" indicates. However, those who find fault with too close of a connection between the poet and the poem seldom question biographical impulses that might propel a work. Apparently, these impulses do not undermine the value of the poetry. However, as feminist scholarship has revealed, the cultural production of women often suffers marginalization because this production seems too embodied. Thus works that seem too womanly also seem to adhere too closely to the (female) body, which mires them in sentiment, sensibility, or silliness. Specifically referencing Millay, Sandra Gilbert identifies one of the difficulties facing early twentieth-century women poets as the "inescapable link between female anatomy and literary destiny, between the perceived body of the 'feminine' poet and the body of her work" (299). Certainly, it proves nearly impossible to discuss Millay's work without attention to Millay as the person with all her physical attributes and her carefully crafted presentation of those attributes.

Although I will, indeed, address these elements in the following pages, I will attempt to keep in place some distance between the "real" Millay and her poetic personae. The biographical connections to the poems that make up Millay's "body" of work do prove interesting. Yet these connections can map intentionality onto the poems in such a way as to limit the larger significance of the poetry itself. Thus, at times in this analysis, I will keep in mind C. C. Barfoot's point that "ultimately it does not matter [if we identify the poet with the speaker] as long as we pay due regard to the poetic speech itself. As long as the poetry sustains the passions and resolve that it expresses, we do not need to seek its grounds or cause in biography" (98). Conversely, among scholars of Millay's work, all readings, interpretations, analyses, and explanations carry with them knowledge of Millay's biography as well as a clear picture of the poet herself.

Ironically, the scholarship on Millay gets caught up in the very paradigms in which and against which Millay struggled: how to write about the body when the only language available to do so carries with it the cultural biases regarding the body itself or, perhaps more accurately, how to represent (in Millay's case) and to theorize (in my case) the body without essentializing the representation or theorization. This dilemma arises directly from the mind-body dichotomy that underwrites the transcendent-immanent, active-passive, male-female, masculine-feminine, voyeur-exhibitionist, and sadistic-masochistic binaries, all of which prove relevant to Millay's poetics of the body. Millay's use of the body as metaphor, her representations of the body, and the womanliness that often manifests in her poetry destabilize these binaries while simultaneously reinforcing them. Because her poetry seems to both challenge and reinscribe dominant ideologies regarding gender as did her self-presentations, no certainty exists regarding the place of the body in Millay's work. The resistance to disciplining systems, I believe, arises not from Millay's literal or figurative "doing of gender." Gender performance itself does not necessarily challenge or resist notions of the fixedness of gender; rather, the *ambiguity* of the performance creates the resistance. In the case of Millay, when confronted with the hyperfeminine, one can never be sure whether the performance, the poetic voice, or poetic body signals internalization of patriarchy's construction of woman *or* mockery of that construction. I argue that it is this inability to know, this uncertainty, that challenges notions of gender and sexuality. In Millay's poetry, then, the body, with its attendant desires, needs, and behaviors, becomes a place of intersection. Resistance and compliance merge in Millay's poetic body, therefore holding all certainties regarding gender in suspension.

My arguments regarding Millay and body poetics do not generate from a desire to prove Millay's intentional resistance to hegemonic ideologies. Drawing on the work of Carole-Anne Tyler, I approach Millay with the following questions in mind: Can we ever identify resistance or subversiveness beyond intention? If Millay intends resistance and *we* miss it, is the work resistive? If Millay presents the hyperfeminine because she trusts its "naturalness" and value *within* patriarchy and *we* read hyperfemininity as a strategy to expose the constructedness of femininity *by* patriarchy, is the work subversive? Despite these questions and the opposing theoretical perspectives they suggest, I propose that Millay's representations of the body open a space for dialogue beyond intentionality—the intentions of the poet and of the critic (Does she intend to be subversive or does she not? Am I imposing my intentions or hers on the work?). I believe that ultimately Millay's poetic bodies do indeed threaten gender ideologies in part because the body in her poetry resists *and* complies. Millay's ability to out-fetishize male fetishism with her poetic representations of the body puts into question masculinity itself.

Millay often presents the female body as the object of the male gaze and as the fetishized object, and, as Cheryl Walker so brilliantly argues, Millay also presents the female body as the object of exchange. These presentations can exemplify internalized oppression or sexism if we read these poetic representations as depictions of Millay's own body. Of course, this reading involves conflating the poet and her artistic creations, a move that restricts female artistic production to the person of the artist. However, in most instances,

Millay's presentations of the body generate from the perspective or voice of
what Gilbert calls the "female female impersonator." In other words, Mil-
lay often offers the body from the subject position of the hyperfeminine.
This hyperfemininity co-opts the power of the male to objectify, fetishize,
and commodify the female body (under the terms of patriarchy, this power
both defines and bolsters masculinity). In some ways, this co-option renders
the masculine as superfluous. Admittedly, the body that emerges here does
not look much different than the female body in much of male discourse;
however, a careful reading—one that perceives some critical distance between
Millay the poet and the speaker of the poems—reveals this fetishization,
objectification, and commodification as artificial or artifice rather than natu-
ral. In other words, these poems exhibit a play with the body and its attendant
sexualities, a play usually lacking in male descriptions of the female body and
female sexuality. Although some of the poetic bodies that Millay presents
fall into the Madonna/whore paradigm, most do not. Instead, Millay gives a
multitude of bodies: sexualized, gendered, virgin, sexually experienced, exces-
sive, restrained, aging, disguised, veiled, clothed, unclothed, fetishized, objec-
tified, female female, desiring, desired, iconic.

These bodies appear and reappear throughout most of Millay's poetry. The
following poems, however, seem to most clearly illustrate Millay's poetics of
the body: "The Witch Wife" from *Renascence* (1917); "First Fig" and "Sec-
ond Fig" from *A Few Figs from Thistles* (1920); "I being born a woman and
distressed" and "Oh, oh you will be sorry for that word!" from *The Harp-
Weaver* (1923); various sonnets from *Fatal Interview* (1931); and "The Plaid
Dress" from *Huntsman, What Quarry?* (1939). While I cannot in this present
study provide an in-depth analysis of all the aforementioned poems, each
does emerge in what follows, and although I introduced these poems in the
chronology of their publication, my analysis and close readings do not neces-
sarily address the poems chronologically. Finally, before turning to Millay's
poetry itself, I look first at instances of Millay's self-presentation.

In his biography of Millay, Daniel Epstein relates that "one night
[in 1920] Millay [along with Edmund Wilson and John Peale Bishop]
decided to write comic self-portraits" (135). Millay's contribution echoes
her earlier description of the famous 1913 Arnold Geneth photograph
of a very young Millay "standing among the magnolia blossoms [that]
would become the blaze in American poetry as [Millay's] own" (Mil-
ford 117). Millay wrote of this photo, "Besides having beautiful hair, an
extraordinary good forehead in spite of the freckles, an impudent, aggres-
sive, & critical nose, and a mysterious mouth . . . I have, artistically, &
even technically, an unusually beautiful throat" (qtd. in Milford 117).[2] In
1920, Millay offered the following description of her person:

E. St. V. M.

> Hair which she still devoutly trusts is red . . .
> A large mouth
> Lascivious,
> Asceticized by blasphemies.
> A long throat,
> Which will someday
> Be strangled . . .
> A small body,
> Unexclamatory
> But which,
> Were it the fashion to wear no clothes,
> Would be as well dressed
> As any. (*Letters* 99–100)

In her analysis of this self-portrait, Walker comments that "Millay's positive body-consciousness at first seems a cause for celebration," and she sees "self-irony" in Millay's reference to "the throat which will one day 'be strangled'" (*Masks* 138–39). Walker then proceeds to show how the self-description fails as a celebratory moment by identifying "two peculiar aspects in [Millay's] self-portrait": violence that indicates "the vulnerability of women under patriarchy" and the suggestion "that women are 'on the market,' objects to be scrutinized" (*Masks* 138–39). I would like to extend the implications of Walker's first two insights and argue that in this self-depiction Millay presents the (her) body as ironic and ambiguous, and ultimately very threatening.

Twenty-eight at the time, Millay unabashedly offers a self-portrait that focuses on the body as desirous and desiring: "Lascivious" indicates a mouth inclined to lustfulness *and* capable of arousing sexual desire. The next line, "Asceticized by blasphemies," initiates the ambiguity that I believe dominates the rest of Millay's self-description, a description that begins straightforwardly with reference to that famous red hair. What implications, however, arise here? Millay's words can refer to both speech and behavior. What utterances have enforced abstinence (asceticism) on the mouth, or what behaviors have moved this mouth to self-mortification? This ambiguity that withholds an "answer" reflects the female body's fraught position within a disciplinary system predicated on sexual difference. In such a system, the female body must behave (present itself) in ways to invite desire while simultaneously assuming a position of self-abasement or masochism. The female mouth must open to ingest patriarchal dictates, and it must abstain from irreverent utterances against masculine prerogatives.

Indeed, Millay seemingly complies with these mandates as she suggests censure, offers her throat—the location of voice—up for slaughter, and makes clear her "small body['s]" inability to cry out. However, Millay undercuts this seeming compliance with the word "but." Millay evokes the metaphor of fashion—dressing the body to *undress* the body. This notion of undressing recurs in Millay's poem "The Plaid Dress," written much later, which I will address at length later in this chapter. In the closing lines of the self-portrait, Millay ironizes the notion of covering the body as she presents a body dressed in nakedness, and as the last two lines clearly state, she feels no shame in the body itself (and in this case, the body *is* Millay's as she *chooses* to present it). In this sense then, this self-portrait does celebrate the body and its power of self-presentation. Furthermore, Millay may describe a body open to the male gaze, a lustful and seductive mouth, a vulnerable throat, and a nude body; however, the mouth is big, the throat long, and the body small. The threat then to the male gaze rests in the excess (bigness and length) of voice. Millay the poet and Millay the body speak, and as a speaker, she or it claims agency within a system that seeks to deny such agency and to silence such "mouthiness." The ambiguity, which the words and phrases of this description suggest, opens a space to read against the grain while also recognizing the elements that disturb Walker (*Masks* 139).

Within this space Millay can flaunt her body, yet even here, in this self-portrait not for public consumption, she plays with words, choosing and placing them to confuse and ironize their meaning. In this description Millay, as she did throughout her life, strikes a pose. This posing or self-styling highlights the artifice of the white female body and white femininity. Does Millay then speak as a female female impersonator, and does she present a female female body? Does she here work through the masquerade as Suzanne Clark suggests in "Uncanny Millay"? In order to answer these questions, I must clarify the terms. In "Female Female Impersonator: Millay and the Theater of Personality," Gilbert argues that both Millay and Marianne Moore "translated the 'handicap' of 'femininity' into aesthetic advantage" albeit in very different ways (297). Millay, Gilbert insists, "generally presented herself as a prototypical *femme fatale*," which I take to mean Millay both seduces and betrays. Within the conventional understanding of femme fatale, the seduction and betrayal often initiates chaos for the male. However, ultimately they result in the death or punishment of the "bad woman," the one who attempts to use her femininity to her advantage. Casting Millay as the femme fatale seems to condemn her to the same fate.[3] Gilbert seems to use the terms "femme fatale" and "female female impersonator" interchangeably although the female female impersonator does not seem to suggest the ultimate down-fall of the poser herself. The female female impersonator does, in Gilbert's view, utilize "the feminine masquerade as a response to the feminization-as-trivialization with which contemporary literary culture greeted [Millay and Moore]" (300), and as such, female female impersonation translates into a strategy whereby a woman consciously dons femininity in order to claim legitimacy *as* a woman. In other words, a woman takes on another layer of femininity thus doubling it or becoming hyperfeminine. As Tyler notes, however, impersonation contains within it seeds of narcissism, and "female impersonation is conformity and critique, paradoxically suggesting there is something *beyond* it that is *within* it" (4, emphasis in original). Millay's "masquerade," her female female impersonation, or her presentation of the femme fatale involves this very paradox: she must be female to "play" female, to posit something outside femaleness. She then evokes a hyperfemininity that works on the level of paradox subverting and reinforcing sexual difference. Millay's poetic bodies perpetuate this paradox. Importantly, however, the paradox in and of itself becomes the resistance because its existence bespeaks uncertainty, and this uncertainty upends gender certainties.

In both "First Fig" and "Second Fig," Millay presents the body through metaphor, a candle in the former and a house in the latter. Both poems resonate with a defiance of conventionality, and readers of "First Fig" instantly align both the defiance and the candle with the poet herself.[4] After all, this "It-girl" embodied the independence and spirit of the Jazz Age as she flirted with bohemianism, paraded her promiscuity, and mocked public morality. Apparently, this "self-projection . . . stole the show . . . [and] suited a loud and raucous jazz-age temper" (Stanbrough 213). In "First Fig" the speaker proclaims,

> My candle burns at both ends;
>
> It will not last the night;
> But ah, my foes, and oh, my friends—
>
> It gives a lovely light! (127)

This poem, suggestive of hedonistic pleasure or, at the very least, unrestrained pleasure, acknowledges the results of "giving into one's body." The "ah" and "oh" may signal regret, but the last line with its ending exclamation point negates this notion. Obviously, pleasure outweighs consequences, and this stance marks the body as masochistic hence female. Herein, however, lies the paradox: despite the passivity implied by masochism, acting on and fulfilling her desires constructs the speaker as the agent of her own pleasure. This body then becomes hypercompliant thus hyperfeminine in order to actively claim pleasure. Walker tells us that "taken literally, the candle that burns at both ends is a stick of dynamite" (*Masks* 138). Although the results might be the same, a candle burning at both ends disintegrates much more slowly than does a stick of dynamite, and the candle "gives a lovely light" rather than a blinding flash.

In "Second Fig," Millay extends the idea of loveliness and its connection to the ephemeral and impermanent:

> Safe upon the solid rock the ugly houses stand;
> Come and see my shining palace built upon the sand! (127)

As she does in "First Fig," Millay ends this poem with an exclamation point that marks the body as exclamatory in contrast to the "unexclamatory" one that she described in her self-portrait. This sense of exuberance, suggested by the ending punctuation, indicates a celebration of the body. However, the celebration, like the body itself with its attendant pleasures and beauty, proves fleeting.

In these two very brief poems, Millay craftily seduces and betrays, a la the femme fatale. The speaker of "Second Fig" invites the gaze—"Come and see"—and both poems work on the level of the visual, light and looking. Millay presents a body enticing in its "shining" brilliance or seductive in its "lovely light." Although both poems delineate the destruction of the body, they simultaneously indicate annihilation directed outward from the body. If, indeed, the candle burning at both ends can be read as dynamite, then no one in its vicinity is safe. Here self-destruction promises collateral damage.[5] In the second poem, the palace built on sand will surely collapse, and in so doing, it will destroy not only itself but also anyone who enters it. These metaphors then (candle and house) present the body as masochistic, seductive, and duplicitous (read feminine), and this presentation upholds femininity as constructed by male desire and anxiety. The body in "First Fig" and "Second Fig" also challenges and threatens the foundations of masculinity in two ways: first, these two poems posit some agency in these positions, and second, the poems suggest the possibility of disrupting patriarchy through compliancy. Thus can masculinity remain intact if femininity is only an act with the potential to explode or collapse? These two poems raise this question, but they do not necessarily answer it. "First Fig" and "Second Fig" present a body that both complies and threatens gender ideologies. This ambiguity marks the female body as suspect within a system dependent on stabilized and coherent gender identities. The onlooker or reader can never quite be sure of the performance or representation of femininity in Millay's poetry.

Another critical element emerges from the complicated layering of femininity that takes place in Millay's poetry—mimicry. Is Millay mimicking femininity that suggests a *doing*, or is she donning it which suggest a *presentation*? Again I turn to Tyler, who asks, "What makes mimicry different from masquerade or feminine identity if [feminine identity] is also an alienated and alienating relation to an image of the self?" (24). This question proves crucial in arguing for the body's function in Millay's poetry. On the one hand, Gilbert, Clark, and Walker as well as I must assume that female female impersonation, masquerade, and self-commodification create a distance between woman (Millay) and her feminine identity, but, as Tyler points out, that identity is itself a distance from the "self" *and* it enacts a distance. On the other hand, I argue that the impossibility of resolving the paradox of femininity as it exists within a system founded on sexual difference generates resistance. If femininity always positions the woman estranged from her image of the self, then female female impersonation, masquerade, and mimicry provide the illusion that the female creates the distance or that these strategies widen the gap in order to give women room to move.

Both theorists of mimicry and of masquerade perceive resistance and agency in each strategy, and each group privileges one over the other. Tyler explains the slight variance between mimicry and masquerade: "The female mimic—self-aware, self-conscious—apparently knows what she is up to. She is up to her neck in patriarchy, but her head is clear . . . The female masquerader, equally bogged down in patriarchy . . . flaunts but apparently does not flout her femininity, and so remains mired in masculinism" (28). However, Tyler argues that ultimately mimicry does not prove any more liberating, subversive, or effective than masquerade: "The best intentions guarantee nothing. A woman's intending to repeat the feminine with a difference may enable her to have a different relationship to femininity but may have no such effect on men—or other women for that matter" (28).

Tyler's arguments return us to the question of intention and intentionality's relation to resistance. Through her poetic bodies, does Millay deliberately seek to create a distance between a woman's image of the self and heterosexual patriarchy's image of woman? To restate the question a bit differently, are the moments of mimicry, masquerade, and female female impersonation, which we identify in both Millay's poetry and her performance of her poems, empty gestures, strategies to foreclose the alienating aspects of feminine identity, or examples of internalized heterosexism, genderism, or sexism? I believe that Millay's poetics of the body signals her acceptance of the terms of white femininity constructed within and by patriarchy, *and* her poetics disrupts, subverts, and threatens these terms. I can no more pin down Millay's intentions than I can pin down her poetics bodies, nor do I seek to do either. Rather, I wish to point out instances where mimicry, masquerade, and female female impersonation manifest in Millay's poems and to posit that these instances provide keen insight into the body's defiance *and* compliance in systems of desire, exchange, and sexual difference.

Although the body serves as a nexus of desire, exchange, and difference in "The Plaid Dress," it stands in stark contrast to the body Millay presents in "First Fig" and "Second Fig." Certainly by the time "The Plaid Dress" appears in 1939, Millay experienced and understood her body differently than she did in the 1920s. Typical of early reviews of Millay's work, the following comments from *Bookman* (1922) illustrate the public fascination with the poet's youth and body: "Edna St. Vincent Millay is a slim young person with chestnut-brown hair shot with glints of bronze and copper . . . ; a slightly snub nose, and freckles; a child mouth, a cool grave voice; and grey-green eyes . . . When reading her poetry, she will seem to be the awed spectator a fragile little girl with apple blossom face" (107). More tellingly, writing in 1950 after Millay's death, John Ciardi explains the faltering of Millay's literary and public reputation, and he explicitly ties her fall from favor to her loss of youth: "Symbolically, Edna Millay's power to thrill and carry the reader seemed to end with [the 1920s]. For what made the poems immediate was the passionate youngness of their author. And suddenly it was years later and the youngness had fled . . . The simple fact seems to be that, having outgrown her youth, Edna Millay had outgrown the one subject she could make exciting" (160). Apparently, as Millay matured, as her body aged, she was no longer capable of captivating readers, and, according to Ciardi's assessment, only while "inhabiting" a young body is the female poet able to write exciting poetry. Millay understood this cult of youth, and she used her youth, body, and femininity to her advantage early in her career.

Millay, as many scholars note, found great currency in her body. In her public appearances and readings, she presented herself as spectacle—as the embodiment of a poetess: "Her reading appearances . . . [became] triumphs of trailing gowns and far-flung gestures" (Ciardi 157). In fact, Millay "would act her poems with her whole body" (Kennedy 97). Clark provides the following details regarding Millay's public persona: "She would appear in a long gown for readings, her voice dramatic, her form girlish and attractive, more like a diva than like the gray-suited male poet" (5).

Walker likens Millay's public exploitation and self-commodification of her body to Madonna's self-marketing and self-objectification.[6] Unlike Madonna, however, Millay failed to repackage the public image as she aged. Epstein presents a harsh description of the poet at age forty-seven: "The image she saw in the mirror was disturbing. Alcohol and drugs had taken a fateful, undeniable toll. Her body sagged, her lips shriveled, her teeth were discolored, and pain had engraved her face" (255). Thus Walker's observation that the tone of many of the poems in *Huntsman, What Quarry?* "vacillates between irate defensiveness and despondency" proves insightful and accurate ("The Female Body" 85).

"The Plaid Dress" opens with the speaker's plea to the sun to bleach the colors from the dress she wears. This dress of purple, red, yellow, and green plaid cannot be "unmade" nor can it be taken off. Instead, it remains unseen, "lining the [speaker's] subtle gown" (348). This dress lies underneath the clothes, and the poem puts into question "the very substance of the body" (Walker, "The Female Body" 86). "The Plaid Dress" also foregrounds the speaker's ambivalence toward her body, and, by extension, Millay once again presents a body that refuses definition. The poem offers a body marked by violence while simultaneously marking the body as angry, ashamed, treacherous, passive, and rash:

> This violent plaid
> Of purple angers and red shames; the yellow stripe
> Of thin but valid treacheries; the flashy green of kind deeds done
> Through indolence, high judgments given in haste;
> The recurring checker of the serious breach of taste? (348)

A system of exchange, commodification, and desire where the body's worth and value depend on the spectacle of the body itself guarantees disappointment, frustration, and anger. Ultimately, the body will indeed lose its luster; inevitably, its appeal will wane, its usefulness diminish— such is the nature of the physical body, although perhaps not of one's self–body image. I believe, however, that the last line of the stanza undercuts the tone of "middle-aged dissatisfaction," which Walker identifies in the first stanza of "The Plaid Dress" ("The Female Body" 86). Millay of the earlier poems appears here with the tongue-in-cheek observation about the body's violation of taste. Does the plaid dress (aging body) present an affront to good taste, style, class, sophistication, refinement, elegance, or judgment, or to all these things? Thus Millay highlights the body's audacity here. This moment of irony precludes one interpretation of the body in this poem. Although the speaker may not like the body's disruptive quality here, she finds some humor in it, and the poem does offer a body defiant of restrictions and decorum.

The unreliability of the body and its "undefinability" points to the paradox of predicating gender on the body. Although the body in "The Plaid Dress" retrains some of the attributes of ideal femininity, passivity, and perhaps, shame, it seems to have shed many of the markers of that ideal. Is the body in this poem no longer feminine, no longer the exhibitionist object of the male gaze? Typical of Millay's poetics of the body, this poem troubles our attempts to "pin down the body." However, I do see fetishism at work here. In a psychoanalytical register, fetishism refers to a substitution, specifically putting something in place to mask a loss, the loss of the phallus. The speaker of "The Plaid Dress," cannot bear to confront the absence of her firm flesh; therefore, she dresses the body. She covers its nakedness with the plaid dress; however, this dressing becomes the body while simultaneously distancing the woman from the body and from her image of the self. The speaker fetishizes the covering in order to avoid looking at the loss. In this sense, the poem presents the paradox of femininity: femininity itself is both alienating and an alienation.

Whereas in her self-portrait, Millay claims nakedness itself *as* fashion, in this poem, she costumes the body in nakedness. In "The Plaid Dress," nakedness does not reveal; rather, it covers:

> No more uncoloured than unmade,
> I fear, can be this garment that I may not doff;
> Confession does not strip it off,
> To send me homeward eased and bare;
> All though the formal, unoffending evening under the clean
> Bright hair,
> Lining the subtle gown . . . it is not seen,
> But it is there. (348)

The speaker cannot lay bare the body, perhaps because she cannot bear the sight of it; however, the poem does present a description of the body. The speaker describes what she sees, so the body emerges as the object of the gaze. The question then becomes, whose gaze? The poem certainly posits a woman speaker. However, can a woman see her body free from the mediation of the patriarchal gaze? "The Plaid Dress" seems to suggest no. The speaker sees a body through the mediation of patriarchal ideals regarding beauty, youth, and the body and reads her body as a text created by male prerogatives and written on by male discourse. However, I believe that the irony of the body's "breach of taste" underscores its unreliability in the very system that seeks to essentialize it and render it immobile. Disciplining systems can cast the body as female, can mark it as feminine, can gender it and sexualize it, but Millay repeatedly acknowledges the body's potential to misbehave—to breach the limits of decorum. In reading the body in "The Plaid Dress," we must not forget that the body unseen, but there, is that same body that, despite violence, anger, and shame, refuses to conform. This body, like the bodies in "First Fig" and "Second Fig," carries a threat, a threat that generates by its seeming acquiescence in its devaluation.

Even at their most enchanting, Millay's poetic bodies taunt, tantalize, and threaten. The male speaker of "Witch-Wife" acknowledges that his wife can "never be all [his]" because she is neither this nor that, "neither pink nor pale" (46). Interestingly, one could read this reference to skin color as a rejection of white femininity, perhaps suggesting a stain on racial purity. Clearly, the woman in this poem refuses categorization and relegation to an either-or paradigm, and this refusal implies the inability both of male discourse and gaze to delineate and contain femininity or female sexuality. The male in the poem can identify what the female *is not* but has difficulty identifying what she *is*. In this space of nondefinition, the female body generates unease in the male, a discomfort caused by a fully exposed excessiveness:

> She has more hair than she needs;
> In the sun 'tis a woe to me! (46)

In this poem Millay utilizes the realm of the spectacular to present the body. Excessive female sexuality, femininity, or femaleness remains in view, and importantly, the spectacle of the female body does not function as a male fetish because rather than alleviate anxiety, the spectacle of too much femininity *becomes* the male's anguish. This distress occurs because the male cannot control the image; he cannot fetishize the woman. The witch-wife possesses more hair than the male deems necessary, and this surplus disrupts the masking power of the fetish, instead revealing the male's inability to contain the excess or to fully posses the woman.

The body in "Witch-Wife," as it does in much of Millay's poetics of the body, complies with patriarchal dictates. However, here again, this compliance contains noncompliance:

> She loves me all that she can,
>
> And her ways to my ways resign;
> But she was not made for any man,
>
> And she never will be mine. (46)

Does the resignation of the woman signal acceptance and acquiescence, or merely an acknowledgment of gender expectations? Clearly, the speaker sees slippage in the woman's compliance. He recognizes that this witch-wife withholds complete submission. Something (her sexuality, her desire, her "self," her image of the self) exceeds the male's grasps; something escapes patriarchal censure.

In the opening stanza, the speaker explains that this witch-wife "learned her hands in a fairy-tale, / And her mouth on a valentine," thereby pointing to gender socialization (46). The woman heard the stories of princesses waiting for prince charming and learned the words of romanticized love. However, "witch" suggests that the woman attended more closely to the stories of women outside the feminine ideal, women holding power to disrupt and challenge male authority—witches. Perhaps, the woman also recognized the sentimental presentation of romanticized and ideal love—lacy valentines offering only clichés—and realized that patriarchal discourse imbues the language of love with empty words meant to trivialize and infantilize emotions. Obviously, then the lessons of patriarchy failed because the woman learned to read against the grain. The witch-wife becomes adept at acting a part, the part of dutiful wife. The last two lines give rise to yet another ambiguity: if not made for any man, is the witch-wife perhaps made for a woman? While subtle, this alternative further complicates the presentation of the female body. "Witch-wife" marks the body as ironic and paradoxical, and these markings open a space for us to read resistance in Millay's poetry whether or not she intends this resistance.

As I noted in the opening of this chapter, analysis of Millay's work almost always carries with it knowledge of Millay's public performances of her poetry. In those public moments, the poetry became a specific body as Millay presented *her* body to the audience. Thus, when Millay recited, "I, being born a woman and distressed," or "What lips my lips have kissed," her listeners often understood the "I" to be Millay. As spectacle, Millay literally offered a material body and, in so doing, moves the body from the realm of the universal to that of the particular. Rather than signifying the category of "woman," Millay's literal and figurative body points to *this woman* and to a femininity specific to *this* performing body at *this* particular moment. However, in the register of performativity, slippage once again occurs.

In her readings, Millay performs both her poetry and her femininity. In donning her "loose velvet gown with red-and-gold braid . . . [and] black velvet cape" (Kennedy 97), Millay puts on her persona of poet—woman poet. This "putting on" involves both masquerade and mimicry:

costuming her body and imitating femininity. Certainly we can read intentionality in both of these acts. Millay intends to play a part. Whether that part indicates complicity with or resistance to the hegemonic and interlocking systems of patriarchy and capitalism does not necessarily depend on intention. The mere act of performing denotes an acting of a part and connotes a distance from the "real." The performative aspect means performing an act by the very fact of uttering. Therefore, to read Millay's public presentations of herself and her poetry within a framework of the performative collapses presenting, saying, and being into one another. Millay's readings evoke all of these aspects of performance. By *acting* the part of a woman poet, Millay simultaneously becomes that poet and renders "woman poet" a creation of the acting, and when she utters, "I, being a woman born," she enacts woman. My point here is that the body that Millay puts on display resists interpretation as much as the bodies in her poetry do. The Millay onstage may *be* the essence of white femininity, or she may be *doing* femininity in order to ironize the notion of gender itself. Both her material performing body and her poetic bodies potentially blur the boundary between compliance and resistance. This potential combined with the paradox, which I argue proves characteristic of Millay's poetic bodies, positions the body as a place of tension in her poetry. The existence of this tension generating from the body's indecipherability in Millay's work continually challenges a system that privileges masculinity over femininity. The body that circulates throughout Millay's poetry vacillates between submissiveness and rebelliousness. Moreover, Millay's wit and irony undercut the stasis of the body within systems predicated on sexual difference and reveal, instead, the dynamics of the body. She dresses both her material (real) body and her poetic bodies in layers of costume that may or may not construct, deconstruct, or *be* the body itself.

As many scholars argue, Millay's bodily performance and the body in her poetry suggest the epitome of femininity, the female female impersonator, masquerade, mimicry, and (self) commodification. Now, I add drag to the list. Derek Furr relates that at least one viewer of a Millay reading labeled it a drag performance.[7] After a 1925 reading by Millay at Bowdoin College, "an undergraduate reporter . . . argues that [she] has essentially duped 'a predominately masculine audience.' Her 'femininity, charm, graciousness, good acting' are a 'subtle drag'" (99), and this reporter goes on to express indignantly that "the dean of the college . . . critics and the public . . . would dare compare the poetess to 'Byron himself'" (99). Furr goes on to argue that Millay, indeed, invokes a comparison to Byron because "like her romantic precursor, Millay embodied an ideal of the poet and the poetic. She was intentionally feminine, enchanting, and dramatic, as he was masculine, melancholy, and daring . . . To suggest, however, that the act was insincere is to miss the point. Millay and Byron *were* their performances of themselves" (99–100). Then, in a footnote, Furr points out that "Millay was clearly aware of her Byronism. Her visit to Albania in 1921 is recorded in a photo that invokes the famous Phillips portrait of Byron in Albanian dress" (108). Given these various impersonations, I wonder just what Millay's drag entailed. Was Millay the ultimate drag performer "doing" femininity, or was she Byron "doing" femininity, or was she Millay "doing" Byron "doing" femininity? Her ability to engage in these complex impersonations and our inability to recognize a lone gender performance disturbs systems that depend on fixed gender categories for stability. Millay, however, literally entered the world confusing accepted and acceptable markers of gender.

Writing about Millay's birth, Milford relates that Millay's Aunt Clem wrote, "We have named the little one Edna St. Vincent Millay . . . Nell would have called it 'Vincent' if it had been a boy." Milford then notes, "They called her Vincent anyway" (18). Throughout her childhood and beyond, then, Millay answered to and claimed a "boy's" name. By all accounts, she was well aware of the impropriety of her name, and she also seemed aware of the freedom conferred by maleness. When one of Millay's grammar school teachers, Mr. Wilbur (also the school's principal) felt that her questions challenged his authority, he ridiculed her first name, Vincent: "He called her Violet, Veronica, Vivienne, Valerie, any name beginning with a V but her own" (Milford 5). The twelve-year-old Vincent refused to relinquish her moniker: "Yes, Mr. Wilbur. But my name is Vincent" (qtd. in Milford 5). Ironically, however, Vincent presented a very feminine appearance. A female teacher described Millay as "small and frail for a twelve-year-old . . . Her mane of red hair and enormous gray-green eyes added to the impression of her frailty, and her stubborn mouth and chin made her seem austere, almost to the point of grimness" (qtd. in Milford 5). As a prepubescent girl, Millay manifested the same ambiguity regarding femininity as she did in her later poetry readings and in her poetry itself. This teacher describes an "impression" of frailty that seems incongruous with the "stubborn mouth and chin." The contradiction that arises in this description, frail but stubborn, further frustrates attempts to pin down Millay's bodily self-presentation and her poetic representations of the female body. On one hand, Millay embodied ideal femininity—small, vulnerable, and inviting. She relished and exaggerated this embodiment. On the other hand, the poet acted aggressively, determinedly, and single-mindedly (unfeminine?). The hyperfeminine body and the masculine actions often occur simultaneously in both Millay's gender performances and poetry.

Indeed, as Stacy Carson Hubbard notes, Millay adopts "both masculine and feminine roles in [her use of] the sonnet" (102). Specifically, this critic points to the tradition of the carpe diem sonnet and the discourse of love associated with the sonnet tradition, in general, arguing that these elements "do not so much *veil* Millay's identity as a woman as make possible its performance, in the process revealing the instabilities of both gender and poetic authority" (101). Hubbard identifies an element of masquerade in the sonnet tradition itself: male desire "was always a masquerade of feminine weakness and sentimentality; wan, beseeching, and consumed by desire" (113). This masquerading becomes complicated when looking at Millay's poetry. Hubbard posits Millay's use of the sonnet also as a form of masquerade (although I see this move as transgendered or transvestism at the least): "Millay [the woman poet] masquerades as a male poet masquerading as a lovesick woman" (113). So, much like her "Byronism," Millay's sonnet writing presents complex layers of doing gender or gender performances.[8] This complexity remains whether one reads the process as masquerade, mimicry, or drag. A further complication arises in *Fatal Interview*: in assuming various poses throughout the sonnet cycle, "Millay filters her speaker's feelings through an array of often oblique, usually *paradoxical* metaphors based upon traditional, male-defined sexual protocols" (Peppe 52, emphasis added).

Regardless of their specific approach to or argument about *Fatal Interview*, scholars all, on some level, note the contradictions regarding the body, woman, and femininity that emerge from the poems. Milford finds Sonnet 47 both "revealing" and "covert"; the speaker "is both wounded and defiant" (332). Throughout the entire sonnet cycle, Holly Peppe sees "Millay's own *ambivalence* [regarding] male-female romantic relationships" (53, emphasis added). Robert Wiltenburg positions "mixed motives and effects at the heart of *Fatal Interview*" (289), and Ernest Smith writes of "the dialectic of commitment and self-emergence" (47). Although Walker begins her treatment of *Fatal Interview* by asserting that Millay's sonnet cycle "reflects that her body is a marked-down commodity unable to tear itself loose from the larger system of values that govern her culture,"[9] she ends her analysis with a list that implies the ambiguity of the body that circulates through these poems: "innocent and guilty," "aggressive and passive," "consumer and consumed" (*Masks* 157, 160). Walker concludes that Millay "tries to blot out half of each of these pairs of oppositions, making the female object wholly innocent, wholly passive, consumed by her madness" (160). Walker identifies failure in this attempt. Millay's attempt fails because the ambiguity of the gender performances in *Fatal Interview* makes it impossible to know if Millay's presentation of the body, femininity, and woman signals essentialism or constructionism.

Fatal Interview, generally acknowledged as Millay's most highly regarded collection, draws on the legend of Selene and Endymion.[10] Daniel Epstein writes, "Endymion's dreams have always been a symbol of the poet's vision, as Selene's kiss has been a symbol of the desire to posses the beloved for all time in the fullness of his beauty" (204). Within the framework of eternal desire and anguish then, the fifty-two sonnet cycle details a love affair from a woman's point of view (but as Hubbard argues, Millay presents this account through the conventions of the sonnet, a form typically aligned with *male* desire and discourse). Paradox, contradiction, and ambiguity mark the sonnets that comprise *Fatal Interview*, and in what follows, I will argue that within this collection, Millay's poetics refuses to present a body easily read as compliant or resistive; instead, *Fatal Interview* presents an uninterpretable body. This denial of interpretation reconstitutes effective resistance *as* that which refuses clear identification *as* resistance. This ambiguity, an ambiguity of the gender performance in the sonnets, makes it difficult to identify the object (body) in need of discipline and punishment.

Millay presents love as the subject of *Fatal Interview*, and by situating love in relation to the story of Selene and Endymion, she implies the aggressiveness of the female and the unawareness of the of the male beloved, an unawareness that renders the man incapable of reciprocity.[11] This framework, however, adds to the paradoxes that circulate through the sonnets. The story itself has several versions, one at least casting Selene as an enchantress and another presenting her as driven mad by Endymion's inability to consciously desire her. *Fatal Interview* manifests the same contradictions (women as agent of her desire or woman destroyed by male [in]action). Does Millay celebrate female sexual desire? Does she present a model of female resistance by rejecting the censure of female sexuality that exceeds the limits of that sexuality as delineated by patriarchy? Does she threaten masculinity itself by co-opting attributes of male sexuality? Does Millay punish woman for her sexual desires by rendering them as illnesses? Does she represent woman as essentially masochistic? Do these sonnets, the story of a woman's love and desire, illustrate internalized sexism? Millay does all these things, and she does so through metaphors of the body and representations of the body itself. Ultimately, *Fatal Interview* does not resolve the contradictions that it presents. Because the poems hold in suspension the celebratory and the abject, the defiant and the compliant, the constructed and the essentialized body, they both sustain and challenge a gender hierarchy predicated on sexual difference. Furthermore, I believe the inability to recognize clear resistance or compliance in Millay's poetics of the body poses the greatest threat here.

The unknowability itself creates a space of resistance because the inability to know means the inability to be certain. Uncertainty initiates anxiety, in this case, uncertainty and anxiety about female desire and sexuality. The speaker of *Fatal Interview* implicitly and explicitly expresses sexual desire and often initiates the sexual encounters or aligns herself with mythical women who do so. She bemoans her lover's attention to the tales of courtly love[12] and asks him to "shift [his] concern to living bones instead," and without subtlety, she articulates her sexual desire:

> More bland the ichor of a ghost should run
> Along your dubious veins than the rude sea
> Of passion pounding all day long in me. (635)

The speaker claims a sexual desire that surpasses that of the male, his "bland" and dead, hers oceanic and powerful. These lines simultaneously relegate the woman to the stereotypically feminine position of loving more *and* place her in the traditional position of the persona of the male sonneteer, "wan, beseeching, and consumed by desire" (to return to Hubbard's point). These lines also posit a female sexuality more vigorous than that of the male.

In Sonnet 39, the woman admits to insatiate desire: "I drank and thirsted still" (668), and in a later sonnet in the sequence, she graphically describes the psychical and emotional intensity of her desires:

> Mistake me not—unto my inmost core
> I do desire your kiss upon my mouth;
> They have not craved a cup of water more
> That bleach upon the deserts of the south. (674)

The metaphor of thirst configures sexual desire as an essential physical need, and in these poems, Millay locates this need in the female body. Here, as throughout *Fatal Interview*, the speaker actively and blatantly claims her sexual desires, and she displays excessive sexuality without tempering that presentation with guile or coyness. She legitimizes her desires by claiming a connection to the women of myth, and she sees in herself the

> unregenerate passions of a day
> When treacherous queens
> Heedless and wilful took their knights to bed. (655)

"Unregenerate," "treacherous," "heedless," and "wilful" point to the speaker's understanding of the transgressive aspects of her desires and actions. In these lines, we can read an open resistance to patriarchal mandates regarding appropriate female behavior, *or* we can discern internalization of those mandates. The contradictions that mark the sonnets in *Fatal Interview* clearly emerge here: does Millay merely present and reinforce the Madonna/whore dichotomy or does she challenge that split? Her intention as well as a definitive reading proves irrelevant; rather, the uncertainty itself disturbs the binary. This ambiguity combined with Millay's poetic transgendered voice (that of a woman impersonating the persona of the male sonneteer speaking as a woman) puts into question regulatory systems that place women in either-or positions that insist on the fixity of gender and that freely discipline the female body.

Traditional gender ideologies attempt to restrain, contain, and at times, punish female sexual aggressiveness as well as excessive female sexuality. These same ideologies also configure women as masochistic, as desiring objects of male sexual aggression. Millay seems to uphold these traditional models of femininity as she renders the woman the willing "victim of love" at the mercy of a "beast." In these poems the speaker emerges as a woman brutalized by her longing, a longing so intense it causes bodily harm, wounding and scaring the body. Evoking the metaphor of fire, the speaker's desire causes a "fever," indicating both passion and illness and, in either case, causing destruction to the body. In Sonnet 4, Millay continues this metaphor of the ill body:

> Nay, learnèd doctor, these fine leeches fresh
> From the pond's edge my cause cannot remove. (633)

Although Millay pathologizes female sexual desire, it resists the "cures" offered by patriarchy, and although "a sick disorder in [the] flesh," female desire proves "deeper than [a doctor's] skill" (633). However, the incurability of female desire (disease) hints at the contaminating aspects of unrestrained female sexuality. This "disease" must be cordoned off, relegated to the fringes, deemed abnormal, and labeled madness. Thus quarantined, excessive female desire and sexuality destroys only the carrier (the mad Selene of legend or the madwoman in the attic).

In *Fatal Interview*, Millay evokes and continues these stories of transgressive and threatening female desire. The speaker likens love and desire to a prison inhabited with those who fill "the dungeon with their piteous woes" (643).[13] However, she holds herself apart from those others unwillingly incarcerated and straining for freedom. Instead, the woman finds

> that [her] chains throughout their iron length
> make such a golden clank upon [her] ear. (634)

The picture of a shackled woman "loving" her chains invokes images of sadomasochism that render the female body bound and passive. The speaker in these sonnets declares that even if she possessed the strength to escape, she would not do so. Millay depicts a body willingly imprisoned by desire, and although she suggests power in that willingness, she also makes clear that the body lacks agency (strength) to free itself. Whatever control the speaker claims here diminishes as the female body becomes the masochistic one "drowned in love and weedily washed ashore" (636). Millay renders the female body passive,

> fretted by the drag and shove
> At the tide's edge. (636)

Despite the speaker's sexual bravado and her forthright acknowledgments of sexual passion, these images reinscribe the feminine as the place of abjection. They further reinforce perceptions of femininity as essentially passive and submissive, women essentially reliant upon male desire, and female sexuality always in need of containment. Unable to represent a female sexuality outside of male influence, Millay cannot sustain the transgressive aspects of the speaker's sexuality. By using the tropes of illness, imprisonment, and bondage, she offers representations of a body capable of only brief and temporary resistance. The masochistic, passive, and bound body that Millay presents manifests as one essentialized within male discourse.

However, read within a framework of the hyperfeminine (masquerade, mimicry, and female female impersonation), this same body becomes an exaggeration. These images viewed as revelations of patriarchy's punishment of the transgressive female sexual body rather than as acquiescence in and internalization of an essentialized white femininity allow us to read the body as *seemingly* disciplined and compliant. Indeed, *Fatal Interview* presents the female speaker as disciplined and compliant *and* as unrepentant and defiant.

Walker's claim that the speaker's "occasional defiance . . . does not ring true" (*Masks* 159) is correct. Rather than finding this untruth crucial to understanding how Millay's poetics of the body ultimately fails to successfully resist patriarchal constructions of gender, I view this untruth as the very thing that offers a place of destabilization to the certainty of those constructions. In *Fatal Interview*, as she does throughout her work, Millay presents an unreliable poetic voice. As readers of these sonnets, we cannot be sure of what the speaker "really" means. Do we take her at face value? Does she relate a story of a woman besotted by love and sexual desire who finds strength and triumph in suffering for love as she asserts in Sonnet 26? Do we disregard this assertion understanding that it leaves her "defenseless" as Walker argues (*Masks* 158)? Does *Fatal Interview* present Millay's personal struggle to come to terms with her aging body, a body rapidly losing currency in a system that values youth? Conversely, can we read the body with its attendant sexuality and desires as an ironized one? Does Millay's poetics depict the body as disruptive and resistive in its ability to accept discipline while simultaneously suggesting the falseness of its compliance? Do these sonnets give us a glimpse of the body's resistive potential through its changeability, by overtly complying while covertly withholding complete acquiesce? Indeed, we can and do read *Fatal Interview* in all these ways, and I believe that because so many possibilities of interpretation exist, in some sense, the body, female sexuality, and desires, as Millay presents them, also remain uninterpretable. By uninterpretable, I do not argue for woman as lack of meaning or even as beyond representation; rather, I suggest, in Millay's poetics of the body, the body itself and female sexuality and desires confuse the issues of resistance and compliance. *Fatal Interview*, after all, relates a love affair in sonnet form from a woman's perspective and posits an actively desiring and sexually aggressive woman. In addition, after the break with the lover, the speaker survives.

The break occurs in Sonnet 39:

> Love me no more, now let the god depart
> If love be grown so bitter to your tongue. (668)

The speaker admits that her

> kisses are sand against [her lover's] mouth
> teeth against his palms and pennies in his eyes. (668)

These realizations underscore the male's rejection of the female and his inability to reciprocate her passion, and they lead the speaker to end the affair. Although close to tears, she will "stiffen up [her] back" in order to confront future memories and the years alone. The following sonnet reveals the process of sorting through and making sense of the end of a love affair as well as of the love itself. The first two lines encapsulate the entire affair and show the speaker's attempt to "let it go" and "let it be":

> "You loved me not all, but let it go;
> I loved you more than life, but let it be. (669)

Claiming her position "as the more injured party," the speaker asserts her right to the "hour's amenities . . . / [t]he choice of weapons" (669). Characteristically, an ambiguity arises here as the speaker does not make clear if the weapons signify self-destruction or revenge. Regardless of the potential use of the weapons, the speaker chooses not to use them, thus continuing the perception of choice that began in the preceding sonnet (the speaker chooses to end the affair and now chooses not to kill herself or, perhaps, her lover). The speaker makes very clear that she "will meet the morning standing"; however, she will be apart from both "heaven and earth," from anyone who thinks that he or she has ownership of his or her soul, and from "gods" and "children" (669). Survival seems to depend upon the speaker consciously repressing her love for the man and the pain of the break:

> And you will leave me, and I shall entomb
> What's cold by then in an adjoining room. (669)

This sonnet reconfigures the masochistic and prostrate lover who previously "lightly to [her] heart / . . . took [his] thrust, whereby [she] since [is] slain . . . A sodden thing bedrenched by tears and rain" into a woman claiming agency (646).

In some sense, this agency, however, proves misleading. The end of the affair was inevitable, a fact the speaker articulates in Sonnet 41:

> I said in the beginning, did I not?—
> Prophetic of the end, though unaware
> How light you took me, ignorant that you thought
> I spoke to see my breath upon the air. (670)[14]

The deterministic aspect here undermines the possibility of "pure" choice. Instead, the inevitability introduces a sense of fatalism suggesting the woman really had no choice.[15] The lines quoted above also represent a reading back, as only in retrospect can the woman see the inequalities in the relationship: the man's dismissal of the woman's utterances.

Despite the speaker's feminine posturing, the images of a bound and masochistic body, and the presentation of a submissive and passive femininity, Millay posits a woman in control of the narrative. In addition, a certain irony seems evident. First, the beginnings of all narratives contain an ending. After all, narratives are always a retelling. Second, this story unfolds through the woman's voice, the "breath upon the air." She controls the plot and the images rendering the male beloved at the mercy of her words. In Sonnet 47, the speaker acknowledges this authority and magnanimously tells the beloved that he need not fear her words:

> Should I outlive this anguish—and men do—
> I shall have only good to say of you. (676)

I perceive Millay's double voice here and another instance of ambiguity. The words bespeak sincerity, but the aside that interrupts the sentence ("and men do") undercuts this earnestness. Indeed, later in the sequence, the speaker tempers the inevitability of the collapse of the love affair and reasserts her agency. In this sonnet (45), she also very directly identifies her authority as speaker of the narrative:

> I know my mind and I have made my choice;
> Not from your temper does my doom depend;
> Love me or not, you have no voice
> In this, which is my portion to the end. (674)

Whether we *choose* to distrust and discount the speaker's assertion of choice, I believe that we must accept the legitimacy of her statement about voice: his is silent; hers tells the story. Clearly, the female voice exceeds patriarchal control regardless of the seeming compliance of the body to patriarchy's mandates regarding normative (white) female sexuality and desires. The ironic voice destabilizes certainty about the femininity displayed by the speaker throughout *Fatal Interview*. Furthermore, the irony invites distrust of the speaker's words and, by extension, hints at the hypocrisy of the gender performances. This suggestion renders tone, language, meaning, and the female body shaky and difficult to pin down. This elusiveness opens up a space in which to read resistance, and the vagueness or uninterpretability of intention becomes the resistance in *Fatal Interview*, as it does in many of Millay's poems and, as I have argued, in her public readings. If meaning and intention remain obscure, how, then, can one censure, discipline, or contain the speaker or actor?

Although the intervening sonnets describe the speaker's anguish, her desire to banish all seasons except winter ("that season which is no man's friend" [Sonnet 43]), her endless and empty days ("that have no meaning and no end" [Sonnet 43]), her journey back from the memories and pain (that seems "steeper" and "stonier" [Sonnet 48]), by Sonnet 51, the speaker declares that the male's worth generated from *her* love, not from the inherent worth of masculinity itself. *She* held him the "noblest among mortal-kind" (680), and *she* further wonders if her love could "restore [the male] somewhat to [his] former pride?" (680). These lines imply that female desire raises men to the stature of the gods, and female love, as rendered by patriarchy (adoring and submissive), bolsters masculinity. The ending couplet grants tremendous power to the woman:

> Indeed I think this memory, even then,
> Must rise you high among the run of men. (680)

This stance, blatant, bold, and brash, clearly sounds a challenge to masculinity itself and renders it impotent, unable to stand erect without femininity to support it. With *Fatal Interview* Millay reveals a femininity that carries an insidious rebellion as she poses the following questions: What happens if the stability of the prop on which masculinity depends proves illusionary? What happens if resistance is read only in overt challenges? How can regulatory systems such as patriarchy contain the threat of female sexuality if that sexuality looks like what patriarchy demands? How can disciplining regimes punish the body if they cannot interpret the body's meanings or actions? Read through this lens, this cycle of sonnets becomes a resistive and subversive text.

However, the volume does not end with Sonnet 51; it closes with a return to the legend of Selene and Endymion. With this return, Millay obviates the speaker's assertion of power. The sonnet's famous opening lines remind us that Selene's desires will go unrecognized and unmet:

> Oh, sleep forever in the Latmian cave
> Mortal Endymion, darling of the Moon! (681)

Although both the legend and the sonnet imply that sexual intercourse occurs, Endymion does not *consciously desire* Selene, nor does he *consciously act* on that desire:

> Whom earthen you, by deathless lips adored,
> Wild-eyed and stammering to the grasses thrust,
> And deep into her crystal body poured
> The hot and sorrowful sweetness of the dust. (681)

Without the conscious desire of males, Millay suggests, women disintegrate, driven mad both by rejection and by the invisibility within patriarchy of female passion. In Sonnet 52, instead of a woman proclaiming the potency of her desires and power of her narrative voice, Millay offers Selene, goddess of the moon, rendered powerless by her desires. Selene, scattered and crazed,

wanders mad, being all unfit
For mortal love, that might not die of it. (681)

Once again, Millay depicts the consequences of excessive female sexuality, and once again, we can read an internalization of patriarchal dictates. We can interpret Millay's depiction of the mad Selene as self-hatred of a body rejected and discarded because it no longer meets the standards of youth and beauty or as Millay's inability to break free from the restraints placed on female sexuality. We can also read this return to Selene as a masquerade, a costume donned by the speaker of the poem to mask the phallic power she revealed in the preceding sonnet, the power to control the discourse about sexuality. Throughout her body of work and in her public appearances, Millay confused the line between compliance and resistance, and she repeatedly offered the body as both the vehicle and the means to challenge the parameters of femininity.

Undoubtedly, Millay understood how femininity should look and sound as her public readings clearly indicated, as does Sonnet 31 from *The Harp-Weaver* (1923). The sonnet—which begins "Oh, oh you will be sorry for that word!"—plays with and within the rigid boundaries of acceptable femininity. In this poem Millay offers the female body as a shield to deflect the verbal barbs of patriarchal discourse and as armor to protect female creativity:

> Oh, oh, you will be sorry for that word!
> Give back my book and take my kiss instead.
> Was it my enemy or my friend I heard,
> "What a big book for such a little head!" (591).

In these lines the speaker would rather relinquish her body ("take my kiss instead") than she would her work ("book"). The poem posits the body as a means of exchange within a system that places value on the female body but not on the female mind, and within such a system, the creative work of females also holds little or no value. The speaker clearly understands the "rules of the game," and she uses this knowledge to her advantage in order to initiate a sense of complacency in the male. Within the realm of the performative, the speaker bolsters the male's sense of mastery and control. However, the self-conscious and deliberate use of her body affords the speaker a space in which to claim creativity and agency.

In "Oh, oh you will be sorry for that word," Millay presents gender performance at its best:

> Come, I will show now my newest hat,
> And you may watch me purse my mouth and prink! (591)

These lines underscore the shallowness of femininity as constructed by patriarchy as the speaker reassures the male that her "real" concern lies with fashion and beauty. "Prink" places the female body in front of a mirror with the speaker fussing over her adornment of the body. This performance directs the male's attention to the person of the speaker and away from her creative and intellectual potential. The lips held up to a kiss and the pursed mouth reassure a nervous patriarch that the speaker is indeed a "woman," one who understands her place within patriarchy (the narcissist in front of the mirror and the object of the male gaze). This woman not only knows how to deck herself out as the male watches, but she also knows how to speak the language of patriarchy: "Oh, I shall love you still, and all of that" (591). The characteristic Millay wit emerges here in the suspiciously flippant tone of "and all of that." Like the witch-wife, the speaker of this poem glibly mouths the words demanded of her *as* a woman.

However, at this point in the poem, Millay makes very clear that women often employ femininity as a strategy of resistance. They put on and speak femininity in order to alleviate male fears of female rebellion:

> I never again shall tell you what I think.
> I shall be sweet and crafty, soft and sly. (591)

On the one hand, "sweet and crafty, soft and sly" reinforce stereotypical characteristics of womanliness. Male discourse has for a very long time relegated women to just such binaries: good woman (sweet and soft) or bad woman (crafty and sly). In this sense, then, by evoking these oppositions, Millay ascribes to the either-or paradigm that upholds a gender hierarchy. On the other hand, "Oh, oh you will be sorry for that word," refuses the either-or model by having the speaker be both good and bad. The speaker will, by her own admission, "be called a wife to pattern by" (591). By the end of the poem, this model wife, this paragon of femininity, will "be gone," and all the male can do is "whistle" for her. Thus, by playing the good woman, the woman visibly embracing femininity, the speaker creates a means of escape. The body, then, provides the screen on which to project compliance while simultaneously being the vehicle of the speaker's independence. This poem blatantly reveals what poems such as "First Fig," "Second Fig," and "The Plaid Dress" "slantly" say: compliance masks repudiation and opposition. The speaker tells the truth in the opening lines—the male will be sorry. However, one can never be sure of the *truth* of femininity in Millay's poetry.

Chapter 3

"Dress Up! Dress Up and Dance at Carnival!"

Elizabeth Bishop's Poetic Bodies

The body in many of Elizabeth Bishop's poems remains tantalizingly elusive, an elusiveness that proves both seductive and frustrating. In her work, the body emerges as ambiguous and problematic as it slips between metaphoric and metonymic representations often occupying liminal spaces.[1] Within an ontological and epistemological matrix, Bishop's poetics of the body explores the intersection of gender, sex, and sexuality with ways of knowing and being. Whether explicitly or implicitly, Bishop posits the body as the "thing" that can bolster or fell the subject, subjectivity, and our understanding of both, and in so doing, she also challenges disciplining structures. Paradoxically, with Bishop, the poems that most strongly suggest body often lack direct and material description of that body. Instead, these poems depict the body through its overdetermination ("In the Waiting Room"), the distorting reflection of a mirror ("The Gentleman of Shalott"), a description of a bodily process ("O Breath"), a blurring of gender lines ("Exchanging Hats"), or the abject body of a dog ("Pink Dog").

However, this seeming disembodiment actually does materialize the body, and this apparent absence of the body in Bishop's published work functions within the Derridian notions regarding absence, presence, and play.[2] In her poems, Bishop does not represent a fixed, coherent, or easily identifiable, body, and, in addition, it often functions a bit like what Jacques Derrida calls the supplement underpinning the subject of the poem, subjects such as loss, love, nostalgia, subjectivity, or knowledge. Because the body supplements the subject, it becomes something *more than* the subject, something excessive, something that the subject needs.

The body, then, implies the insufficiency of the subject—and, by extension, subjectivity—and it involves both presence and absence. Bishop's poetics of the body depends on multiple metonymic and metaphoric substitutions, surplus signification, and often on a conspicuous absence of the material body itself. This absence, however, keeps the body enticingly in view, and although ambivalent about the body, Bishop uses it strategically within her poetry. The body becomes a contested site because it serves as the nexus between Bishop's conflicting desires to embrace and deny it just as she disavows both loss and selfhood in many of her poems. This conflict results in representations of the body as coded and disguised; however, disguise ultimately flaunts rather than conceals the body just as fragmentation and distortion result in its overdetermination.

Bishop's attention to multiple perspectives and multifaceted views often seem to work within binaries, which Eve Sedgwick identifies as "sites that are *peculiarly* densely charged with lasting potentials for powerful manipulation" (10). Because Bishop's poetry often evidences an awareness of this potential, I believe that her use of oppositions points to the dangers of the either-or conditions that binaries demand, and ultimately, Bishop's seeming reliance on binarisms exposes them as unnatural and constructed. Potentially the most powerful, and perhaps the most dangerous, manipulative element of Western binaries resides in the male-female split. Because this opposition underwrites the mind-body binary and because Bishop seems intent on valorizing the mind, it proves tempting to suggest that she does not want to muddy up her writing with female sexuality—with the female body.

Female sexuality and the female body do, however, circulate within Bishop's poetry. This manifestation occurs amid contradictions, paradoxes, and ambiguities as her poetry relentlessly redefines, reconfigures, and reconstructs both sexuality and the body within and in reaction to traditional epistemological paradigms. These redefinitions occur because "the body" in Bishop's poems becomes bodies. Although no one universalized or essentialized body materializes in the poems under discussion because they present multiple and particularized bodies, race and ethnicity is seldom a specific marker in Bishop's representation of the body. In fact, in the poems under discussion, the bodies are unmarked racially and ethnically. This lack of racial markings, then, assumes a white body, and in this sense, Bishop evokes an essentialist and universalist standpoint regarding the body. Furthermore, this position echoes the traditional stance within Western philosophy regarding whiteness, masculinity, and achievement. These "dynamics," according to Kincheloe and Steinberg, "have been naturalized and universalized" (6). In addition, Renée Curry points out that although "in letters to friends, lovers, family members, and colleagues, Bishop demonstrates that whiteness is the standard of being in multiple ways . . . [her] poetry provides a much more thought-out and self-reflective language" regarding racial ethnic others. Curry argues that this disjunction between Bishop's letters and poetry raises suspicions regarding "Bishop's racism and/or awareness of white privilege" (*White Women* 76). To the extent, however, that Bishop does particularize the body, her poems often undo the ties among gender, sexuality, and body, and they problematize traditional notions of knowledge, truth, and subjectivity.

Seemingly, Bishop's poetry echoes the Platonic notion of body as an "albatross." Indeed, her alcoholic asthmatic body often failed her. Bishop, however, remained acutely aware of the body, a "self-realization" that occurred through and on the body itself, for example, in the manifestations of her eczema, her attacks of asthma, the bruises and broken bones precipitated by her alcoholism, and the shaking of her hands as she wrote her poetry.[3] On one level, Bishop refuses to put the body on display, be that the lesbian, asthmatic, or alcoholic body, yet on another level, such bodies do manifest in her work. Bishop's poetics of the body simultaneously conceals and reveals bodies that emerge as distorted and disguised in order to survive in a world hostile to the "deviant" body, one that strays from *and* exposes cultural norms.

Disguises and distorted perceptions of the body provide a space from which one can challenge prescribed gender behaviors. Of course, disguise involves changing one's appearance and altering the way one's body looks, and a skewed perception of the body means changing how one looks at the body. Neither, however, involves erasing the body; instead, the body becomes the *necessary* element for both as well as for masquerade and mimicry. Bishop presents these disguised and distorted bodies in order to upend our certainties about sex, gender, and sexuality.[4] Her poetics of the body destabilizes these certainties because it suggests the body's potential for rearrangement and ambiguity and its ability to occupy in-between spaces. The body with its attendant sexuality rearranges and confuses the viability of the subject—male, female, heterosexual, homosexual, and all points in between—in Bishop's work.

According to Judith Butler, questions regarding a universalized and essentialized female subject reside at this "site of contest [woman]" and these "troublesome term[s]" provoke anxiety (*Gender Trouble* 3). In an effort to negotiate this anxiousness, Gayatri Chakrovorty Spivak argues for a strategic essentialism, and she finds value in strategically retaining essentialism *as it relates to the body*. However, as have many feminists,

Butler questions the efficacy of any kind of essentialism, strategic or not, "for strategies always have meanings that exceed the purposes for which they are intended" (*Gender Trouble* 4). Just as this idea of excess "troubles" both gender and the body in feminist politics and theories, excess also becomes a troublemaker in several of Bishop's poems ("Questions of Travel" provides a good example with its "too many waterfalls," "streams hurry too rapidly," and "so many clouds"). In addition, this excessiveness marks the representations of sexuality and the body in the poems under discussion—in either an overabundance of disguise and distortion or overdetermination of the body itself.

In "In the Waiting Room," Bishop plays with the present-nonpresent body as she examines the connection between the self and the body. She complicates this connection by presenting distorted images of the body as well as depicting the effects of denying one's bodily existence. The waiting room of the dentist's office crowded with adults, sundry outerwear, lights, and "magazines" overwhelms the poem's speaker, six-year-old Elizabeth. Clearly, she feels the presence of the adults around her just as she feels the absence of her aunt for whom the child waits. Surrounded by bodies, the speaker's sense of her own material existence seems to fade as she distances herself from the overcrowded waiting room. She turns her attention to a copy of the *National Geographic* and "read[s] it straight through," yet Bishop does not describe what the child reads; rather, Bishop describes what Elizabeth sees: "Osa and Martin Johnson" and their clothing ("breeches," "boots and pith helmets"), "a dead man slung on a pole," "babies with . . . heads" misshapen by string," "black, naked women with necks" elongated by "wire," and the women's "horrifying breasts" (159). These pictures offer bodies fragmented and distorted by clothing or by custom. Images of the body become overdetermined and overpowering, and they initiate an ontological crisis in the speaker.

The child issues a cry, "oh," which at first she attributes to her aunt. However, this cry comes from the child herself, and this realization proves unsettling. Caught in this multitude of bodies and pictures of them, Elizabeth loses her equilibrium and feels as though she were descending into the "cold" dark void of "space." Paradoxically, the child has lost a sense of herself while simultaneously becoming aware of her being-ness. Drawn to the images of bodies, bodies that both horrify and fascinate, Elizabeth recognizes her connection to those bodies, a recognition that she disavows with the following question: "*Why* should you be one, too?" (160). This disavowal hinges on the speaker's utterance of her name, "Elizabeth," and her reluctance to recognize the "what" of her being-ness. The child, however, cannot escape the body. As she looks for grounding, she does not see the bodies of those around her; instead, she fixates on their clothing. This strategy parallels the child's focus, when reading the *National Geographic*, on the clothing of the Johnsons. In the earlier incident, the nakedness of the nonwhite bodies overwhelmed the speaker. In this instance, the clothing distracts the child from the awareness or her own body. Using clothing as metonymic markers of the body, Bishop clearly embodies subjectivity while simultaneously locating the body at the border of stability. Subjectivity involves an awareness of the body; however, the body precipitates instability. The body, then, becomes the thing that both grounds and upends the subject.

Young Elizabeth, in "In the Waiting Room," seeks to understand what makes her *her*. In this poem, Bishop presents a defining moment of ontological awareness—acknowledging one's selfhood. The moment depends on understanding "similarities," and Bishop locates these similarities in the corporal: "boots, hands, the family voice, and those awful hanging breasts" (160). This recognition of similarities invites several interpretations. Curry identifies "In the Waiting Room" as an important poem for "understanding Bishop's ideological framework regarding whiteness and connections among women," and she asserts that Elizabeth's comprehension of the connection between herself and the black women "brings on a feeling of being drowned in blackness" (*White Women* 118). Curry's argument also suggests that, in this poem, Bishop tacitly understands that awareness of oneself *as* a self depends on one's awareness of racial differences and similarities manifested on the body. Susan McCabe argues that the child's "terrifying, yet homoerotic, identification with other women signals the loss of an ungendered, atemporal being in the world, but she also discovers that the self is always a matter of shifting, and that to define where it begins and ends is an act of language, self-naming" (3). Through her recognition that she is indeed "one of them" ("homoerotic identification" based on the body), Elizabeth also realizes some agency—"self-naming." Bishop's "In the Waiting Room" clearly implicates the body in the process of becoming a gendered and active subject. However, the ontological crisis arises not only with the child's terror of "becoming a woman" and resolves not only with the power to call herself "Elizabeth." Rather, this moment of self-awareness occurs amid an overdetermination—an excess of the bodies, an awareness of those bodies, a moment of disembodiment, and finally, a return to the body. I do not argue that here Bishop denies the body; rather, I suggest that she acknowledges the very materiality of the body and the necessity of recognizing its role in selfhood. In this poem, the body resides, once again, in some liminal space, at the limits of immanence or, perhaps, transcendence.

While "In the Waiting Room" works within a framework of overdetermination of the body, an excessive absence of the *material or real* body does mark several of Bishop's poems. "The Gentleman of Shalott," offers an intriguing, as well as paradoxical, textual example of Bishop's treatment of the body. The poem details a body distorted by a mirror and presents a reflected male image. In addition, body and mirror are positioned so that the mirror rests against the center of the man's body. Through this positioning, Bishop represents the body as half-mirrored reflection. The body *seems* material or real; however, the poem immediately raises questions regarding materiality, reality, and perspective, opening with two questions regarding the distinction between "real" body parts—eyes and limbs—and their reflections. A complicated layering of perspective occurs as the speaker of the poem "sees" both a "real" and reflected body, yet the gentleman cannot distinguish which is which as real and reflection conflate. The speaker cannot tell what is and is not reflection and acknowledges that nothing tangible exists to substantiate either the real or image. In addition, the reader sees both the speaker and the gentleman seeing. In "The Gentleman of Shalott," Bishop plays with perspective and questions our understanding of both the body and mind by positioning the body in front of a mirror. The man in the mirror considers the implications of his position in regards to his ability to think because he *sees* only half a head. Although in actuality the speaker's head is indeed whole, the speaker's realization that what he sees is merely a reflection opens a gap between mind and body. In "The Gentleman of Shalott," Bishop implies that the mind-body split may be only a matter of perception, and the poem also denies any certainty regarding what is or is not "real," what is or is not material, and what is or is not body. This uncertainty suggests the fluidity of the body itself and Bishop's unwillingness to represent an identifiable body as well as her reluctance to totally display the body. In other words, because the poem presents the body through the distorting properties of a mirror, "The Gentleman of Shalott," describes an *image* of the body rather than the body itself. The mirror then becomes the body's disguise by displaying it as a reflection.

Paradoxically, the speaker acknowledges his incompleteness while simultaneously viewing a potentially "doubled" body. Thus, the poem hints at an excess of the material body, or at least, at an excessive reflection of that body. The man perceives his body as he *sees* it as "half-looking glass" rather than as doubled (9). Indeed, why should he "be doubled?"—a question that the poem raises but does not answer. Although the poem does not depict the gentleman as double, the modest claim of half "material" and "half looking-glass" combines to form a whole as long as the speaker does not move. In other words, as long as the body remains fixed and poised in front of the mirror or as long as the speaker possesses awareness of his location in front of a mirror, he can *claim* coherence. The body must remain unmoving, pinned down by cultural definitions of embodiment, corporeality, and the body itself. This poem also suggests the Lacanian process of misrecognition in the formation of subjectivity to include the misrecognition in the cultural construction of the body. The body, like subjectivity, generates from the distorting surface of a mirror.

Unlike the mirror in Tennyson's "The Lady of Shallot," which reflects and constructs the lady's world, the mirror in Bishop's poem functions both as the vehicle to a perceived coherent body and as the device that can literally halve that body "if the glass slips" (9). Unlike Tennyson's lady, Bishop's gentleman does not see the world in his mirror; rather, he sees himself, and unlike the mirror in Lacan's theory, the mirror in "The Gentleman of Shalott" does not solidify the phallic power; instead, this mirror threatens castration. It places the body along with gender and sex in jeopardy. The "gentleman" retains his "manhood" only as long as he does not move and only as long as the mirror does not slip. Bishop closes the poem with humor and play along with her typical move toward uncertainty. The unsureness and precariousness of his position seems to energize the man and a "sense of constant re-adjustment" to please him (10). This "constant re-adjustment" can refer only to a readjustment of perspective because as the poem makes clear any physical readjustment will deny the subject a stable position and a unified subjectivity, and it will quite literally separate that subject from the power of the phallus. The same sense of modesty and meekness that opens the second stanza resonates in the poem's closing line: "Half is enough."

Although the gentleman proclaims that "half is enough," he makes this statement from his location in front of a mirror that presents him with a reflection of wholeness, and as the gentleman suggested in the second stanza, the mirror possesses the potential to double the existing body. Thus Bishop suggests that maleness expects wholeness and will claim it even in a state of "half-ness" or incompleteness (the state of femininity?). The gentleman can utter these words because he *is* male, which guarantees his wholeness (despite appearances). While simultaneously granting the male body a perception of wholeness, Bishop blatantly places the male in a fixed location: in front of a mirror that threatens the integrity of the body. The position of this "doubled" and or "halved" body in "The Gentleman of Shalott" demands immobility and immanence. The poem places the male body in the traditionally and culturally assigned location of the female body, yet the speaker articulates his maleness. Bishop suggests that maleness alone confers transcendence, despite the fact that males, like females, posses a body (that pesky "albatross"): the gentleman's masculinity, although threatened, remains intact. Maleness can be "pinned down" only momentarily as masculinity seems able to transcend the body in ways that femininity cannot. In this rewriting of Tennyson's poem, Bishop depicts the ridiculousness of the gentleman of Shallot's failure to recognize his powerlessness. Her substitution of the male who views his body in the mirror for the female who views the world beyond in the mirror exposes the absurdity of unexamined social restrictions.

Body in "The Gentleman of Shalott" depends on location and distortion and on an unmoving relationship to both. A positional shift literally reconfigures the body. The wholeness of the gendered, sexed (male) body then depends on a strict adherence to social and cultural mandates. Of course, the gentleman fails to see things that way. He *claims* coherence regardless of his immobility and regardless of the fact that he can see only half his body. The reality of his circumstances does not destabilize *his* (read male) understanding of masculinity or his certainty in the privileges of his maleness, as he retains the prerogative to claim wholeness and transcendence—although those circumstances certainly destabilize the readers' perceptions of masculinity. In this poem, Bishop exposes the illusions on which the certainty of male privilege rests. It is in her telling all smoke and mirrors.

The *male* body in "The Gentleman of Shalott" exemplifies what Grosz calls "*the* cultural product" (*Volatile Bodies* 23), and as such, the body can claim neither wholeness nor fragmentation, stability nor instability, mobility nor immobility, lack nor excess because to do so denies the contradictions of the body itself. The poetic body rests at the site of liminality, poised between material and illusion. The poem appears to present a body, yet one never quite materializes or at least one unitary body fails to manifest; instead, its wholeness depends on the gentleman's proclamation. This poem renders the male body as the object of scrutiny as it depicts it as feminine without the speaker ever seeing it as such. The body, in this poem, disrupts the transcendent-immanent binary through Bishop's depiction of a body literally straddling the bar. The body appears on both sides of the / (slash), becoming the site and moment of deconstruction, the deconstructive object. Finally, by inverting the cultural location of maleness and femaleness in the story of Shalott, Bishop reveals the discursive and fictitious aspects of masculinity, femininity, and the body itself.

In her poem "O Breath" (the last of "Four Poems," a sequence of lesbian erotic poems), Bishop fragments the body differently than she does in "The Gentleman of Shalott." In the former, although fragmented, the body pulses with life, and the poem depends on movement. Anne Colwell reads "O Breath" as "the speaker's search for a means of connection . . . through the same kind of passionate attention to another's body that Bishop explored in 'The Fish'" (84). However, "The Fish" presents a detailed description of the fish's body: "tremendous," "a grunting weight," "brown skin," "speckled with barnacles," large, shallow, yellow, "sullen face," "mechanism of his jaw," "a lip." No such concrete details fill "O Breath"; instead, Bishop describes a biological process—breathing. Marilyn Lombardi writes that "'O Breath' is one of [Bishop's] only published poems about the eroticized female body" (33). Although one never sees the entire body and despite the lack of a clear description of the body, "O Breath" does indeed represent the female body.

The opening lines of "O Breath" promise a description of a beloved body: "Beneath that loved and celebrated breast . . ." (79). Yet the promise of those lines never quite materializes because Bishop does not offer a tangible, coherent body. Rather, the representation that emerges generates from the fragmentation of that body through metonymic markers: "breast," "black hairs," "nipple." Susan Bordo rightly points out that language mediates the body, and this mediation means that "we have no direct, innocent, or unconstructed knowledge of our bodies; rather, we are always reading our bodies according to various interpretive schemes" (289). "O Breath" offers both metonymy and metaphor as elements of an interpretive scheme for reading the body. Metonymy genders the poetic body female. What can signify *female* more blatantly than the words "nipple" and "breast"—particularly a "loved and celebrated breast"? Furthermore, the body emerges both from the speaker's metonymic descriptions and in her pauses for breath. The struggle for breath becomes the speaker's and reader's, and as such, the poem foregrounds the natural processes of the body. The struggle for breath embodies the apparent disembodiment of the poem as reader and speaker experience the poem through bodily sensations.[5]

While the metonymic elements in "O Breath" mark the poetic body as woman, metaphor sexualizes the poetic body as lesbian as metaphor closes the gap between Bishop, the poet, and the first-person "I." The poem's title identifies the subject of the poem as breath, and the poem's construction—meter and punctuation—simulates a struggle to breathe. Most critics read "O Breath" as Bishop's poem "to her asthma and the negotiations it demanded" (Millier 231). This reading suggests that Bishop translated her own bodily sensations into poetic language. This biographical link clearly identifies the speaker of the poem as female, thus particularizing both the writing subject and the poetic body as lesbian.[6]

The subject, breath, metaphorically becomes, according to Colwell, "the only visible external indication of commonality, of the possibility for connection for equivalence" (86): a commonality and equivalence that takes place between lovers. Brett Millier more clearly explicates the metaphoric possibilities of "O Breath": "As the title suggests, the poem is also an apostrophe of breathing itself, and the asthma . . . becomes a symbol for the cautious, constrained relationship" (232). Lombardi offers yet another metaphoric possibility: "'O Breath' is a captivatingly ambiguous love poem that plays with the narrow passageway for authorized speech permitted a woman of [Bishop's] class and education in 1955" (33). Extending Lombardi's reading of the poem as metaphor for Bishop's struggle as a female poet, I suggest that this struggle also involves the desire both to conceal and to reveal the lesbian body, sexuality, and desire.[7]

This concealment and revelation depend on the movement of inhaling and exhaling. Millier writes that Bishop "struggled with the meter and punctuation of 'O Breath' to reflect the lung capacity and speaking pace of an asthma suffer" (231). The pauses and lines break also suggest the sounds of sexual intercourse, the hesitations, inhalations, and exhalations of physical lovemaking. Explaining the function of the caesura in "O Breath," Colwell writes, "The alliterative verse form, used so often in heroic poetry to portray the clash of actual battle, here depicts a more figurative war, the desire to storm the walls of the other to conquer, and comprehend the interior" (85). This "desire to storm the walls of the other and to conquer, and comprehend the interior" becomes in Bishop's poem the desire *for* the other and *for* the other's body. The speaker's desires are not only to know the other's inner self but also to know the other's body inside and out. Although identifying the theme of the poem as "the boundary between the self and the other" (85), Colwell's explanation also suggests that when lovers' bodies touch the boundary between self and other collapses. Bodies enact connection.[8]

This "ambiguous love poem," which articulates desire for "commonality" and "equivalence," emerges as a metaphoric representation of sexual connection between lesbian lovers. In *A Desire for Women*, Suzanne Juhasz asserts that while the word lesbian connotes desire, it also "signifies a sexuality, an identity, a love relationship, and/or lifestyle." She also sees desire as the primary and necessary "but not sufficient condition that conditions all of the rest" (143). Juhasz's point proves relevant to my argument that "O Breath" represents a kind of lesbian erotics represented by bodily processes that both signal and conceal that desire. The poem plays within the framework of a lesbian desire that Juhasz calls "a fantasy—a hope, a belief, a longing, and a thrill—about complementary identification between partners: a longing to be and to have, to share sameness and difference" (145). The model that Juhasz offers carries with it tension and contradiction (being and having, sameness and difference). I believe that Bishop's poem exhibits similar contradictions. One such tension resides in the poem's pauses. Besides replicating the struggle to breath, these literal gaps in the lines function as liminal spaces—the locations of claiming and deflecting desire. The speaker discerns movement in the beloved's body, yet that movement remains invisible. Despite its invisibility, that movement does lay within the body. At the moment that the poem seems to offer some certainty regarding the material body, the description shifts from exterior to interior, to something "beneath": a beating heart, laboring lungs. Lombardi identifies this moving force as desire"—something caged within that body as surely as a clamoring heart or a pair of wheezing lungs" (35). The speaker of the poem then does not seek only a commonality and equivalence between herself and her lover, but she also attempts both to unleash and to harness the force of desire. The poem's construction underwrites this dilemma as the pauses simultaneously move toward and defer desire.

In addition to locating this desire "beneath that loved and celebrated breast," Bishop situates desire at the site of paradox between "clamor" and "restrained." All definitions of *clamor* include some sense of excess: "a loud uproar"; "a vehement expression of desire or dissatisfaction"; "popular outcry"; "any loud continued noise." In "O Breath," the body itself restrains the "clamor" of the heart, of the lungs, and ultimately, of desire, for the speaker can sense movement—invitation or response—in the beloved, but she cannot *see* it. While the body *is* the site of desire, it also restrains it. Here again the poem evidences the conflict between celebrating the body and rejecting its excesses. Therefore, the poem both demands and constrains excess and, as Sedgwick has made clear, sexuality has very much to do with excess (29). "O Breath" presents a poetic body in motion, clamoring but "restrained," a body both desired and desiring. The poem sets forth an economy of desire that involves visible and invisible differences as well as visible and invisible sameness, and within this economy, Bishop writes desire both on and within the body. Furthermore, the processes of the body strategically camouflage desire as well as the body itself. The camouflage, however, does not prove entirely successful

The speaker of "O Breath" inscribes meaning on the body of her lover because Bishop both reads and writes connection, commonality, and equivalents on the poetic bodies. The longing for commonality and equivalents becomes, as Colwell suggests, a desire for connection (84–87). The desire that circulates within the poem and the desire that resides in the long pauses also become markers of lesbian desire and sexuality. The speaker claims a commonality between the lovers, but according to Colwell, Bishop's "play on 'equivocal' and 'equivalent' reveals the struggle both to connect and to avoid connecting, to discover equivalence without becoming equal to, losing identity" (86). *Equivocal* suggests not only uncertainty and ambiguity, but it also denotes the possibility of a double interpretation. While Bishop's poem may indeed express a longing for connection, it also, and simultaneously, acknowledges that sameness (equivalence) does not ensure "peace." Bishop does not idealize lesbian desire; rather, she presents this desire as dangerous and contested, and the body becomes the ground of this contest. The speaker recognizes an undetermined something (desire, body), something that the two lovers share. Whatever commonality exists between the lovers—femaleness, lesbian desire, and sexuality—generates a need, in the speaker, for negotiation rather than easy acceptance. The speaker must negotiate with this commonality, and the peace that may result resides "beneath" and "within" rather than "with." In other words, Bishop situates this "peace" in relation to some unnamed thing (again, I suggest both desire and body). Furthermore, this relational aspect depends on depth and interiority. "Beneath" and "within" continue the poem's focus on the body's internal workings, and it situates desire deep within the confines of the body.

Both "O Breath" and "The Gentleman of Shalott" contest the rigid separation between inside and outside, interiority and exteriority, and body and not body. Joseph Boone suggests that "surface and depth alike are continually inundated by those psychosexual currents that provide a meeting point between individual subjectivity and social formations" (9). As these poems challenge the depth-surface or mind-body binarisms, they also place the sex-gender distinction in jeopardy by locating this distinction in social formations.[9] Many feminists insist that, like gender, the body, sex, and sexuality emerge as social construction. Bishop's poem "Exchanging Hats" challenges but does not collapse the sex-gender binary; rather, the poem points to the *artificiality* of the binarism itself by exposing the constructedness of gender. More importantly, the poem presents the danger of ignoring that constructedness. Here I veer slightly from Kathryn Kent's argument regarding the power of cross-dressing that Bishop presents in "Exchanging Hats."[10] She asserts that in the poem "Bishop recognizes the power *and* the danger of occupying [the position of a cross-dresser]" (206). I wish to amplify Kent's reading by suggesting that Bishop uses this cross-dressing in order to "trouble" (to borrow a term from Butler) the gender, sex, sexuality, and body connection; to expose the absurdity of masculinity and femininity; and to "undo" (to borrow another term from Butler) epistemological and ontological understandings of gender, sex, sexuality, and body. In addition, this undoing occurs because of the changeability of the body and its presentation. Paradoxically, one seems to need a body in order to disconnect it from gender, sex, and sexuality.

"Exchanging Hats" unfixes gender from its adherence to the sexed body through the exchange of clothes and through moments of transvestitism. "Exchanging Hats" both genders and sexualizes the body through the taking off and the putting on of the accouterments of gender and by simultaneously hiding and exposing the body. The hats, or rather, the exchange of hats, enact gender, and the incongruity between hat and wearer ("unfunny uncles" and ladies' hats, "anandrous aunts" and "yachtsmen's caps") draws attention to the body itself. Once again Bishop relies on elements of metonymy in order to represent gender, sex, and the body, without depicting a naked, sexed, and essentialized body. Thus the hats function as metonymic markers of a body inscribed by cultural, patriarchal, and heterosexual norms. However, these markers do not possess signification in and of themselves, and meaning occurs not only because of conventional understandings of sex and gender but because one can take off, give away, and put on the items that cover the body. Gender and sexuality signify because they are processes or strategies rather than fixed entities.

The doing in the poem enacts the being. "Exchanging Hats" challenges a coherent gender identity as it complicates notions of the sexed body through its depiction of what Butler calls gender performativity.[11] Taken to the extreme (as in drag or cross-dressing), gender performances render normative sexuality (masculinity and femininity) ridiculous. Gender performance disrupts notions of a natural sexed body, and the resulting detachment of gender from sex dispels traditional understandings of the body as a fixed and immutable object. "Exchanging Hats" presents a mutable poetic body, one *temporarily* unfixed from cultural mandates, gender expectations, and a coherent sexual identity. The poetic bodies manifest as male playing female, female playing male, as dead bodies and as transvestite bodies.

The transvestite performances of the aunts and uncles in "Exchanging Hats" demonstrate the parodic and perfomative aspects of gender and sexual identity while at the same time complicating the notion of parody. Both the males and the females in the poem attempt to take on, by literally putting on, alternative gender roles. However, the uncles prove "unfunny" in their attempt to act out or to assume femaleness through costume;

"the joke" fails because no joke exists. In one sense, all gendered identities depend on parody and performance: "The parodic repetition of 'the original' . . . reveals the original to be nothing other than a parody of the *idea* of the natural and the original" (*Gender Trouble* 31). Yet parody itself suggests the existence of an original. However, Bishop seems well aware of the illusions that propel the desire to claim an original and natural sexed body or a coherent gender identity. The poem exhibits a more postmodern pastiche that clearly recognizes the dangers to the self of demanding a unitary identity either sexual or gendered and the benefits to disciplining systems of keeping a sexual and gendered identity fixed and unchanging. The speaker of the poem acknowledges that this game playing and gender switching takes on serious implications within a context of complexity based on clothing and mores. The uncles cause embarrassment; their experimentation with cross-dressing makes them an unfunny joke. The adjective "anandrous" (lacking stems) identifies the aunts as perpetually cut off from phallic power, despite their insistence on wearing "yachtsmen's caps." Although the textual ruptures become moments of postmodern pastiche, because they continually and repetitively underscore the nonexistence of an original and bounded sexual identity, the poem makes clear the rigidity of socially and culturally constructed sexualities. The speaker's acknowledgment regarding the complexity of the relationship between clothing and social conventions underwrites Bishop's ambiguity about overt displays of the body. Deviant behavior, even poetic deviance, results in discipline to real bodies.

However, Carole-Anne Tyler asks an important question in her work on female impersonation: "But if all identities are alienated and fictional, what makes one credible and the other incredible, an obvious fake?" She offers an answer: "The answer, it seems, is the author's intention: parody is legible in the drama of gender performance *if* someone meant to script it, intending it to be there" (102, emphasis added). I believe that Bishop does deliberately script the "drama of gender performance" in "Exchanging Hats." The poem does not contain any subtleness regarding Bishop's play with gender, and critics often point to the satiric and parodic tone of "Exchanging Hats." Indeed, the poem offers a satiric and irreverent look at gender roles and the institutions that put those roles in place. Costello writes that "Exchanging Hats" "describes an anxiety about social roles as well as creative deviance. The 'hats' we wear, the social identities we take on, are inherently insecure" (*Elizabeth Bishop* 83). "Exchanging Hats," however, does more than articulate an anxiety regarding social roles or argue for the insecurity of those roles. The poem also exposes the "constructedness" and instability of *any* gender coherence as it confronts the deviance mandated by the regulatory practices of heterosexuality. The "hatter" implicitly fashions culture ("opera hats"), politics ("crowns"), and religion ("miter"), all of which attempt to govern sexual practices. The speaker acknowledges that all these institutions result *from* perversity and madness and that all *contain* the instability of the perverse and the mad. Moreover, as Michel Foucault argues in *The History of Sexuality*, the disciplining of "peripheral sexualities" produces perversions (36–47). Within "Exchanging Hats," these disciplining institutions generate transvestite aunts and uncles, who, according to Kent, "may in fact destabilize the social order" (203).[12]

The cross-dressing "does" gender, and it "does" sexuality, and by extension, it "does" the body. "Exchanging Hats" evokes the multiple meanings of "performativity" and "performative." According to Cathy Davidson and Linda Wagner-Martin in the *Oxford Companion to Women's Writing in the United States*, "Performativity refers to the *doing* of language. It focuses on language as action and on meaning as provisional, contingent" (657). Webster's New Universal Unabridged Dictionary defines "performative" as "performing an act by the very fact of being uttered." "Exchanging Hats" utilizes language to enact an uncoupling of gender from the sexed body and, in so doing, puts both terms in question. The meaning of gender resides in the clothing, in hats, in transvestitism, in perversities, in exhibitionism, and in excess. All these elements demand a body, yet none of them *is* the body. The poem locates gender as adornment on the body, as markers on the surface of the body, or as poses and behaviors *of* the body. Thus both the language and the images in the poem disrupt the traditional discursive constructions of gender as they simultaneously expose those very constructions. The challenge to cultural gender expectations through transvestitism in "Exchanging Hats" functions similarly to what Butler describes as the role of drag: "*In imitating gender, drag implicitly reveals the imitative structure of gender itself—as well as its contingency*" (*Gender Trouble* 137). The aunts and uncles in the poem *imitate* masculine and feminine, and they *imitate* effeminate men and phallic women. I perceive the poem's depiction of gender performance as perhaps the most threatening to traditional heterosexual mandates regarding gender and sexuality, not because, as Tyler rightly asserts, "drag routines generally reveal the body beneath the clothes, which is made to serve as the ground of identity," (95), but because in "Exchanging Hats" all performances fail, including so-called normative performances.[13] The exchanging of hats in the poem materializes the body, but this exchange and its resultant "experiment" with gender never unclothes the body. Bishop grants the phallus to neither the uncles nor the aunts because she never reveals the body as either male or female; the poem presents masculinity and femininity through both normative and deviant (transvestite) performances. In so doing, she places the body at the *border* of gender performance rather than at the *center* of gender.

In her reading of "Exchanging Hats," Costello rightly points out that the poem "describes a world of sexual anxiety" and argues that the poem depicts a world "where men become effeminate and women become the captains" (*Elizabeth Bishop* 83). However, the uncles only *act* effeminate in their ladies' hats. Their performance proves embarrassing because it can only be performance. The uncles cannot become female; they can only "experiment." The aunts remain stemless, and, despite the "yachtsmen's caps," these women shriek from the position of the exhibitionist, a position most often thought of in terms of the feminine. Rather than suggest that indeed gender adheres to the body, these failed performances imply the failure of all attempts to reconcile the discontinuities of gender *within a patriarchal and heterosexual paradigm*. The poem makes clear that no other paradigm apparently exists in which to situate sexual difference.

Just as the markers of social institutions may break down or become insubstantial, the sexed and gendered bodies in "Exchanging Hats," disintegrate. The poem closes with questions asked of dead aunts and uncles, with queries directed at dead bodies. Although returning to the opening description of the uncles as "unfunny," the penultimate stanza presents an uncle too male, with "a hat too big" who also experimented too much, a man who wore "one too many" hats. This uncle embodies both a monolithic maleness and the discontinuities of that maleness. The "aunt exemplary and slim" in the last stanza emerges as commendable, as a warning, as a model, or perhaps as typical. "Exemplary" invokes all these meanings, and like the uncle who wears one big hat as well as too many hats, this aunt embodies contradictions and ambiguities. Ultimately, the poem traps both uncle and aunt inside of their hats, the metonymic markers of gender and sex, enacting gender long after the body has decayed.

Bishop's playfulness in this poem makes more striking the near impossibility of reconfiguring gender, sex, sexuality, and the body *within heterosexual constructs* although she does reconfigure our understanding of all four. "Exchanging Hats" offers a glimpse of gender play, but this play seems, at best, ineffectual or, at worst, destructive to the individual. Significantly, the markers of the poetic body remain as the material body vanishes. Male, female, masculine, and feminine continue to signify without a body, yet these terms implicitly demand the body because it acts as prop and supplement to gender and sexuality as they are socially and culturally constructed. Specifically, "Exchanging Hats," exposes the paradox

of this interdependence as it exists within the regimen of regulatory het-
erosexual mandates: gender performativity both blurs and solidifies the
body-sex binarism.

Whereas "Exchanging Hats" hints at the difficulty of resisting such
practices, Bishop's poem "Pink Dog" emerges as a blatant warning regard-
ing the dangers of overtly flaunting the body, particularly an "unnatural"
or deviant one. Yet this poem also makes clear that the attempt at hid-
ing, disguising, or disavowing the body ultimately, like the gender per-
formances in "Exchanging Hats," ends in failure. "Pink Dog" exemplifies
more clearly than any of Bishop's other poems a fascination with the
expressions of sexuality and gender as they play out on and through the
body. Lombardi argues that the "plight of the 'depilated' animal Bishop
describes in 'Pink Dog' suggests the degree of dread that Bishop felt at the
prospect of parading her body before the world" and that "Bishop uses the
theatricality of verse to simultaneously unveil and disguise her unortho-
dox identity" (65). Lombardi's argument closes the gap between Bishop
and the speaker of the poem, a gap that I believe fluctuates—narrowing
at times but never closing. Rather than view Bishop's "poetic personae—
her masks [as] necessary" to shield her from the "world's contempt" (65)
as Lombardi does, I argue that these poetic personae, masks, masquerades,
and performances are necessary to Bishop's poetics of the body. Specifically
in "Pink Dog," Bishop places the poetic body in the realm of the grotesque,
a site that ultimately produces the abject female body. Significantly, within
the poem, the abject female body's insistence on visibility and invisibility,
as well as marginality and centrality, disturbs notions of natural bodies
and coherent sexual identities while seemingly reinforcing both the natu-
ralness of the body and the coherence of sexual identities. Paradoxically,
the body in "Pink Dog" challenges the regulating practices of the status
quo while it simultaneously reveals the illusions of the celebratory aspects
of either the grotesque or the spectacle.[14]

In this poem, the body, sexuality, and gender all signify the mon-
strous and the grotesque. Bernard McElroy identifies the grotesque as
"something exceptional, something set apart or aberrant, and in its most
extreme forms situated in the realm of fantasy, dream, or hallucination"
(6). The representation of the body that emerges through the images in
"Pink Dog" moves from the exceptional, a "naked," hairless dog, through
the aberrant, a scabies-covered dog, to the fantastic, "a dog in *máscara*."
Costello notes that "in 'Pink Dog' Bishop makes her most complete and
successful use of the grotesque; its style, its imagery, and its tone are all
intensely ambivalent" (*Questions* 86). This intense ambivalence not only

attaches to style, imagery, and tone, but it also marks the poetic body and the speaker's attitude toward it.

Although the body in "Pink Dog" circulates within the realm of the grotesque and manifests many attributes of the grotesque, it does not *become* the grotesque body. Peter Stallybrass and Allon White point out that "the grotesque body is emphasized as a mobile, split, multiple self, a subject of pleasure in processes of exchange; and it is never closed off from either its social or ecosystemic context" (22). Bishop makes clear the intersection of the body and the "social or ecosystemic context" as she utilizes the realm of the grotesque both to expose and cover the body. The body, however, is not "a subject of pleasure in processes of exchange"; rather, it remains, what Grosz calls, "a most peculiar 'thing' . . . never quite reducible to being merely a thing; nor does it ever quite manage to rise above the status of thing. Thus it is both a thing and a nonthing" (*Volatile Bodies* xi). The incongruity and inconsistency of this thing or nonthing accentuates both the dynamic aspects of the body and its position of liminality within "Pink Dog." In locating the dog (body) in a liminal space, Bishop can have it both ways: the body can be a culturally inscribed thing, and it can shed its "thing-ness" and become a subject with the potential to resist stasis.

Bishop emphasizes the mobility, mutability, and materiality of the body in the image of the poem's pink and naked dog. The body is "naked and pink," a carrier of disease and contagion—"rabies" and "scabies,"—and "a nursing mother." In addition, the representation of the body in "Pink Dog" presents a metaphoric connection between the female body and the body of a female dog, and it places that female body, in all its perceived grotesqueness, in plain sight. The body's dependence on excess visibility propels it to the limits of both the grotesque and the spectacle and into the realm of abjection.

The grotesque's reliance on excess, multiplicity, distention, disproportion, and exorbitance exaggerates the specular aspects of the body (Stallybrass and White 8, 23). The body, albeit a bitch's body, in "Pink Dog," both repels and attracts. The people on the street stare at the hairless creature while simultaneously avoiding it. The people who pass the dog shrink from her in order to distance themselves from or to prevent physical contact with the deviant body as they demand the spectacle of that body. As Guy Debord makes clear, the spectacle functions as a "means of unification," thus implying the existence of division and separation. Although Debord posits that "the spectacle appears at once as society [and] as a part of society," he does not argue for the marginalization of the spectacle (12). Indeed, the spectacle takes on the characteristics and the functions of the center as defined by structuralism. This spectacle as center governs the structure and limits the possibility of play within the totality. However, Debord goes on to stress that the spectacle places in view the mere appearance of human and social life: "The spectacle proclaims the predominance of appearances . . . [I]t [is] a visible negation of life" (14). The spectacle, then, contains and enacts conflicting realities and illusions. Thus the specular aspect of the body in "Pink Dog" engenders the repulsion and attraction felt by the passersby as it substantiates and negates the reality of the body. In presenting the passersby's need to look and not look, Bishop highlights the necessity of deviance against which to solidify normativity.

However, the very excessiveness of both the spectacle and the grotesque body draws on aspects of voyeurism and exhibitionism.[15] I locate the move from the grotesque to the abject in the need to see and to be seen. The poetic body in the poem emerges as a site of irresolution, a place that occupies both inside and outside, a location of shifting desires. Bishop uses the grotesque to present conflicting desires without any attempt to reconcile those desires: the desire both to reveal and conceal abjection, celebrate and denigrate the body, and claim and refuse the center. The speaker of the poem seems well aware of society's insistence on the visibility of the physical body while simultaneously abhorring intimate physical contact with the body. Costello argues that "the grotesque style brings together (without resolution) the categories that our minds and our culture like to keep apart but that constantly converge in nature and in experience" ("Attractive Mortality" 126). "Pink Dog," however, refuses this moment of convergence by widening the gap between culture and the body, because Bishop refuses the celebratory and collective aspect of the grotesque and instead presents a particularized body that remains necessary to, but shunned by, the collective. The body in the poem challenges social conventions not as a grotesque body but rather as an abject being that refuses invisibility by inhabiting the limits of the visible.

The pink dog defies cultural and social conventions by wandering the streets, refusing to hide her femaleness as her clearly visible teats serve as a constant reminder that the naked body, in the poem, is female. Within the Bakhtinian paradigm, the grotesque concerns itself "with the lower stratum of the body, the life of the belly and the reproductive organs; it therefore relates to acts of defecation and copulation, conception, pregnancy and birth" (21). However, Bakhtin does not identify the grotesque as female per se. His concept of the lower stratum refers not to a particularized or even a universalized female body; rather, Bakhtin's lower stratum concerns "the fruitful earth and the womb," or in other words, the lower stratum suggests the procreative function of the female—what the female body *does*, not what it *is* (21). The grotesque body within the Bakhtinian model represents the regeneration of life through processes of exchange, specifically through the cycles of birth and death. However, in "Pink Dog," this naked nursing mother materializes the grotesque body as a female body. By particularizing rather than universalizing the grotesque body, Bishop rejects the celebratory aspect the grotesque.

Scholarship on "Pink Dog," almost without exception, identifies the elements of the grotesque in the poem, and Bishop scholars (Axelrod, Costello, Lombardi, and McCabe) examine Bishop's use of the grotesque along two lines. They identify a subversive aspect in the grotesque, and they argue for the marginalization—and Bishop's identification with that marginalization—of the grotesque. A perception of the grotesque as marginal calls for a redefinition of the grotesque, and it calls for a rethinking of the function of the body in "Pink Dog." Lombardi places Bishop "on the border between male and female, right and wrong, life and death" (49), and McCabe argues that "as a poet who lived and wrote as exile, Bishop translates the marginal" (15). Costello argues Bishop "writes from the margins, on the divide between culture and nature, a creature of both" (*Elizabeth Bishop* 85),[16] and views the grotesque figure as a misfit, an outsider, and she insists on assigning Bishop that same outsider status. However, as Bakhtin points out, this notion of the grotesque as alien generates from Romanticism's perversion of the grotesque. These arguments also insist on the marginalization of the grotesque by locating the grotesque body on the periphery of society. However, the pink dog brazenly walks down the street in the blazing sun. The dog, as a particularized, naked, female body, refuses the margins; rather, the poem suggests that the marginal always already exists within the center.

Bakhtin does not marginalize the grotesque; instead, he finds it a means of materializing the "high, spiritual, ideal [and the] abstract" (19–20).[17] As he disallows the marginal status of the grotesque, Bakhtin provides a way to read the grotesque as celebratory and offers the carnival as a mode of liberation. However, he also points out that while the carnival breaks down established order and suspends "hierarchical rank, privileges, norms and prohibitions," the liberation proves temporary (10). Bakhtin does offer a model through which to situate both carnival and the grotesque in "Pink Dog." I suggest that the poem, while representing some aspects of the grotesque ultimately, does not place the body exclusively within that realm. The poem does not depict a universalized or cosmic body, and it makes clear that any attempt to dismantle the status quo, however temporary, proves futile. The body in "Pink Dog" becomes a very particularized body, one that refuses the generative aspect of the grotesque. While Bakhtin insists that "in grotesque realism . . . the bodily element is deeply positive" (19) because the grotesque body represents regeneration, rebirth, and renewal, the body in "Pink Dog" seems neither positive nor generative. Instead, disease, contagion, and the feminine conflate in the naked body of the pink dog. At this intersection of fear of disease (rabies) and contaminated body (scabies), the abject female body emerges. The poem, then, does not present a marginalized grotesque body; rather, it represents an abject body that inhabits both margin and center simultaneously or, perhaps more accurately, the spaces at the parameters of both.

According to Butler, subject formation demands nonsubjects, "abject beings" who both construct and remain outside of the "domain [of] the subject" in order to demarcate the parameters of that domain (*Bodies* 3). Butler stresses that subject formation "requires an identification with the normative phantasm of 'sex'" (3). This identification materializes the body, as well as placing sex and gender within regulatory and compulsory heterosexual practices. Subject formation and a sexed and gendered identity also depend on a "repudiation which produces the domain of abjection" (3). The subject must cast away what becomes unthinkable and unlivable, thus suggesting the centrality of the abjection to the subject.[18] The domain of abjection contains all that the regulatory practices of patriarchy and heterosexuality prohibit. This abject material comes from within the body, must be cast from the body, but more importantly, this refuse must remain visible. The body in "Pink Dog" does remain visible, and its visibility becomes a reminder of a failed attempt to construct and control gender and sexuality. The abject female body in the poem carries with it not just the threat of disease and contagion but also the threat of social upheaval.

In addition, the body complicates the binary structures of mind-body, sex-gender, male-female, and culture-nature because, as the abject body, it collapses meaning, signifies liminality, and refuses stasis. In her work on abjection, Julia Kristeva examines the construction of a proper social body within a psychological and subjective register. Although she argues that "the abject has only one quality of the object—that of being opposed to *I*" (1), for Kristeva, abjection "does not have, properly speaking, a definable *object*" (1). However, in "Pink Dog," Bishop does imbue abjection with a representable, if not definable, object, the body. Kristeva's theory of the abjection locates the body, or more specifically, the orifices and products of these orifices, on the boundary between inside and outside. The abjection disrupts identity, disturbs order, and destabilizes systems.[19] The abject body also circulates in that Derridian space of play and *différance*.[20] Significantly, play's reliance on supplement suggests a disruption or deferral of meaning, and it points to potentially endless and multiple meanings, and more importantly, the supplement destroys the notion of binary oppositions. Abjection, or even more specifically, Bishop's naked dog, operates as a supplement as its visibility and nakedness centers the marginal. Bishop's dog rejects the governing function of the spectacle to unify by presenting the appearance of life. The naked, scabies-encrusted dog disturbs this presentation by moving "not-life" (the abjection)—placing *herself* in full view—front and center.

Bishop's pink dog parades in plain view and functions as a visual marker of a nonsubject, an abject being. However, this very visibility and the dog's refusal to occupy the margins prompt the speaker of the poem to offer both a solution (wear a costume) and a warning (your nakedness emerges as both threatening and vulnerable). Bishop seems here aware of what Adriana Cavarero identifies as crucial to what she calls "horrorism": "The uniqueness that characterizes the ontological status of humans is also in fact a constitutive vulnerability, especially when understood in corporeal terms" (*Horrorism* 20). I suggest that much is at stake in this warning: first, the dog's visible vulnerability exposes the fragility of the body itself and by extension of an ontological existence; second, within the poem, the pink dog poses a threat to the domain of the bounded and fixed subject and to any certainty regarding a coherent sexual identity. Paradoxically, the advice to cover the body through masquerade further destabilizes subjectivity, gender, and sexual identity, as well as traditional understandings of the body. "Masking is," as Steven Axelrod notes, "metalepis, a figural substitution" (76). In addition, a dog in costume becomes more noticeable as Costello humorously notes, "If a depilated dog does not look attractive, one in mascara, dressed up and dancing, is truly obscene" (86). However, obscenity does not threaten the sex-gender connection; this challenge comes from the costuming or masquerade of the dog.

"Masquerade" suggests several possibilities: a disguise worn at a festive gathering, a false outward showing, or a going about under false pretenses. In "Pink Dog," the speaker advises the animal to don masquerade in order to become invisible. The dog must cloak the body in invisibility in order to remove from view the threat of chaos and disorder that the abject female body implies. By covering the dog's nakedness, the *fantasía* that the speaker proposes should disguise the feminine abjection. However, the costume fails to mitigate the threat of the abjection as it merely offers an illusion of conformity. Masquerade cannot and does not eliminate the chaotic or the disorderly; rather, it veils the threat in acceptability.

Masquerade serves yet another function as it unfixes gender from sex and sex from the body. Butler raises several questions regarding the link between masquerade and femininity. Her questions move toward unfixing gender from the body and toward complicating notions of a coherent sexual identity. They also articulate the threat of the feminine, and perhaps the masquerade, to the stability of masculinity: "Does [masquerade] serve primarily to conceal or express a pregiven femininity, a feminine desire which would establish an insubordinate alterity to the masculine subject and expose the necessary failure of masculinity? Or is masquerade the means which femininity itself is *first* established?" (*Gender Trouble* 48). The body, of course, emerges as the site on which, and through which, the expression of either masculinity or femininity occurs. Masquerade, however, offers an alternative to the body as a location for these articulations. In other words, the masquerade can enact gender independent from the sexed body. It can both conceal and express a sexed or gendered identity; this concealment and expression, however, rarely indicates a coherent or stable sexual identity.[21] In "Pink Dog," masquerade serves to camouflage *and* to exhibit the body with its attendant sexualities. Significantly, masquerade hides female genitalia—the female body—while simultaneously amplifying performed femininity.

The speaker insists that the dog cover her nakedness, her threat of contagion, and her femaleness. Simultaneously, however, the speaker of the poem commands the pink dog to perform, to express her femininity through dance: "Dress up! Dress up and dance at Carnival!" (191). In "Pink Dog," survival depends on the dog's ability to "dress up" and on her ability to "dance at Carnival." The dog must assume a disguise and must also blatantly perform acceptable femininity while in that disguise. The speaker understands that through this performance the female body remains hidden, yet the performance moves abjection to the center for all to see.

Although, in "Pink Dog," Bishop explicitly acknowledges the need for costume in order to render the abject female body invisible, she implies that the masquerade renders female sexuality and desire visible. However, without the masquerade, the visibility of the body seems to threaten males within the Symbolic Order.[22] Within a psychoanalytical register, the feminine, "naked and pink," must be covered; unmasked, this femaleness reminds males that they stand in danger of losing the phallus. Masquerade involves rejecting aspects of femininity in order for a woman to be "the signifier of the desire of the Other": "It is in order to be the phallus, that is to say, the signifier of the desire of the Other, that a woman will reject an essential part of femininity, namely all her attributes in the masquerade" (Lacan 209). This explanation suggests that the Other can desire the woman only when she hides the reminder of castration, by masking both the female body and its sexuality. Unmasked female sexuality and desire pose too great a threat to the male and, by extension, to normative sexuality. Masquerade hides the female body, thus allowing that body to stand in for the phallus, the signifier of desire, ultimately reinforcing the stability of masculinity and a system predicated on sexual difference.

However, as Butler points out, having the phallus generates from an impossible ideal and from an anxiety of masculinity. The dog in Bishop's poem dons masquerade in order to lessen gender anxiety and to cover any reminders of loss (lack or castration), yet the attempt fails. The naked and pink dog, walking the streets during the carnival in Brazil, symbolizes both loss and abjection. The dog's presence, therefore, "represents for the subject the risk to which the very symbolic order is permanently exposed, to the extent that [filth] is a device of discriminations, of differences" (Kristeva 69). In "Pink Dog," loss, abjection, and filth all adhere to and construct the body (female); however, those elements are not the body. Kristeva makes clear that the abjection becomes "the jettisoned object [and] is radically excluded," and she locates abjection within the realm of desire (2). More specifically, the abjection must remain in its place of "non-existence and hallucination" in order to keep intact the illusion of a unified subjectivity.[23] Abjection also serves to stabilize the social order by siphoning off all bodies, all sexualities that exceed the limits imposed by cultural mandates.

"Pink Dog" foregrounds the dangers of excess within a society predicated on both patriarchy and heterosexuality. The warning the speaker issues to the hairless dog generates from an awareness of what Brazilian society does with those abject beings who insist on visibility: "They take and throw them in tidal rivers" (190). Those whom society attempts to confine to the margins, as well as the feminine, in "Pink Dog," become "the jettisoned object" as they bob "in the ebbing sewage," in the domain of the abjection.[24] In "Pink Dog," the feminine (exposed and disguised), as Bishop represents it in the abject body of a nursing naked dog, both threatens and solidifies culture, society, heterosexuality, patriarchy, and subjectivity.

The speaker's insistence that the dog don a costume carries with it an awareness of the cultural pressures to contain, control, and discipline the abject body and its excesses. However, with this carefully chosen word—*fantasía*—Bishop brings to the poem a consciousness that costume, masquerade, and performance do not harness the body, sexuality, or desire. Rather, the disguise and performance become the strategies of desire, sexuality, and the body. According to Carmen L. Oliveira, *fantasía* possesses a double meaning in Portuguese. It means both costume and illusion. This double meaning suggests masquerade always involves illusion, and, therefore, any attempt to cover the body becomes mere fantasy. Consequently, the body always remains visible. Ultimately, "Pink Dog" suggests the visibility of the body, and it points to the fantasy that underwrites notions of an unmediated body and to the fiction that insists on a coherent sexual identity. A *fantasía* becomes the apparel par excellence of the body inhabiting that liminal space where real meets unreal, self meets other, and normativity meets resistance.

CHAPTER 4

WRITING THE BODY PALIMPSEST

MARILYN CHIN

MARILYN CHIN WRITES WITHIN SEVERAL POETIC TRADITIONS—AMERICAN, Chinese, and Asian American.[1] At times, within her poetry, these traditions collide in jarring and unsettling ways, and at other times, they gently and subtly overlap. However, regardless of how these traditions manifest, they form the framework within and against which Chin writes. The body often serves as the visual site of this collision or overlap because the body as depicted by Chin must continually negotiate among various cultures—American, Chinese, and Chinese American. Because of this continual negotiation and because of the bicultural aspects of being an immigrant in white America, the body manifests as a palimpsest, in both senses of the word. Chin often marks her poetic bodies with multiple layers of inscriptions, and previous experiences remain legible and readable. The body also becomes the object that reflects personal, familial, and cultural histories. Thus, in Chin's poetry, we read history, dislocation, grief, anger, as well as subjectivity both on the body and through the body. In addition, Chin presents a body neither white nor black.

This poet does not write with the color blindness of whiteness that both Millay and Bishop often evoke.[2] Although the body in Chin's poetry occupies the threshold of white and not white, Chin simultaneously complicates that notion by marking the body as not quite white and not quite *non*white. Paradoxically, however, as many scholars argue, Chinese in America often served as the object(s) by which to solidify "the naturalization and centrality" of whiteness (Lowe 32).[3] Chin's focus on the Chinese immigrant experience evokes the legal formation, through the Chinese Exclusion Act, of the Chinese as racialized other. Her poetry echoes Mae Ngai's assertion that "exclusion informed the Chinese American historical experience in many ways. It codified Chinese as the racial 'other' in America—unwanted, unassimilable, ineligible to citizenship" (3). However, Chin also draws on a long history of the fraught position of Asians in the United States. The idea that Asian Americans have "come to occupy a curious place in the American racial imaginary, embodying both delight and repugnance" (Cheng 23), proves implicit in much of Chin's poetry.[4] Anne Cheng points specifically to "the notion of the 'model minority,' the figure who has not only assimilated but also euphorically sings the praises of the American way" (23). In "How I Got That Name," Chin directly addresses the insidiousness of this idea of the model minority by keeping the Asian American body in view—a body that does not look like the white American one or the African American, one

> neither black nor white,
> neither cherished nor vanquished. (18)

Whereas Bishop demonstrates some ambiguity *regarding* the body, Chin depicts an *ambiguous* body, one offering multiple interpretations as well as indicating confusion. I suggest that this confusion parallels the cultural confusion of the Asian American experience and the subjective disavowal demanded by assimilation. Repeatedly, Chin represents a subjectivity predicated on an ontological and corporeal denial. In other words, understanding oneself as an Asian American often involves denying one's cultural and racial being—both of which Chin locates on the body. On one hand, Chin's focus on the cultural displacement of the body and the loss that Asian American immigrants suffer *as* immigrants confronted by the demands of assimilation aligns with the concerns of most first-generation Asian American poets. On the other hand, Chin disrupts these expectations by depicting the body as the site where time and generations merge or intersect, and, in the Diana Toy poems, Chin demonstrates the collapse of existence when one refuses to swallow negation.[5] These two aspects of the body, the nexus between past and present and the place of ultimate resistance, emerge most blatantly in "How I Got That Name" and the Diana Toy poems in *The Phoenix Gone, The Terrace Empty.* However, before turning to these poems, I will investigate the ways in which the body responds to and disrupts normative and disciplining structures in several of Chin's other poems.

Just as she constructs a poetic hybridity, Chin often renders a corporeal and cultural hybridity. The speaker in "We Are Americans Now, We Live in the Tundra" lives in San Francisco but faces "seaward / toward China" (*Dwarf Bamboo* 28). In this poem, Chin offers a body relocated through immigration, yet despite its physical location, this body cannot turn away from its homeland. The body, then, becomes the vehicle and marker of the confusion often engendered by the bicultural experience. Although the Chinese immigrant body cannot literally lose the physical characteristics of being Chinese, Chin makes clear that cultural hybridity can threaten a Chinese American's sense of his or her "Chinese" self (if indeed one can identify racial and ethnic separate selves). In "That Half Is Almost Gone," the speaker laments the loss of

> the Chinese half,
> the fair side of a peach,
> darkened by the knife of time,
> fades like a cruel sun. (*Rhapsody in Plain Yellow* 17)

Rhapsody opens with "Blues on Yellow," which describes the pain and confusion of living Chinese in white America, and besides other things, this poem suggests the historical circumstances of being yellow. The third stanza begins with the image of a cracked egg with the yolk bleeding into the white, an image that Chin repeats in the second line, and then the speaker proclaims, "*Run, run, sweet little Puritan, yellow will ooze into white*" (13, emphasis in original). Although the speaker may indeed be "singing the blues," these lines convey a defiance of total assimilation (the yellow threatens the white). In addition to this reminder of the rhetoric of the "Yellow Peril," the poem also points to the real dangers faced by Chinese immigrants—violence to the body: "*If you cut my yellow fists, I'll teach my yellow feet to fight*" (13, emphasis in original). "Blues on Yellow" makes clear that violence to the body begets resistance. Chin's poetics of the body evidences layers of complications as the body that emerges serves as the nexus among personal and cultural histories. It becomes the constant reminder of the difficulty of living within and between two or more cultures.

Chin often uses flora and Southern California landscapes to represent the convergence of these cultures; usually, but not exclusively, these representations deal with Chinese and American vegetation. Direct inclusion of the body or its parts, as well as metaphors of the body, also marks these "landscape poems." Although "Where We Live Now (Vol 3, #4): *eternal noonscape*," also from *Rhapsody*, is a love poem addressed to the absent body of the speaker's lover, Chin's juxtaposition of human and plant bodies within the poem underscores the presence of cultural hybridity on American soil. The speaker of "Where We Live Now" notes the appearance of the "exotic seedlings" among the "local flora," claiming that the exotic has "invaded" the indigenous and cultivated landscape. "Seedlings" suggests that although the exotic must take root and that its survival is not assured, the exotic is indeed visible ("imperial cherries"; 64). The landscape then becomes a space clearly marked by cultural mixing.

These lines follow the speaker "naming" herself "Ms. Lookeast" and identifying herself as both bicultural and culturally displaced. Although she considers her "mother . . . the right hand of Buddha," the speaker positions herself as the "left hand of darkness." Then she ruminates on other body parts, nose, hair, and a "5 o'clock shadow," which the speaker deems unbecoming "on a Chinese woman" (64). Thus Chin addresses the difficulties of cultural identity through what the speaker considers appropriate to the Chinese American female body. The body becomes the thing that signals and solidifies cultural location and dislocation, much like a landscape comprised of cacti, cherries, wildflowers, and store-bought roses. In this instance, the body emerges as natural and exotic, uncultivated and cultivated.

Throughout "Where We Live Now," Chin offers depictions of the body or bodies, and then moves to descriptions of flora and fauna. This shift from human to plant or animal reinforces the psychic and emotional layering that occurs as the immigrant body moves from one cultural location to another. This body not only must adapt to "foreign" landscapes, but it also alters the landscapes into which it ventures. This alteration often engenders a sense of unease and unsettledness in both the foreign other and the dominant culture—certainly, white hegemony consolidates to combat this "invasion." Following the description of the yard, the poem breaks into white space. In the next section, the speaker makes very clear that just as the seedlings have mixed with the existing flora, she, the Chinese American, has entered a white neighborhood:

> A Chink has moved into their neighborhood
> and there's nothing they can do about it. (64)

Despite this claim that her neighbors can do nothing about her presence, earlier in the poem, she hints at the threat that always exists—the possibility that the neighbors will indeed attempt to do something:

> my skinhead neighbor says
> that he believes in segregation
> in racial purity . . . (61)

Of course, the racial purity of which the skinhead speaks is white because "being White [means] possessing the privilege of being uncontaminated by any other bloodline" (Kincheloe and Steinberg 6). In this poem, Chin challenges white hegemony's certainty of its pureness by presenting landscapes comprised of the foreign, the exotic, and the nonnative, and these landscapes serve as metonymic markers of the body.

However, the metonymic aspect of the body does not open the poem; rather, it emerges as the poem unfolds. Chin begins the poem by using metaphor to describe the body, in this instance, presumably that of a male. The speaker maps images of nature onto the corporeal using adjectives such as "savage," "pale," "fragrant," "sun-spectred," and "sliver-timbred" to describe her lover (57). This immediate conflation of body and nature signals the relationship between the body and the various images and descriptions of flora throughout the poem. Chin does not offer a traditional love poem in which the speaker "reads" nature in the body of the beloved in order to ruminate on his beauty. Rather, Chin's "savage" landscapes result in spaces where purple "jacarandas," "lantana," "geckos," "Korean grass," "horses," "motorcycles," "oleander," "jasmine," "forsythia," "verbena," and "hibiscus" "dance around" Mother Earth (57–58). This landscape emerges as one dependent on the savagery of variety. This section of the poem opens with the human body and ends with the body of Mother Earth. This movement from body to nature structures the poem, suggesting a body that must be constantly rethought and reconfigured because it is a body always out of place.

This "out-of-place-ness" seems most blatant in the section devoted to the speaker's mother. In this section, consisting of seven italicized lines, the speaker speculates that in painting bamboo her mother left the corporal, or more accurately, the body became the bamboo or vice versa. In this displacement, body/self into bamboo, the mother experiences liberation and celebration as she sings, *"one with the forest"* (63, emphasis in original).

Chin repeats the seven italicized lines, however, she does so with a difference, without using italics: "When / my / mother / painted / bamboo /" (63). Here the slashes do not represent line breaks; rather, Chin includes a slash after each word. Whereas, the italicized lines invite a fluid reading, the lines broken by the slash result in a labored reading, which, I suggest, foregrounds the disconnection the mother feels from her body. In both instances, however, Chin offers a poetic body split from any notion of subjectivity and from artistic creation: the mother cannot see herself in her artistic production. The body that emerges in these lines bespeaks the inability of the immigrant mother to claim a place of rootedness except as a disembodied voice within the landscape. However, this oneness with nature demands a loss of self as well as a denial of the body, both of which manifest more starkly in the drawn-out and belabored lines disrupted with slashes. Unlike the previous images of flora, these lines do not suggest a cultural hybridity; rather, they suggest the loss that often defines the immigrant experience. The body here is not one written and rewritten upon. This body remains "hardened," leaving it susceptible to breakage.

In "A Chinaman's Chance" from *Dwarf Bamboo*, Chin presents the image of literal dismemberment while simultaneously offering a metaphoric severing of cultural and ethnic identity from one's subjectivity:

> The railroad killed your great-grandfather.
> His arms, here his legs there. . . .
> *How can we remake ourselves in his image?* (29, ellipsis and italics in original)

Addressing a third- or fourth-generation Chinese American, the speaker draws on the history of Chinese immigrants on the West Coast. These lines delineate the part that Chinese labor played in the history of the United States, and they make clear the material conditions of life for Chinese immigrants.

Although not specifically addressed in this poem or in the other poems that I discuss in this chapter, the fact that the Chinese immigrant population was overwhelmingly male and remained so well into the twentieth century emerges as a crucial aspect of the lived reality of the Chinese immigrant. The sexual imbalance in this population occurred for several reasons. First, the Chinese concept of family bound a married woman to her *husband's family*, which discouraged women from emigrating with her husband. Second, most Chinese males came to America as sojourners with a view to returning home. However, George Peffer points to the 1875 Page Law (which preceded the Chinese Exclusion Act of 1882) as a key factor in keeping sexual imbalance in place within the Chinese population. This law "authorized American officials to prohibit the immigration of Chinese whom they suspected of coming for 'immoral' or other 'lewd' purposes" (8). In other words, the Page Law sought to keep out Chinese prostitutes and, in so doing, literally interpellated most Chinese females *as* prostitutes. Under this law, the female Chinese body could be read only as "immoral" and "lewd," thus in need of containment. Peffer convincingly argues that official census takers "ignored the existence of women who were not prostitutes. The apparent objectivity of their reports had, in turn, further obscured the presence of all but the prostitutes and reinforced the stereotypical images of the Chinese women who immigrated to the United States before 1882. Thus, the mysteries surrounding Chinese female immigration share a common thread of 'invisibility'" (9–10).

In "A Chinaman's Chance," as the lines quoted previously illustrate, the effects of violence on the Chinese immigrant body are *not* invisible. Chin offers the body as the ultimate sacrifice for life in America, and she also uses the trauma to the body to suggest the ontological wound of cultural and ethnic alienation for Chinese men *and* women: identity predicated on disavowal *is like* a body disconnected—dismembered—from itself. Chin insists that assimilation demands a forgetting, or negation, of the past. No references exist for the immigrant struggling to reconcile being Chinese in white America ("*How can we remake ourselves in his image?*").

Although "A Chinaman's Chance" moves away from the violence of a body torn to pieces, it continues to use the body as the visual marker of the history of Chinese labor in the United States. In addition, the body becomes the link between the then and now:

> Your father worked his knuckles black,
> So you might have pink cheeks. (29)

The juxtaposition of black knuckles and "pink cheeks" tells us that to understand the marks on the body is to understand the history of generations. Generally, succeeding generations of immigrants live lives "better than" those of the earlier generations. Although this poem suggests this improvement as evidenced on the body, it speaks to the psychic cost of becoming American (assimilation):

> Your father was happy, he was charred by the sun,
> *Danced and sang until he died at twenty-one.* (29, emphasis in orginal)

Once again, death becomes the ultimate price one must pay in order to reap the benefits of America. I suggest that these deaths function metaphorically to concretize the death of identity demanded by assimilation. By linking physical and psychic violence, Chin allows the body to disrupt the idealist discourse of the American dream *as the dominant culture presents that discourse to immigrants.*

Chin's commitment to writing poetry of activism, of keeping the material reality of immigration in view, means that she also renders bodies particularized by time and place. She refuses to present a universal or theorized body devoid of a personal and cultural history. For example, "The Last Woman with Lotus Feet," also from *Dwarf Bamboo*, identifies the setting as Locke, California, and the time as 1983, and the title specifies a body marked by the intersection of violence, beauty, and tradition. Locke, founded in 1915 after the Chinese section of Walnut Grove, California, burned, is the only U.S. town built by and *for* Chinese immigrants. In "Last Woman," Chinese history and tradition merge with immigrant experiences, and in this poem, the female body functions as the site of this convergence. The poem carries through the immigrant theme so prevalent in Chin's early poetry while simultaneously addressing issues specific to women regardless of their race or ethnicity. The poem opens with the effects of foot binding: "She hobbled down to tell us about the widows" (33). The image of a body bearing the story of ancient Chinese tradition gives way to the telling of more recent Chinese American history:

> of gold-diggers no taller than you and me, women
> who dragged their men out from under oxcarts and
> wheelbarrows. (33)

As in "A Chinaman's Chance," "Last Woman" highlights the violence enacted on immigrant bodies as it depicts the material cost of the dreams of "Gold Mountain."

However, by evoking the tradition of foot binding, Chin also presents the violence generated by culturally constructed notions of female beauty and femininity. While the last woman with lotus feet tells her listeners of the horrors of gold mining, of bodies crushed, the poem's images depict the horrors enacted in the name of idealized feminine beauty: an old and hobbling woman, "still virgin." In many ways, the woman in the poem seems caged—wings clipped—keeping her bound to place and trapped in time. "The bandage darkening around her ankles" (33) offers a bloody reminder that beauty ideals literally mark and eroticize women's bodies. Although Wang Ping locates female empowerment in the foot binding tradition because it helped form female communities,[6] she also acknowledges both the shame and eroticism attached to the bound foot. In an interview, she explains, "Chinese lotus feet have always been the object of eroticism, not only for Chinese, but also for the West. In the West, such a fascination is also mixed with the notion of exotic, mysterious, and the other" (Kawano). Wang makes clear the contradictory nature of the tradition and the varying perspectives regarding it: "A pair of perfectly bound feet must meet seven qualifications—small, slim, pointed, arched, fragrant, soft, and straight—in order to become a piece of art, an object of erotic desire. Such beauty is created, however, through sheer violence" (3). In "Last Woman," certainly words and phrases such as "hobbled," "still virgin," and "bandage darkening around her ankle" lead us to read foot binding as a brutal process that demonstrates violent means to dictate feminine beauty and control female sexuality. In this sense, then, "The Last Woman with Lotus Feet" resonates with other processes that violate a woman's body in the name of beauty and or chastity, and it disavows the eroticism associated with the demure, alluring, Chinese woman with bound feet.[7]

However, "The Last Woman with Lotus Feet" offers both male and female bodies particularized by race and gender. In this poem the weight of the American dream destroys the male body, and the demands of physical beauty disable the female one. Foot binding may have "hobbled" the woman in the poem, but she can and does bear testimony to the experiences of Chinese women as well as those of Chinese immigrants in general. She tells the story of suffering and loss of the early Chinese in America. The poem illustrates the convergence of various histories through a telling and through visual evidence (the woman's bound feet). Thus the poem posits the body as a crucial element in a cultural understanding of and for the Chinese American immigrant. The poem's closing line, "There was more to tell now, less to show," insists on the urgency of telling and retelling the stories that constitute the immigrant experience.

This telling and retelling emerges most overtly and directly in Chin's narrative poem, "How I Got That Name: An Essay on Assimilation," from her second volume of poems, *The Phoenix Gone, The Terrace Empty* (16–18). From the beginning of a narrative (poem), the telling is always a retelling because, as Paul Ricoeur reminds us, "when someone, whether storyteller, or historian, starts recounting, everything is already spread out in time" (171). The beginning has already occurred, and it already contains the events that will occur: The opening "I" in "How I Got That Name" is already Marilyn Mei Ling Chin; Marilyn Mei Ling Chin is already an I; migration has already taken place as has the renaming. The "events" of the succeeding sections also reside in the "I am" and constitute the subject: the speaker's recognition and resistance to Asian American stereotypes ("But the 'Model Minority' is a tease"); her lament regarding a lack of cultural belonging ("Oh, God, where have we gone wrong? / We have no inner resources!"; from section 2); and her inadequacy as *authentically* Chinese (from section 3):

> Then, one redolent spring morning
> the Great Patriarch Chin
> peered down from his kiosk in heaven
> and saw that his descendants were ugly.
> . . . .
> And I, his least favorite—
> "not quite boiled, not quite cooked,"
> a plump pomfret simmering in my juices—
> too listless to fight for my people's destiny. (17)

In "How I Got That Name," poetic time seems to make past and future equivalent. The "future" events of the narrative have already occurred; future, in narrative, *is* past. What implications regarding being arise from this seemingly collapse of boundaries between past and future, and how does this collapse implicate the body (specifically for Chin the immigrant body)?

In this poem Chin uses the body in two distinct ways: first, as the site of convergence of both time and generation, and second, as the particular marker of immigrant and gender experiences that tend to be both homogenized and marginalized. Again I will evoke the term palimpsest in order to describe how the body functions in "How I Got That Name." Webster's New Universal Unabridged Dictionary offers the following definition for "palimpsest": "(1) a manuscript, typically of papyrus or parchment that has been written on more than once, with the earlier writing incompletely erased and often legible; (2) an object, place, or area that reflects its history." Throughout this narrative poem, the body or person of Marilyn Mei Ling Chin evidences an earlier "existence" "incompletely erased and often legible," and it also emerges as the object "that reflects its history." In this poem the body and its temporal and special location underscore the instability of subjectivities constructed within multiple hegemonic structures such as Chinese *and* Chinese American cultural traditions and both Chinese and white patriarchy.

Many critics have commented on Chin's use of time; however, they discuss time in the context of generational dialogue and, for the most part, argue that Chin's use of cultural and familial pasts depicts the elements necessary for the immigrant to recognize his or her authentic subjectivity. Mary Slowik typifies critical approaches to this issue, arguing that Chin and other cross-cultural poets articulate the fear and necessity of looking back at one's home country, cultural and familial histories, and the event of migration. Slowik locates this looking back in these poets' use of the dialogic form, "the give-and-take of conversation . . . where the voice in the poem is not wholly the poet's own but shifts between family members and moves across time" (236). I, however, believe that Chin's poetry moves beyond the restrictions implied by authenticity. Many of Chin's poems, especially the poems under discussion, disrupt notions of authenticity. The body, as Chin presents it in her poetry, makes "real" immigrant experiences because it emerges as the visual and "real" location of cultural disconnection and violence. However, Chin's poetic bodies reveal the subtext of national and cultural narratives thus highlighting the illusions of order, rationality, and coherent subjectivity necessary to disciplining regimes.

The question, for me, becomes, how does Chin situate the body in the crossing of time to which Slowik refers? Although this crossing of time does indeed fracture the poetic voice into voices of the past and present as well as of the future, it also reinscribes time as continually present by offering a body testifying to the past while negotiating the present, a body "not quite boiled, not quite cooked." Chin's poem collapses the distinction between past and present by keeping in view cultural, familial, and personal histories as those histories manifest in the person of Marilyn Mei Ling Chin, yet "How I Got That Name" neither obliterates the present nor reifies the past. Rather, the poem positions the immigrant body in the now continually, albeit undercooked, looking back and peering forward.

Chin's poetry locates time within an ontological register by forging a link between time and being, certainly not a new endeavor. Many of Chin's poems do indeed constitute subjectivity through a play with time, and very often, these poems suggest that one cannot *be* unless one recognizes and acknowledges the "present-ness" of the past. However, because Chin perceives the present as crucial to selfhood, she does not simply replicate in poetry Heidegger's arguments regarding time and being.[8] Instead, she gives us a body that stabilizes *and* destabilizes connections among past, present, and future as well as between ideology and material existence.

Clearly, when Chin collapses the temporal distance between past and present, she seemingly reinforces Heidegger's notions regarding *Dasein*, the unified or authentic self. Indeed, when past and present merge in her poems, a movement toward future possibility emerges. For example, "How I Got That Name" opens with the first-person singular, "I," which implies a fixed subject—one rooted in time and space, in the "here and now," and "I" further indicates a self-knowing, an authority of presence. However, the "I" that the speaker claims proves much more complicated than a unified and authentic self. The name that follows this "I" immediately fragments the "I" through a convergence of Chinese and American names, and by line ten, the speaker acknowledges the factuality, or pastness, of the present (I am):

> I am Marilyn Mei Ling Chin
> Oh, how I love the resoluteness
> of that first person singular
> followed by that stalwart indicative
> of "be," without the uncertain i-n-g
> of "becoming." Of course,
> the name had been changed somewhere between Angel Island and the sea,
> when my father the paperson
> in the late 1950s
> obsessed with a bombshell blonde
> transliterated "Mei Ling" to "Marilyn." (16)

The "I" of the first line already carries within itself preexisting situations (factuality or past): migration and renaming. The "I am" (Marilyn Mei Ling Chin) is always already an "I was" (Mei Ling Chin) and an "I will be" (Marilyn Chin, Mei Ling Chin, *and* Marilyn Mei Ling Chin). Clearly, ontological concerns circulate in these opening lines. Beginning at a place of firmness, the speaker claims a "stalwart" existence—which defines both physical and psychic strength—and denies the ambiguity of subjectivity as process. However, the next lines completely upend the speaker's proclamation of resoluteness. The ironic "Of course" points precisely to the unsteadiness of the "I," and I suggest that these lines also rely on the body as the thing that actualizes or makes visible ontological instability.

The name change occurs during a physical relocation—the body literally moves from one place to another. In the course of that move, loss of name and renaming take place. Suspended in the oceanic—that Freudian place of limitlessness where the ego feels unbounded—the speaker of "How I Got That Name" literally loses a delineated ego as her father, "the paperson," renames her. "Paperson" refers to the Chinese immigrants who established their right to enter the United States through a paper trail. These men and, rarely but occasionally, women carried with them papers that identified them, often fraudulently, as sons and daughters of American citizens. Ngai argues that "the widespread practice of paper immigration during the exclusion period . . . exacerbated the stigma of illegitimacy associated with exclusion" (3). More importantly, however, paper immigration solidified the racial otherness of Chinese immigrants because "culturally, it contributed to a racialized view of Chinese as unscrupulous, devious, and immoral" (Ngai 6). These papersons often invented family connections, family histories.

Marilyn Mei Ling Chin's father lacked the body of the father; therefore, he proved paternal linage through marks on a paper. Marilyn Mei Ling becomes the text on which her father writes the cultural and familial history of Chinese immigration. Through his obsession with "a bombshell blonde," Chin bestows on his daughter a name that *embodies* whiteness and sexuality—it quite literally embodies the body. Thus the renaming carries with it both excess and lack. The *Marilyn* in Marilyn Mei Ling Chin signifies 1950s white America's ideal femininity while simultaneously signifying Mei Ling's fundamental lack in relation to that ideal—whiteness. The body, then, sits at this point of convergence between excess and lack. It, in fact, denies assimilation; however, this denial or the body's disruptive element does not generate only from the body. Instead, the "impulse" that "nobody dared question" places Mei Ling in an untenable position, and the body (her body) becomes the visible marker of this instability. It also bespeaks the irony inherent in the naming:

> And there I was, a wayward pink baby,
> named after some tragic white woman
> swollen with gin and Nembutal. (16)

Chin's ironic tone acknowledges the "psychical complications for people living within a ruling episteme that privileges that which they never can be" (Cheng 7). Marilyn Mei Ling Chin cannot *be* white nor can she ever be the iconic representation of that whiteness. Her Chinese American body disallows both.

While recognizing that "the minority subject" does indeed develop strategies that become both self-affirming and sustaining, Cheng maintains that the "injunctive ideal" initiates for the minority subject "a painful negotiation . . . with the demands of that social ideality, the reality of that always—insisted-on-difference" (7). The second section of "How I Got That Name" illustrates this negotiation, and this section depicts the anger and anguish of assimilating into white America. In this section the speaker names and challenges the position allotted to Asian Americans by a "ruling episteme":

> Oh, how trustworthy our daughters,
> how thrifty our sons!
> How we've managed to fool the experts
> in education, statistics and demography—
> We're not very creative but not adverse to rote-learning.
> Indeed, the can *use* us.
> But the "Model Minority" is a tease.
> . . . .
> The further west we go, we'll hit east;
> the deeper down we dig, we'll find China.
> . . . .
> Oh God, where have we gone wrong?
> We have no inner resources! (17, emphasis in original)

The speaker begins in a place of defiance; however, the tone shifts to one of confusion and pain.[9]

Cheng identifies the pain and confusion that emerges in this poem as symptomatic of the "history of Asian abjection" in relation to the American dream (23). Indeed, Chin's poem through its depiction of Mei Ling's father, the representation of the "trustworthy daughters [and] thrifty sons," and the inclusion of the "Model Minority" does evoke, what

Cheng terms, the Asian immigrant's "manic relation" to this dream (23). *Manic* denotes both excess and violence, and "A Chinaman's Chance" and "The Last Woman with Lotus Feet" offer the body as the visual marker of both. Cheng concludes that "to racially assimilate (in the senses of blending *and* taking in) implies an act of private and subjective dissimulation" (126, emphasis in original). "How I Got That Name" more closely ties the "history of Asian abjection" to subjectivity than do the other two poems previously discussed.

Although I believe that this notion of "private and subjective dissimulation" underwrites many of Chin's poems, "How I Got That Name" more directly delineates the subjective processes implicated in being Asian American. As the poem's subtitle, "An Essay on Assimilation," indicates, subjectivity for Asian Americans involves incorporation of, adaptation to, and absorption into white America. In an interview with Calvin Bedient, Chin makes clear the loss that assimilation entails: "The loss of China, the loss of being part of that world . . . My poetry is about the fear of assimilation, of being incorporated by the Western world" (12). The dissembling that Cheng identifies as an element in assimilation for the Asian American demands that the individual pretend *to be*. The question becomes, *to be what*? White? A *real* American? The model minority? This ontological confusion becomes clarified through and on the body in Chin's poems because the body cannot pretend to be anything other than what it *is*. Although the being-ness of the body does, according to contemporary theories of the body, arise from cultural, social, and personal constructions and understandings of it, the immigrant Asian American body as rendered by Chin cannot be other than what it is—an embodiment of otherness. I do not argue that all Asian immigrants are essentially other. Instead, I suggest that white America's reliance on the centrality and normativity of unexamined whiteness casts all nonwhite bodies as other. The Asian body, in this instance, becomes culturally constructed and understood *as* other by hegemonic whiteness. Chin herself acknowledges her experience with otherness: "In America, I'm always reminded of my difference" (Bedient 12). Thus this body is physically different from that of a white American, and it *performs* differently than does the body of an "authentically" Chinese because most often the body in Chin's poems is a body living a bicultural existence.

"How I Got That Name" presents a body that does not look American and does not act Chinese, does not behave according to Chinese cultural mandates; rather, the body is Chinese American. The body as it emerges in Chin's poems slides along a continuum of Asian-ness and American-ness— not Chinese enough for the Great Patriarch Chin and certainly not white enough for white America. Chin adorns the body in "a too-tight / laven-der kimono" in "Night Visit" and in a Mandarin frock in "I Confess . . ." (both from *Dwarf Bamboo*), and she decorates the body with tattoos and eyeliner in these poems. Chin fragments the body—offering it piece by piece (eyes, lips, hair, arms, thighs, back)—in "Unrequited Love," and she gives us a face scarred with reticence in "Beauty, My Sister, Is Not Regalia." Chin renders into poetry young and old bodies, growing and aging ones, the bodies of grandmothers and mothers, of wives and lovers, of brides and widows, of musicians and singers, of poets and painters, and of prin-cesses and prostitutes. Chin does not depict a universalized or essentialized Asian (American) body because she cannot—such a body does not exist. She does, however, through her poetry, underscore the link between sub-jectivity and the body. Her poetic bodies disrupt the tidy categories that assimilation demands—categories of margin and center, inclusion and exclusion—because the poems present the body as dynamic rather than static. We do not find a fixed and unchanging "other" in Chin's poems; instead, we find subjects under construction. In other words, many of these poems represent the process of becoming and knowing.

Whether or not overtly *about* the body, Chin's poetry continually engages with bodily representations or tropes. The Marilyn Mei Ling Chin of "How I Got That Name" works through the ontological issues of assimilation and subjectivity, and she relies on the body to ground her "sense" of being. She begins by acknowledging that her "Asian" body cannot be the body of the blonde bombshell for whom she is named, nor can it be the black body against which whiteness sustains. However, as Marilyn Mei Ling Chin of "How I Got That Name" confronts and challenges the demands of assimilation and as she describes the psychic cost of assimilating, she appears critically aware of the body as crucial to both—challenging the demands of assimilation and experiencing the wounds of assimilating.

In the last section of the poem, Chin writes of death, which implies the end of the material body. The trope of death works on several levels: first, it ties both subjectivity and the body to concepts of time; second, it reminds us of the materiality of the body. Besides her insistence that both space and time are crucial to our ability to rethink traditional theories of the body, Elizabeth Grosz also makes clear that "bodies are always under-stood within a spatial and temporal context, and space and time remain conceivable only insofar as corporeality provides the basis for our percep-tion and representation of them" (*Space, Time* 84). Grosz outlines the link between time, space, and subjectivity, and she argues for the impor-tance of understanding both the natural and social sciences' discourses on time and space. Finally, Grosz "assess[es] conceptions of space/time from the point of view of the sexually specific embodiment of subjects" (84). Throughout "How I Got That Name," Chin plays with conventional understandings of space and time, and, as I have argued, the immigrant body provides the grounding for both. In other words, Chin conceptualizes space and time through a racially or ethnically specific embodiment of the subject. Ironically, death signals both the collapse of space and time and the corporeality of the body, thus through this trope, Chin reminds us that we negotiate all dimensions of our world as well as our subjectivity on and through an always already decaying body.

In the poem Marilyn Mei Ling Chin waits "for imminent death" but admits that "this death is also metaphorical," which attests to her "lethargy." This literal and metaphorical death suspends the "I" in time (waiting in the present for something in the future) and in space (a site of certainty "imminent death" and a site of instability, or turn—metaphor). However, the last stanza seems to resolve these tensions. The speaker, evoking words usually found etched into a headstone, says, "Here lies Marilyn Mei Ling Chin." Do these lines as well as this closing section signal the literal death of Marilyn Mei Ling Chin, or does Chin give us a metaphorical death? Does the speaker bury the Marilyn Mei Ling Chin who wearily masquerades as wife, granddaughter, daughter, poet, "neither black nor white," or does she offer us a Marilyn Mei Ling Chin who comes *to be* within the gap between past and present, Chinese and Chinese American, American and Chinese American, Chinese and American? I suggest that the poem does the latter.

The space in which Marilyn Mei Ling Chin *is* occurs *in* time "one day" and *in a gap* in time, a chasm with the attributes of blinding whiteness and spectacular "Asian-ness":

> when one day heaven was unmerciful,
> and a chasm opened where she stood.
> Like the jowls of a mighty white whale,
> or the jaws of a metaphysical Godzilla,
> it swallowed her whole. (18)

The allusions of these lines ("a mighty white whale" and "Godzilla") intensify the bicultural aspects and ontological conflicts of being Asian American. They also satirically entwine "high" literary tradition (*Moby Dick*) with "low" popular culture. Significantly, however, in the lines quoted above, Chin works on two levels of time: one quantitative and easily recognizable, "one day"; the other immeasurable and more difficult to discern, a marked interruption of continuity, "chasm." In these lines

Chin places Marilyn Mei Ling Chin not in a coffin underground; rather, she locates her in a *space in time*. In this gap in time, existence is possible. Indeed, I suggest that in "How I Got That Name," Chin posits a subjectivity constituted through past, future, and present, but actualized in the gaps among them.

In the end Marilyn Mei Ling Chin is apparently whole and happy:

> solid as wood, happily
> a little gnawed, tattered, mesmerized
> by all that was lavished upon her
> and all that was taken away. (18)

"Solid" certainly suggests permanence and stability. However, I suspect Chin's characteristic irony here. "Wood" undercuts, or troubles, the suggestion of stability as wood is neither unchanging nor indestructible. Indeed, John Gery asserts that "the end of 'How I Got That Name' balances precariously between, the assimilation into American culture that Chin sees as inevitable, an assimilation that will ultimately eradicate her distinctly Asian heritage" (37). However, I contend that the "I," the Marilyn Mei Ling Chin, that emerges at the end of the retelling exists not within a void of nothingness but rather in a space of possibilities filled with a past open to reinscription "gnawed and tattered," a present spellbound by the violence and benevolence of the past, and a future that can retell the story of Marilyn Mei Ling Chin without the constraints of the present telling.

By the end of "How I Got That Name," the subject and, by extension, the body are marked ("gnawed, tattered") by both abundance ("all that was lavished upon [it]") and lack ("all that was taken away"). This excess and lack, fullness and emptiness, largess and denial propel the poems in the section of *The Phoenix Gone, The Terrace Empty* titled "Homage to Diana Toy" (59–68). These oppositions along with the vanishing body of Diana Toy thematically unite the eight poems. These poems poignantly depict the physical and psychic effects of acculturation, and they represent the extreme of "Asian abjection" while simultaneously detailing the link between beauty ideals and the destruction of the body.

Feminist scholars as well as others have examined and continue to examine what Sharlene Nagy Hesse-Biber terms "the cult of thinness." Most, if not all, of these researchers identify the link between cultural ideals and eating disorders. Hesse-Biber writes that "women's bodies are cultural artifacts, continually molded by history and culture" (45). While certainly not the first to make such a claim, Hesse-Biber does so not within a theoretical framework but rather from within a clinical one. Based on her research, she identifies a clear distinction between clinical eating disorders and culturally induced ones. Hesse-Biber offers the following conclusion: "*Those women who subscribed to the cultural definition of body image were more at risk for developing eating disorders*" than those who followed a medical model (155, emphasis in original). Clearly, perceptions of one's body and its relationship to beauty arise from cultural and historical mandates. In other words, how women "experience being a body" (to borrow a phrase from Hesse-Biber) rests on a process of acculturation or assimilation. Women must be *acculturated* into a patriarchal society and into the cult of thinness.

Although numerous studies exist dealing with eating behaviors and disorders, these reports deal primarily with "Caucasian American adult women with eating disorders who attend college, who are seen in inpatient and outpatient treatment settings, or who live in areas where large university-based research-oriented hospitals operate" (Walcott, Pratt, and Patel 224). However, more recent studies have begun to investigate body image and eating disorders among African American, Asian American, and Hispanic women. Writing for *AsianWeek*, Eunice Park speaks directly to the "myth that eating disorders are only prevalent in white teenagers" noting that "eating disorders have been most rampant in South Korea and China, countries that are undergoing rapid economic change and increasingly Western acculturation." Park reveals that nonwhite women do, in fact, struggle with eating disorders. More importantly, Park links these disorders to acculturation and assimilation: "While Asians living in Asia have to cope with rapid Westernization, it has been suggested that the pressures of discrimination, trying to blend into Western society, and certain stereotypes compound the problem for Asian Americans." Christine Iijima Hall extends this point and adds an ontological component to the discussion: "Devaluation of their homeland by the dominant American culture may cause young women to reject their country of origin," and she continues, "Asian women see many physical disparities between white women and themselves . . . This comparison may lead to 'feelings of inferiority' (Arknoff & Weaver, 1996), self-hatred (Fujitomi & Wong, 1973), and racial self-hate (Sue & Sue, 1971)" (10–11). Finally, Hall acknowledges, "The fear among mental health professionals is that as the new generation of Asian American women becomes more 'acculturated' they may begin to take on 'dysfunctional' behaviors of white American society" (17). In the Diana Toy poems, Chin presents the "story" of a young Chinese American girl's struggle with assimilation, patriarchal and cultural expectations, and male power, and Diana's ultimate death from Diana's refusal to eat.

The body, in these poems, testifies to the dangers confronting non-Western women attempting to adapt to Western ideals of beauty, dangers, of course, that lurk for all women in the face of these ideals. However, Chin's poems, because they situate Diana's struggle within frameworks of assimilation and acculturation, open a theoretical space in which we can think differently about both the ontological and physical effects of these demands. In other words, the female body must always assimilate into patriarchal culture, and in some sense, then, *that* body is always a foreign body. For female immigrants, then, a double assimilation or acculturation must take place as *woman* and as *immigrant*. In addition, as Chin's poems also make clear, this assimilation takes place amid competing patriarchal mandates. These women must be Chinese women as well as American women, and this negotiation often results in ontological confusion. In the Diana Toy poems, Chin reveals the precariousness of subjectivity itself for immigrant women by positioning Diana's anorexic, female, Asian, American body within a matrix of conflicting discourses and ideologies. This position results in Diana's denial, negation, and destruction of the visual marker of her otherness—the body.

Chin, of course, is not the first writer or poet to present images of hunger, starvation, and food in relation to women. Tamar Heller and Patricia Moran point out that "a number of noteworthy studies . . . elaborating on the connection between anorexia and self expression in literary texts [exist] . . . Women writers themselves anticipated this critical work, deliberately making use of tropes of hunger, starvation and eating to explore complex issues of female identity and expression" (4–5). Although not explicitly addressing issues of expression in the Toy poems, Chin does imply the connections among silence, starvation, assimilation, and the body. Indeed, Chin uses the trope of eating and not eating to reveal the physical and psychological effects of refusing to ingest both Chinese and American mandates. Diana literally denies the biological demand of her body, which culminates in its destruction. In addition, during this process of denial, Diana also becomes both an "I" and a "not-I," "a hollow specimen" ("First Lessons, Redux" 64).

In her groundbreaking work on Asian American literature, Cynthia Wong Sau-ling identifies "eating as one of the most biologically deterministic and, at the same time, socially adaptable human acts," (18) and she argues that "ingestion is the physical act that mediates between self and not-self, native essence and foreign matter, the inside and outside . . . [P]sychological survival . . . may demand unusually difficult 'swallowing' to ensure a continued supply of nourishment for the next generation" (26). This "swallowing" refers to internalizing cultural mandates demanded of immigrants by white America. In "Gruel," the first poem in "Homage to Diana Toy," the speaker directs Diana:

> This is the philosophy of your tong:
> you, the child, must learn to understand the universe
> through the port-of-entry, your mouth, (59)

The body becomes the vehicle through which Diana must "learn," and understanding occurs through ingestion, yet as the series of poems makes clear, Diana refuses to "swallow" either food or cultural mandates. Truth for Diana, becomes her "hunger / growing wider as the season darkens" ("The Disorder" 60). Finally, according to Sau-ling, "Swallowing negation creates an unfillable hole in the very core of one's being" (77). The paradox and irony that resides in "swallowing negation" underscores the poignancy of the Diana Toy cycle in *Phoenix*.

The subtitle to "Homage to Diana Toy" identifies Diana's location, and it situates her in time: "Crestwood Psychiatric Hospital, 1983." Diana's confinement disrupts the inside-outside binary by placing her both inside (abnormality) *and* outside (normalcy). Her "'destination [is] elsewhere' / and her 're-entry [is] denied'" ("First Lessons, Redux" 64). In addition, although the subject of the poems, Diana has no voice and, more importantly, no bodily presence. Thus Diana simultaneously inhabits the margins and various centers. The speaker—presumably a woman—of "Gruel," the first poem in the series, names Diana Toy as the subject of the poem, and the speaker reminds Diana of her role as daughter—as Chinese daughter:

> Your name is Diana Toy.
> And all you have for breakfast is rice gruel.
> You can't spit it back into the cauldron for it would be unfilial. (59)

The next two lines repeat "You can't," thus setting a tone of denial and negation. Chin makes clear that, within Chinese cultural mandates, all options are closed to Diana *except for swallowing the gruel.*

Diana emerges not in bodily descriptions; rather, she shimmers with a noncorporality that pervades the rest of the poem:

> even if it's nothing,
> that gruel, that nothingness will shine. (59)

Chin makes nothingness visible. Diana will see it in her "mother's scrap-iron wok," in "the glare of [her] father's cleaver," and finally, nothingness will "dance in [Diana's] porcelain bowl" (59). By the end of "Gruel," Diana and nothingness merge:

> Remember, what they deny you won't hurt you.
> What they spare you, you make shine,
> so shine, shine . . . (59)

This glimmer that constitutes Diana suggests a nonbeing, an ontological absence. As Diana increasingly becomes a nonbody, she also seems to become a nonperson. Ironically, Diana shines through self-negation, the refusal to eat, and through a lack of bodily substance.

The subsequent poems detail the psychology of this negation and denial, and Chin seems intent on linking Diana's refusal to eat to issues of acculturation and assimilation. I believe that, within these poems, anorexia emerges as a material marker, albeit an extreme one, of the ontological confusion that comes from straddling cultures. Susan Bordo contends that "a variety of cultural currents or streams converge in anorexia, find their perfect, precise expression in it" (142). Indeed, in the Diana Toy poems, this disorder seems to function as "the perfect, precise expression" of the liminal or non-place of the Asian American woman in white America. As George Peffer's historical research indicates, Chinese women in America were indeed invisible in official records, and because of both the Page Law and the Exclusion Act, Chinese women were also physically absent. Diana must be Chinese, but she is Chinese within an American context. Her heritage demands that she follow the philosophy of her tong, that she perform her filial duties, and that she embrace the promise of America, yet throughout "Homage to Diana Toy," Diana remains absent, an eerie nonbody:

> Everywhere
> you venture the mirrors whisper,
> the pond's reflections resound your dolor. ("The Disorder" 60)

Chin's poem captures and (re)presents the paradox of anorexia: it is all about body, but, as Bordo stresses, the thin body is "the nonbody" (146). Thus, anorexia serves as an apt metaphor for the paradox of being Asian American—"the model minority," the expert assimilationists, and the foreign other.

In Diana's world, nothing confirms (reflects back) her corporal existence; rather, her sense of self rests on her grief and her diminishing physicality. Diana takes up little space, and, much like Marilyn Mei Ling Chin in "How I Got That Name," she balances on the abyss:

> As you attempt to fill an emptiness
> not filled by the sun, as you wait

for your inevitable fall,
a small child
within you remembers: *so, these, these,*
were the "golden mountains!" (60, emphasis in original)

In these lines Chin makes clear the promise of America, the abundance of the Gold Mountain, and like "A Chinaman's Chance" and "The Last Woman with Lotus Feet," "The Disorder" reinforces the psychic and physical cost of the American Dream. The poem suggests that in order to assimilate—to claim the abundance of the Gold Mountain—the Asian female must empty herself of *herself.* In fact, Sau-ling identifies this necessity to disavow one's Asian-ness as "one of the bitterest necessities for Asian Americans." Sau-ling explains that "Asian Americans [have] to contend with total devaluation of their Asian ethnicity. If they stomach it, they get caught in a crucial bind: to become acceptable to a racist society, one must first reject an integral part of oneself" (77). Obviously, anorexia becomes the marker *par excellence* of this jettisoning of an integral part of selfhood as the disorder mandates a rejection of one's body.

The body that circulates throughout the eight poems comprising "Homage" hardly seems material as it emerges from within the framework of self-starvation. This body, however, is the location of resistance and as such it is also a confined body:

After you get well, Diana,
we'll take that long drive.
. . . .
But today, there are particulars:
bath-time, nap-time, music therapy,
a meeting to condemn contrabands. ("Diana Takes a Nap; Dolores Calls Mia
to Apologize; Mrs. Moorehead Leaves for the Community" 61)

Chin renders a passive body, controlled and regulated by the routines of the hospital, and one implicated within a field of power relations. Most researchers agree that anorexia often arises from the anorexic's desire to assert control. It seems rather ironic that Diana's recovery from this disorder requires that she surrender control. These poems underscore the Foucauldian notions regarding power and the body. According to Foucault, "Power relations have an immediate hold upon [the body]; they invest it, mark it, train it, torture it, force it to carry out tasks, to perform ceremonies, to emit signs . . . [T]he body becomes a useful force only if it is both a productive body and a subjected body" (*Discipline and Punish* 26–27).

Seemingly, within the parameters of a Foucauldian framework, Diana's body is not a useful force. Although a subjected body, it hardly appears as a productive one. However, if this body is the site of resistance, then it *is* indeed productive as it produces resistance to disciplinary regimes. My argument here refers not to a "real" body but to Diana's body as Chin *represents* it in the poems. It is this representation of the body that is productive in the Foucauldian sense. In other words, within her poetry, Chin gives Diana's anorexic, immigrant, Asian body meaning. Through her poetry, Chin presents the body as a productive force—one possessing the potential to disrupt normativity.

Thus Chin uses representations of the body to further her poetry of activism. In "Homage to Diana Toy," she reveals the dangers of assimilation while simultaneously depicting the perils that exist for women within a patriarchal society. Two distinct sets of power relations converge in these poems, and the body provides the nexus for this convergence: immigrant/"real" American and male/female. "The Administrator," the fifth poem in the series of eight poems, details Diana's rape by the hospital administrator and, by extension, her violation by the institutions of patriarchy. The administrator (the "he" of the poem) represents "the other world," a world other than Diana's. He is "the keeper of the gate, the purveyor of keys" (65). The administrator becomes the part for the whole—the metonymic marker of patriarchy, of government control, of "the powers that be." He represents a disciplining force, and through rape he further diminishes Diana's claim to her body:

> He says,
> "You would not bite the hand that feeds you, Diana." And so,
> she succumbs to him . . . and those within chant the song of the prairie:
> the beast does what beasts do as the lion plays with his maw,
> and the carrion teases the condor. (65)

These lines underscore intersecting fields of power: Diana's resistance to the demands of assimilation *and* patriarchy. She has already "bit" the hand that feeds her because she refuses to feed—to ingest patriarchal and cultural mandates.

As she does in "The Last Woman with Lotus Feet" and "A Chinaman's Chance," Chin presents the body as the site of racialized and gendered violence. The anorexic, resisting body that Chin depicts in the Diana Toy poems is not safe from physical assault from others. Diana "succumbs" to the rape of her body—a body that has already become "not her." In "The Administrator," Chin further severs the body and its experiences from the "self" of Diana. In the chant of the prairie,

Chin evokes disassociation, a common occurrence in rape and sexual assault. In order to survive the physical assault, the rape victim disavows the body—to claim it could mean psychic annihilation. With chilling irony, Chin's imagery presents Diana as the food; her starving, shrinking body becomes the substance for patriarchal or governmental power. This poem, devoid of optimism or possibility, sounds a harsh warning regarding a woman's place within the institutions of patriarchy. As Diana ponders and longs for death, silent witnesses chant, "*The State is your conservator; the prairie will be your life!*" (65, emphasis in original). In other words, because Diana refuses to eat from the hand that feeds her, she will be forever confined and devoured. Her escape rests in oblivion and in total destruction of the body.

I believe it important to note the contradictions that arise both in the poem and in my analysis regarding the body as it circulates within "Homage to Diana Toy." On one hand, anorexia often signals a girl's or woman's internalization of white America's beauty ideal, and as such, this behavior seems more subjected or compliant than defiant. On the other hand, anorexia also often signifies girls' or women's assertion of power and control in the face of strong cultural mandates regarding a woman's body. Within patriarchy, certainly, the control or containment of the female body has been and, to a degree, continues to be denied women. I argue that the representations of the body in Chin's poetry carry these contradictions. As Chin gives voice to the experiences of immigrants and to the tensions specific to those experiences, she (consciously or unconsciously) reveals the significance of the body. After all, within white America people of color are simultaneously invisible or *hyper*visible, bodiless or all body, a condition of which Chin seems well aware. Chin does not, however, reduce Diana to body, and although I argue that Diana seems to become a nonperson as her body diminishes, I do not suggest that Chin sees the link between "self" and body as inviolate. Instead, I want to suggest that Chin depicts the interrelation between "self" and body and that very often the body becomes a vehicle for denying *and* claiming subjectivity, for complying with *and* challenging disciplinary mandates, and for celebrating *and* denigrating one's existence.

As the title of the Diana Toy cycle makes clear, these poems serve as a homage to this young woman. They testify to loss and grief often associated with assimilation (into white America, into patriarchy). "Homage to Diana Toy" reiterates the significance of personal and cultural histories and to the ways in which those histories mark bodies. *Homage* denotes deference and honor all of which indicate respect or reverence paid. Chin uses the forms and elements of poetry to pay tribute to immigrants and their experiences. Through the wit, irony, and beauty of her poetic language, she writes of the sadness and sacrifice as well as the "wonderful magic of [assimilation]" (Moyers 69). Throughout the Diana Toy poems, "That Half Is Almost Gone," "Blues on Yellow," "Where We Live Now," "A Chinaman's Chance," "The Last Woman with Lotus Feet," and "How I Got That Name," Chin offers marred, scarred, deformed, and starved bodies, and through her poetry, she presents the body as testament to the complexities of being Asian in America.

CHAPTER 5

NARRATIVE AND DESIRE ON AND THROUGH THE BODY

MARILYN HACKER

IN 1925, FREUD ASKED, "WHAT DOES A WOMAN WANT?" In 1988, Jessica Benjamin offered "that women *want to want*, to have a sense of agency and desire—sexual subjectivity" (qtd. in Elise 125). The poetry of Marilyn Hacker underscores this wanting to want as it pulses with a sense of both agency and desire. "Lesbian lives, women's various relationships with other women, women writer's relationship to forms, frank lyrical portrayals of women's bodies, aging, cancer, and death" comprise the major themes of Hacker's poetry, and "graphic images of sexual love [have] become one of her trademarks" (Curry, "Marilyn Hacker" 159). Hacker develops these themes, most of which play out in the register of desire and sexual subjectivity, through the language *of* the body while simultaneously mapping language *onto* the body. Throughout her oeuvre, she presents us with details and descriptions of the body (how it looks, what it does, and what it wishes to do). For Hacker, language, desire, and body continuously interact, and through this interaction, sexual subjectivities and narratives emerge.[1] Bodies with their attendant sexualities create narratives, and they *are* narratives. Like language, bodies seem to suggest too little or too much.

The body as represented in Hacker's poetry, however, seems always on the edge of excess, constantly straining to exceed containment, with "waves . . . overflow[ing] restraint" ("Eight Days in April" from *Love, Death, and the Changing of the Seasons* 70).[2] Dianne Elise argues that cultural mythology regarding male sexuality as active, visible, and concentrated and female sexuality as passive, hidden, and diffuse "must in some part reflect the actuality of the two bodies" (137). Thus, according to Elise, "anotomical qualities are extended into culturally relevant anatomical metaphors that then lead to a particular view of the body as a 'reality' of anatomy . . . The cultural emphasis is an extension of the two bodies that circles back around to inaccurately define and confine the body" (137). By offering female bodies and sexualities that reject passivity and refuse to be hidden, Hacker challenges this cultural mythology regarding sexuality, and she gives new meaning to cultural metaphors of and for the body. *Love, Death, and the Changing of the Seasons* chronicles the development and end of a lesbian love affair between the narrator, Hack, and Rachel, and this chronicle unfolds through detailed accounts of sexuality and sexual desire. Significantly, the 180 poems in the volume reconstitute female desire as both active and visible. Hack wants Rachel "so much [she] can taste it," and she admits to being "horny as a timber wolf in heat" (6, 10). Hack unabashedly proclaims she wants to "suck," "infiltrate," "tug," "stoke," and "lick" ("Fear of Flying" 22). In "Fear of Flying," Hacker constitutes the speaker's desire as active as Hack explains what *she* wants to *do*.

Although, in a poem located midway through *Love, Death and the Changing of the Seasons*, Hacker blatantly jettisons the dichotomy of gender ("*can* the dichotomy"; 111, emphasis added), she does not, however, simply rewrite the active (male) or passive (female) binary into a lesbian framework. Instead, Hack desires *as* a woman. The sexual desire is the desire of a woman for a woman. As the love affair develops, the poems represent this sexual aggressiveness as shared and fluid. Both women actively desire and *act* on that desire. In the sonnet that begins, "First, I want to make you come in my hand," the speaker uses the phrase "I want" four times clearly articulating her desire, and she details what she wishes to do: "watch," "drink," "hold" (21). However, as Suzanne Juhasz asserts, this "sonnet . . . is formally structured around *reciprocal* identification in/ through erotic desire" (156, emphasis added). Besides identification, this reciprocity indicates that desire itself shifts *along* an active-passive continuum rather that *between* an active-passive split.

Although traditional understandings of active sexual desire map maleness and femaleness onto this continuum, Hacker's poem does not. The bodies involved are female bodies, and the desire is that of women for each other. In the closing lines of this sonnet, Hack's "desire is to be done to—for the lover to do for her what she had done for her lover" (Juhasz 156). Thus Hack desires both to give and receive, which means that Rachel, too, must be both active and passive, and Hack makes this point clear as she tells her lover what she needs and wants from her. Hack demands that Rach "cover" her with Rach's "hands, everywhere," and, with no shades of subtlety, Hack directs, "Make me come" (21). Sexual aggressiveness shifts between the lovers further eschewing any notions of a polarity of masculinity and femininity. In "Saturday Morning," Rachel becomes a "troubadour" who initiates the lovemaking (74). This sonnet casts Rachel as active: the actions are hers; she wakes Hack, catches her, and makes her come.

While it proves tempting to argue that at various times during the relationship each woman takes up a positionality of masculinity, such a claim reinforces the cultural mythologies regarding the body, sexuality, and gender. Juahsz's explanation regarding lesbian desire provides a sound framework in which to ground my reading of a reconfigured cultural understanding of the body in Hacker's work: "Lesbian desire extends the range and definition of *woman* to include gender positions that are neither traditionally feminine nor traditionally masculine, erotic positions that are not heterosexual" (145). Because multiple positions and desires generate from and on the female body, the male-female split crumbles.

Hacker opens the fourteenth poem in *Love, Death, and the Changing of the Seasons* by directly addressing Rachel, calling her a "boy," one who Hack "would have eyeballed at the bar" (17). However, this "boy" body reconfigures by the end of the poem, and although Hack again expresses what she will do, the poem ends in a shared place, a "place [they] both belong" (17). Both the body and desire constitute this place of belonging, and this poem, like many of the poems throughout Hacker's various volumes, constructs desire as active while making clear that it circulates between women. "Conversation in the Park" also foregrounds the body's fluidity, its ability to defy gender classification:

> Honey, you look like a twelve-year-old boy.
> But you go down on me the way, God knows,
> only a girl goes down! (101)

The body in these poems manifests as dynamic, changing, and changeable. It refuses the stasis demanded of it by a fixed, binary system of gender and sexuality. Instead, the body can be boy or girl without restraint.

The collapse of the male-female split as a structuring binary of desire also denies the power-powerless and sadistic-masochistic binaries. This denial occurs within realms both of desire and narrative. Joseph Boone identifies a "sense in which both the act of sex and the art of fiction are not only *overpowering* but expressions of absolute *powerlessness*, enacting the intense human desire to let go—to be released, to yield to an 'other' (a lover, a text)" (1, emphasis in original). In the sonnets previously quoted, Hack's litany of her wants does indeed seem overpowering; the

"I" controls the narrative unfolding of the poems as well as the desire. However, Hack also indicates her intense desire "to yield to an "other": "I want you to make me come" ("Saturday Morning" 74). Many of the poems in *Love, Death, and the Changing of Seasons* represent desire as overpowering *and* powerless, and they depict the desire for surrender as well as for control. Boone offers a crucial warning regarding this issue of submission: "Surrender to otherness on these terms [should not] be confused with masochistic submission to a greater power" (2). Importantly, he identifies the difficulty that exists within our "disciplinary culture . . . to conceptualize acts of surrender that are not acts of submission" (2). The body, in Hacker's poetry, often surrenders (or longs for surrender); however, it never submits.

The body becomes the visible and material register of sexual desire: "My elbow twitched like jumping beans; sweat ran / into my shirtsleeves" ("Runaways Café II" 4); "I kissed her until heat split my spine" ("February 25" 5); "Didn't Sappho say her guts clenched up like this?" (12). The body also *becomes* inseparable from the mind. In *Death, Love, and the Changing of the Seasons*, body and mind merge, and this convergence concretizes desire and longing by designating the body a crucial element in our understanding of both. The body then becomes epistemologically significant in understanding desire, fear, loss, longing, and life. Acknowledging that her and Rachel's minds touch, Hack admits that she desires the intermingling of their minds *and* bodies (111, 36). In "Cancer Winter," the last section of *Winter Numbers*, Hacker chronicles her diagnosis of breast cancer, the mastectomy that followed the diagnosis, and her ultimate survival. Obviously, the body is both the betrayer and the survivor, and Hacker writes that

> to survive
> my body stops dreaming it's twenty-five. (84)

Although in this poem the body must rethink its own location in time and although Hacker seems to open a gap between the body and the "I" (subject), as we read the poem, we understand that Hacker (the subject) rethinks. In other words, this poem admits no distinction between the "I" and the body. How we understand and know desire, loss, longing, and life involves corporeal sensations as well as how we interpret and theorize those sensations through the body *and* the mind.

Through her poetry, Hacker renders the body as the very thing that challenges the mind-body split, an opposition "so ancient as to have become part of our collective unconsciousness" (Mairs 298). Within this paradigm, we understand the body separate from the "I."[3] Nancy Mairs explains that when discussing embodiment, an individual will more likely say, "I *have* a body [rather than] I *am* a body" (298). Such an assertion keeps intact the gap between body and mind. However, Elizabeth Grosz claims that "human subjects never simply *have* a body, the body is always necessarily the object and the subject of attitudes and judgments" (*Volatile Bodies* 81). This distinction proves crucial in understanding the significance of the body in Hacker's poetry. For Hacker, the body is, indeed, both object and subject, and the lesbian body plays a critical role in attitudes and judgments. I do not suggest that lesbian is all body; rather, as I read and theorize the body in Hacker's poetry, I argue that the body (and often the lesbian body) functions as both a reconfigured *epistemological* object and subject and as a redefined *ontological* object and subject. The body becomes the object of our knowing as well as the "I" who knows while simultaneously being constitutive of and constituting that "I" (subjectivity).

The constitutive and constituting aspect of the body manifests in "*La Loubiane*" from *Love, Death, and the Changing of the Seasons*. This poem links subjectivity to the body and to doing—doing desire. At a restaurant in southern France, while attempting to "avert [her] eyes," Hack is keenly aware of the shared caresses of two women (183). Hack, however, must look away because this overt physical expression of desire reminds her of her loneliness, her desire "to touch" Rachel in the same way. Hack admits to being happy to see the two women in the restaurant, and, clearly, she identifies with them. Yet she acknowledges her inability and reluctance to reveal her own lesbianism to the two women. The poem actualizes lesbian desire in the inclusion of the three women—the two lovers who openly express their desire for each other and the onlooker, Hack, who understands this desire and experiences it within a resister of loneliness and longing. The poem inscribes that desire in the physical manifestation of it, the caress. Importantly, the physical act constructs Hack's reality:

> it makes
> my thoughts real when they touch each other. (183)

Thus, desire acted by and on the body makes real a lesbian subjectivity and lesbian desire. The body as subject and object of desire legitimizes Hack's identity as well as her longing for Rachel.

Hacker's poetic investigation of desire continues in "Ghazal" from *Desesperanto* further linking desire and identity. This poetic form proves an apt vehicle for Hacker's poetic renderings of this connection because, traditionally, the ghazal often raised metaphysical questions as it invoked love and longing.[4] In this erotic poem, the recurring rhymes along with the repetition of the word *desire* (ten times in the sixteen-line poem) declare the primacy of sexual urges and appetites. The poem details the necessity of desire itself, and in a rather self-conscious postmodern move, "Ghazal" depicts the desire *for* desire. Like many of the poems in *Love, Death, and the Changing of the Seasons*, it presents female desire as active and aggressive. The opening lines suggest the transgressive nature of such a desire: "She took what wasn't hers to take: desire" (98). The "she" does not wait to be the object of desire; rather, she seizes something forbidden to her. Here Hacker constructs desire as something other to the "I," and she casts it as a circularity: desire as the thing that initiates desire, and in the poem, it also initiates a "quest," raises a "question," and manifests as a seeker. However, "one can't seek desire," nor, according to the speaker of "Ghazal," can desire be unmade, despite attempts to undo it. Desire, it seems, makes up the fabric of life, of an individual's existence, simultaneously pervasive and elusive.

Throughout the poem, Hacker plays with the contradictory nature of desire. In the sixth stanza, *oblique* modifies *desire*. What then is desire here? Slanting? Perverse? This stanza, which begins with an imperative, "Crave nothing," directs that we, you, or she "accept" unsought and "oblique desire" (98). The eroticism of these lines—images of the closed eyes of an unaware sleeper laden with desire—give way in the next stanza to the ontological, transcendental, and perhaps, material consequences of desire. Desire requires acknowledgment ("an answer"), a not-I ("an other"), and a transcendental or metaphysical entity ("a Thou"). The closing clause of this stanza addresses a chilling aspect of desire, "mutilations suffered for [its] sake." In a move typical of Hacker, she writes ambiguity into these lines. Are the mutilations physical ones—bodily disfigurement—or are they psychic ones—psychological maiming? In either case, these lines underscore the significance and consequences of desire in human existence, and finally, in the last stanza Hacker ties desire to the person of the poet. In the tradition of the ghazal, the closing lines include the word "hack," which, of course, echoes "Hack" of *Love, Death, and the Changing of the Seasons*, the lover "horny as a timber wolf." Without desire, the poet remains nameless lacking identity or a sense of being-ness. These lines also end in the same circularity that began the poem—desire *for* desire—one can only speak desire *through* desire. One must possess it in order to expresses it.

"Ghazal" raises questions and makes statements about desire that circulate within a complicated and complex philosophical register that associates desire with issues of recognition, identity, prohibition, and subjection. Desire is seldom as simple as "I want" as Judith Butler makes clear. In *The Psychic Life of Power* (after addressing Hegel's, Freud's, and Nietzsche's theories of desire), she declares, "The desire to desire is a willingness to desire that which would foreclose desire, if only for the possibility of continuing desire" (61). Hacker puts into poetic form Butler's explanation regarding the continuousness of desire itself. The poem acknowledges the endlessness of desire set in motion and the weight of it once we are aware of it:

> Once conscious of desire, we're laden
> with its accountability. (*Squares and Courtyards* 79)

In "Ghazal," Hacker exposes a matrix of desire, and she reveals the interconnections among desire, power, and subjectivity.

Within the tradition of Western metaphysics, many have wrestled, and continue to do so, with the place of desire in relation to the human psychic and the human condition. Additionally, within this tradition, desire, like the body, configures within the active-passive or male-female split. This mapping of desire as male-female and active-passive occurs most overtly in regards to sexual desire and most blatantly within psychoanalytical theory. Freudian psychoanalysis casts women as the objects of desire and female desire *as* the desire *for* passivity. As philosophers and theorists attempt to sort out the complicated role that desire plays in human relationships, they must confront issues of sexuality, of otherness, and of power, as well as the role of the body in these interactions. The body, after all, manifests as the visible marker as well as the active agent of desire, and it is the thing that suffers punishment or restriction in order to contain excessive or inappropriate desires. The body carries extreme significance within the register of sexual desire and sexuality: "The body is quite literally rewritten, traced over, by desire. Desire is based on a veritable cartography of the body (one's own as well as that of the other)" (Grosz, *Volatile Bodies* 56). "March Wind," from *Love, Death, and the Changing of the Seasons*, extends this mapping of the landscape of the body as the poem compares body to a country. Hack's desire propels the exploration as she attempts to "learn [Rachel's] entire country" (47). Hacker renders the body as flora ("flower") and as landscape ("country," "hills"), and she situates these metaphors in relation to intense desire.

The "cartography of the body" also appears in "August Journal," from "Cancer Winter" the last section of *Winter Numbers*; however, in this poem the metaphor solidifies the connection between subjectivity and the body's epistemological and ontological status rather than mapping desire onto the body. Hacker proclaims,

> Upon my body is superimposed
> the map of Europe I never knew. (94)

Here, similar to many of Marilyn Chin's poems, time and generations converge in the body. Hacker, the cancer victim and survivor, writes the history of Holocaust victims and survivors onto her scarred body, and it not only manifests a physical geography, but it also makes visible an identity:

> my olive skin, my eyes, my hips, my nose
> all mark me as an Ashkencizi Jew. (94)

The marked body—prey, victim, and survivor—becomes a location of identification and the vehicle to understanding both a personal history and that of a people.

In some sense, by locating her cancer-scarred body as a place of historical and cultural identification, Hacker evokes the politics of positionality, which involves "devot[ing] special attention to the differing ways individuals from diverse social backgrounds construct knowledge and make meaning" (Kincheloe and Steinberg 3). In Hacker's poetics of the body, the body's position does not relate exclusively to an individual self; instead, she marks the body so as to position it in relation to groups of people. The racial-ethnic body that emerges most visibly throughout Hacker's work is the Jewish one. In "August Journal" and in other poems where this body appears, Hacker implicitly challenges assumptions regarding whiteness and white purity and whiteness's relation to hegemony. "Whiteness cannot be separated from hegemony[,] . . . [but it] is always shifting, always reinscribing itself around changing meanings of race in the larger society" (Kincheloe and Steinberg 4). The Jewish body that circulates throughout Hacker's work echoes this reinscription of racial meaning as it carries with it both insider and outsider status. Indeed, "*Jewish* American, Italian American, and Latinos have, at different times and from varying political standpoints, been viewed as both 'white' and 'nonwhite'" (Frankenberg 11, emphasis added). Thus Hacker's inclusion of the Jewish body adds to the complexity of the body in relation to language, desire, identity, and narrative in her poetry.

In poem after poem, Hacker uses the body as the text and testimony of "the apex of horroism . . . the Nazi death camps" (Cavarero, *Horrorism* 33). In her commitment to her Jewishness and "her horror at both the cruelties imposed historically on her forebears and the cruelties visited today on Palestinians by Israelis" (Biggs 9), Hacker positions the body as the connection between past and present cruelties. In a sonnet from the

"Cancer Winter" section of *Winter Numbers*, she references Etty Hillesum[5] and Anne Frank immediately after identifying both the unknowing-ness of the dying process and her desire to live (88). In this volume, Hacker seeks to mitigate the terror of breast cancer and surgery by remembering the 1940s roundup and interment of Jews. Admitting her own "terror," she also tells herself that her diagnosis and treatment

> isn't the worst horror.
> It's not Auschwitz. It's not the Vel d' Hir. (83)

The tenth sonnet repeats the preceding line and then proceeds to identify cancer as "gratuitous as a massacre" (85). Hacker's cancer spurs her to wonder what "numbered, shaved, emaciated Jew / [she] might have been" (85) as she presents a body under the assault of cancer as manifesting the familiar characteristics of a Jewish body subjected to Nazi ideologies and pogroms. This analogy extends beyond a gratuitous claim of victimhood. In this sonnet, Hacker's "self-betraying body" emerges scarred, and its mastectomy scar will identify her as a cancer survivor. She directly links this visible marker of survival to the tattoos of Nazi concentration camp survivors. This linkage does not, within Hacker's work, shrink the historical into the personal. The body, scarred by breast surgery, that emerges is a *particular* body, the body of an Ashkenazi Jew who carries a *particular* history with it.[6] Thus the present moment of scarring makes visible the past mutilations of Jewish bodies. In this poem, for Hacker, scars on the body directly relate to her sense of being.

Throughout much of her work, the body becomes a crucial element in making sense of *being*, yet Hacker never reduces subjectivity to the body alone. In fact, she never presents an essentialized body. In *The Human Condition*, Hannah Arendt acknowledges the near impossibility of identifying a human nature, an essence of humanness; instead, she asserts that "the human condition is not the same as human nature, and the sum total of human activities and capabilities which corresponds to the human condition does not constitute anything like human nature" (6). As Arendt develops her theories regarding the human condition, she makes clear that humans "are conditioned beings because everything they come in contact with turns immediately into a condition of their existence" (9). Issues of existence emerge as crucial concerns for Hacker, and in her poetry, she presents things such as love, desire, illness, loss, relationships, sex, and sexuality that constitute the human condition, and Arendt maintains that "human existence . . . would be impossible without things" (9). For Arendt, *things* refer to the "objectivity of the world," and she identifies the supplementary relationship between this objectivity and the human condition. Although Arendt insists that we can never fully comprehend what it means to *be* human, understanding the things that make up our world helps us make sense of *how* we exist in this world. Importantly, however, Arendt identifies our longing for the answer to the following question: *Who* are we? Hacker poses this same question in her poetry, and she offers a glimpse of the things that condition our experiences as humans as she attempts to explain what it means to *be*.[7] On some level, Hacker responds to Arendt's assertion that "whatever men do or know or experience can make sense only to the extent it can be spoken about" (4). Hacker speaks knowledge and experience by rendering them into verse. As her poetic images redefine the body, the body, no longer the albatross, the drag on the mind, emerges as the storyteller and the story. It becomes the medium on which and through which knowledge and experience gain meaning.

Drawing on Arendt's theories, Adriana Cavarero elaborates the link between narrative and subjectivity stressing the significance of the corporeal in this relationship. Evoking a long philosophical tradition regarding appearance, Cavarero suggests, "The primacy of appearance constitutes, through the other's gaze, the fundamental corporal aspect of identity" (*Relating Narratives* 21). Cavarero makes three points that prove critical to this study: first, one needs a body to appear; second, a link between body and being exists; third, one must appear to someone else. I suggest that in many of her poems Hacker's display of the body reinforces its ontological significance. Her poetic bodies remain visible because they demand recognition; they demand to be looked at and acknowledged. These bodies become the markers of existence, and they manifest as one of the crucial elements of the human condition. Clearly, for Hacker, being-ness cannot be separated from corporeality. Throughout *Love, Death, and the Changing of the Seasons*, Hack's identity intertwines with the desires of her body. These poems unfold a narrative of desire and being arising from the connection of two bodies as well as the recognition between Hack and Rachel of their individual and shared corporeality. Although cancer does not define Hacker in "Cancer Winter," the effects of cancer on the body intimately affect her sense of self. While acknowledging philosophy's love of separating "—within the subject—the body from the soul," Cavarero insists that "appearance—and the primacy of the visible with which it embraces phenomena—are nonetheless always and everywhere rooted in the materiality of the context" (21). Throughout her poetry, Hacker places meaning and subjectivity in "the materiality of the context" of the body.

"August Journal" opens with a question as the speaker examines the link between subjectivity and the body:

> How does it feel, in this ephemeral flesh
> to be back at my work table, to sit
> looking out the window while a flush
> of late sun brightens scrubbed stone opposite,
> illuminates known neighbors' unknown rooms,
> just as it shone a year, two years ago
> when I, immortal as an eight-year-old,
> looked out in my clean, unscarred, unbroken skin
> (the oily selfhood I'm sequestered in,
> the body I'm not going to leave alive,
> whose guard—I didn't know it yet—was down)? (91)

While acknowledging the transitory aspect of the body, the speaker also identifies the body as selfhood itself. However, these lines also posit an "I" separate from the body *and* selfhood: "the oily selfhood I'm sequestered in" and "whose guard—I didn't know it yet was done." This body/selfhood/I/not-I occurs simultaneously. The speaker is her body and not her body. Rather than moving between being and having, subjectivity means having and being the body at the same time as well as being as self and having a selfhood. Thus the question posed (How does it *feel* to take up daily life understanding how short-lived the life of the body is?) remains unanswered and unanswerable. Instead, Hacker veers from the question and muddles the answer by simultaneously splitting subjectivity from and binding it to the body, "the body [she's] not going to leave alive."

As I suggest above, in Hacker's poetry, the body is both the storyteller and the story. In poem after poem, language folds into the body, which then becomes inseparable from the text. However, both body and text simultaneously remain discrete facets of subjectivity and narrative, and, as Cavarero posits, "a tenacious relation of desire" between identity and narration exists (*Relating Narratives* 32). In Hacker's poetry, the body often reinforces the tenacity of this desire. Cavarero links this desire to self and other by identifying a single desire that binds autobiography and biography together—"the desire to hear one's own story *in life*" (33). Each of us desires to tell our story and to hear it told, and Hacker often complicates this desire for our own stories by connecting it to sexual desire. In "August Journal," Hacker states the obvious: life depends on inhabiting a body. Therefore, it follows that for this poet the narratable self relies on a narratable and narrated body.[8] For example, in "Future Conditional" (in *Love, Death, and the Changing of the Seasons*), Hack identifies Rachel's body as "text" that constructs "the art" (50). In this poem, poetry ("art"), body, text, sexual desire, and subject construction merge into and depend on each other. However, the body *as text*, in this instance, Rachel's body, emerges as the vital component among these elements. Here it becomes the essential need for Hack and for her creative production. Among other meanings, *text* means a written *body* of work—something already written and able to be read. Within a Barthian model, text becomes both readerly and writerly, thus continually producing meaning. *Text* within current literary theory implies the possibilities of endless and excessive signification, and the body, as rendered by Hacker, seems to promise multiple and excessive pleasures, meanings, and narratives. Indeed, as Gail Weis argues, "The body serves as a narrative horizon for all texts, and in particular, for all the stories that we tell about (and which are indistinguishable from) ourselves" (26). Hacker's metaphor (body is text) presents the body as constituted by *and* constitutive of narrative and subjectivity. Hacker does not, however, offer only the beloved's body as text; rather, she once again refuses binary constructions of desire by insisting on reciprocal desires. Hack sees her body as a book, one "made for [Rachel's] hands to read, [her] mouth to use" (50). Although Hack requires Rachel's body to give meaning to her poetry, Hack acknowledges that both bodies offer stories. Her body contains a story, her story, and Hack demands that Rachel read or write it, and Hacker links reading to the body ("hands," "mouth"). Reading, meaning, and narrating depend on the desiring and desired body.

A tension exists in Hacker's poetry caused by a desire, or even a necessity, for endless and unrestrained narrative. Although the body often seems the locus of this tension, Hacker's reliance on traditional or received forms initiates a strain that heightens and curbs the significance of the body in the poetry. In a now seminal 1980 interview with Karla Hammond, Hacker admits to liking "the tension in a poem that comes from the diction of ordinary speech playing against a form" (22). Speaking with Annie Finch in 1996, Hacker sees the struggle to keep form and the poetry in balance "as productive of [her] own best work" (24). Hacker elaborates, "And it's a tension which is most fruitfully and daringly employed by poets who exercise those forms with enough expertise to allow that improvisatory counterform to come into play" (Finch 24). Scholars, critics, and reviewers of Hacker's poetry concur on the skill she displays in her use of form, especially the sonnet.[9] In a 2004 review of *Desesperanto*, Adrian Oktenberg writes that Hacker's "forms are so unobtrusive, call so little attention to themselves, that they seem entirely organic to the poem" (7). Similar to "Future Conditional," where "boundaries dissolve between body and text, poet and book" (Honicker 98), the parameters of forms collapse in Hacker's poetry.

However, form in her poetry parallels the having a selfhood and body and being a self and a body suggested in "August Journal." The poems simultaneously *possess* a form (which implies a distinction between form and content) and *are* the form (which collapses that distinction). In a poem such as "Villanelle," from *Selected Poems: 1965–1990*, the title identifies the poem as a form thus seemingly boundaries between the poem and its form disappear. Yet form, the villanelle in this case, is also something a poet does. Maxine Kumin compares the writing of the villanelle to performing "gymnastics" (316). Hacker proves herself an apt gymnast in "Villanelle" as she creates a balance between the poem and its form. A villanelle depends on two rhymes and builds on two refrains, specifically in "Villanelle": "Every day our bodies separate," and "Not understanding what we celebrate." In "Villanelle," the body as body and as language becomes the thing that confounds and clarifies meaning, and the rules of the villanelle underscore the body's tendency to resist stasis. Through the use of repetition, the poem continually repositions the body, which allows for a constant reexamination of the body and its attendant desires. The rigid form of the poem demands such positioning and repositioning and examination and reexamination. Rather ironically, the form's rigidity allows fluidity.

As the poem develops, the repeated words and phrases take on new meanings depending on their position in each triplet, and despite the formality of the received form, both signification and narrative seem endless. The lovers in the poem are bodies and have bodies, and through having and being bodies, they seek to understand each other and their shared desires. The speaker also attempts to identify where and how she is a self and body separate from that of her lover. In "Villanelle" the separation of bodies is continual and necessary because, despite the desire or feeling of oneness, the lovers are separate individuals, yet the poem posits the act of separation as a violent one that leaves the body "torn and dazed." As the poem unfolds, it becomes clear that this violence occurs in several areas. The lovers literally and physically untangle their bodies, and they reestablish their distinct selves. Finally, the lovers in this poem communicate through touch and "fused limbs and lips"; therefore, bodily separation disrupts communication between them. The body, then, becomes the mode of communication as well as language itself. The lovers, speechless and wordless, "grope through languages." Although, at times, resulting in speechlessness, this fumbling also results in amazement, power, and praise.

On some level in "Villanelle," Hacker gives us a body that transcends language. Words prove inadequate to explain what the lovers celebrate

(ritualize, observe, honor, proclaim, or exalt). The poem represents artic-
ulations beyond words as the lovers seek understanding through and on
bodies. The body, then, not only offers a way to communicate, but it also
serves as a vehicle to knowledge. As Hacker plays within the mandates
of the villanelle placing the second refrain ("Not understanding what we
celebrate") at the end of the third and fifth triplets, the question of the
"what" shifts. In triplet one and two, the lack of comprehension *causes*
the lovers to "grope through languages" leading them to find the answer
with and on their bodies. A subtle shift in meaning occurs in the next two
triplets. The illegible, and perhaps unnamable and unspeakable, "power"
resulting from the body leaves the speaker frightened and out of sync. This
lack of understanding indicates a lack of meaning. The underlying or "real"
questions Hacker poses seem bound to the body: What does it *mean* when
bodies come together, when bodies speak, when bodies convey knowledge,
and when bodies separate? Although the poem does not answer these
questions, it does, however, imply the body's connection to subjectivity,
desire, and language. By the quatrain, the second refrain changes as the
"what" drops out eliminating the vagueness conveyed in the triplets.
Here the speaker questions not *what* the lovers celebrate but "*how* [they]
celebrate [their] bodies" (emphasis added). In "Villanelle," the body
emerges as the celebrated, praised, and worshiped subject. This body's
ability to convey meaning exceeds language's capabilities.

Conversely, one could argue that the body's "language" indicates a pri-
mordial one. However, only reading the body as prelingual runs the risk
of reducing everything to the body and its urges. I am not making such a
move here, nor do I believe that Hacker does so in "Villanelle." Instead,
Hacker, once again, rejects an either-or construction of the body or posi-
tion for it. She depicts the body as transcendent and immanent. In this
poem, the body *tells* the story of the lovers, and it *is* their story. It becomes
a way of knowing and the subject that knows. Hacker also gives us a body
separate from the self or I, one that unties the lovers from the scripts of
their lives (27). However, this separation does not oppose the body to the
self; Hacker's poetics of the body does not advocate ascendancy among
the entities—mind, body, self.

"Sestina," also from *Selected Poems*, evidences this same unmooring of
the body from being, and in this poem, Hacker once again uses the tropes
of body language and body cartography. The bodies of the two lovers
whisper and tell secrets. In this poem, Hacker offers a poetics of the body
that posits one possessing agency independent from that of the "you" and
the "I." The bodies in "Sestina" betray the self by revealing something
the self wishes to keep hidden. Hacker presents a body containing and

sharing knowledge, thus it becomes an alternative way of knowing and speaking. It speaks a language "harder and more tender" than that used by the "you" and the "I."

This poem, like "Villanelle" and the poems that comprise *Love, Death, and the Changing of the Seasons*, focuses on lovers, desire, and reciprocity. Cavarero offers a clear link between narration and eros, and her arguments provide another lens through which to "read" Hacker's poetry: "Love is indeed often characterized by a spontaneous narrative reciprocity. The reciprocal desire of a narratable self . . . is of course part of the narrative . . . On the stage of love, the questions 'who am I?' and 'who are you?' form the beat of body language and the language of storytelling, which maintain a secret rhythm" (*Relating Narratives* 109). In "Sestina," the body puts in motion the "narrative reciprocity," and it asks and attempts to answer the questions that Cavarero identifies regarding self and other. Body language and the language of the story merge *and* separate in this poem. The lovers wake because their bodies "talk," and the lovers find themselves "tangled / dragons on [the bodies'] map." These bodies "have a plan" (25).

As "Sestina" progresses and as the six end words of the first stanza ("whispers," "secrets," "language," "wakes," "tangled," and "plan") repeat, body, language, and cartography continue to intersect. The speaker expresses doubt about the other's language: "You are not speaking your native tongue" (25). This choice to use a language different from one's mother tongue may result in a lack of understanding or a miscommunication. The speaker further worries that his or her lover will have gaps in his or her understanding of the speaker's body. What crucial message will the lover miss because of his or her choice to use a language alien to him or herself? Clearly, then, language often falls short and proves inadequate. However, the language of the body accommodates the shortfall and the inadequacy as it once again "whispers." This need for supplementation implicates the body in language and in signification. The supplementary aspect reveals the illusory nature of a binary that opposes the body to knowledge, meaning, or language. Here, as she does throughout her poetry, Hacker rejects that opposition, but she does not invert the binary. Instead, the body becomes one of several crucial elements in making meaning, telling stories, and constructing selves.

Intensity, violence, betrayal, and sexuality mark the fourth stanza of "Sestina." Desire, language, and the body interact here offering all these elements as essential components of articulation and representation. Within the rigors of the form, Hacker creates a sense of urgency and tension regarding ontological and epistemological questions: The poem asks not only "Who am I?" and "Who are you?" but it also asks "Who are we?" and "How do we know the I, the you, the us?" Hand and hair tangle until "language split like a black fig" (25). The fourth stanza's repeated "s" sound ("split," "suck," "secrets," "skin") adds a sinister tone reinforcing a sense of urgency. Touch disrupts language, and once again the body displays its independence from the self. How does touch enact this disruption, and how does the body declare its independence? "Split" denotes a breaking open or separating. Does touch open language thus making possible meanings beyond language itself, or does it demolish language making it unnecessary? Although we do not know what the speaker learns, we do know how he or she does so. In this stanza, understanding comes from the body thus making words superfluous. Here again the body reveals what the "self" refuses to or, perhaps, what the "self" does not know. However, the poem also acknowledges the transgression in gaining knowledge through the body: "This isn't the plan." Finally, the stanza ends with a warning of caution. Hacker seems to suggest a need to contain the bodily manifestation of desire as well as the body itself. This body language or language of the body threatens to displace the logos or perhaps to disrupt tidy categories of narrative and selfhood.

"Sestina" presents a body that speaks language devoid of remembrance, one "without memory" (26). Memory means "the mental capacity or faculty of retaining and reviving impressions, or of recalling or recognizing previous experiences" (*Webster's New Universal Unabridged Dictionary*). While the poem suggests that lovers must "write" new scripts or love demands that one begin anew, it also disconnects experience from language and thus from knowledge and selfhood. It proves tempting to argue that Hacker rejects postmodern notions regarding language's role in constructing subjectivity and knowledge. However, I see Hacker's insertion of the body into the construction of both as a rejection of the hierarchy implied in the mind-body split. Hacker does not assert an essentialist position, reducing knowledge and subjectivity to the body, nor does she ignore language's constitutive role. Instead, Hacker casts the body as an equal agent, one that possesses a different kind of language, a language without self-conscious memory.

What does it mean to lose the capacity to remember impressions or experiences? The ability to recall and reorganize experiences and retain and revive impressions drives narratives. However, "Sestina" grants the body a significant place in storytelling as well as in how and what we know, and in how we know who we are. To speak a language without memory points to the possibility of new meanings and new stories—perhaps endless ones.

Indeed, Hacker makes clear that the body continually demands and creates narratives, and she indicates the excessiveness of the body's linguistic desires and capabilities by describing "secret places" as "garrulous," which seems oxymoronic. However, as many theorists of narratology argue, secrets create narratives, and they propel the plot. Secrets spawn stories because they demand speculation and retelling. In "Sestina," the body both holds and tells secrets. The body thus is the text already written and the text waiting to be written. In addition, the poem makes equivalent the language of the body with the language of storytelling.[10] Although the body possesses a secret language, the lovers will remember it, and from whispers, secrets, and touch, new stories emerge (26). The language of the body and what we learn from that language alters plans—jettisons them.

As Hacker merges touch and language, she challenges the way we understand self and other. In "Sestina," as throughout *Love, Death, and the Changing of the Seasons*, Hacker presents reciprocity as necessary for desire and subjectivity as well as for narrative. She understands that when lovers touch, each individual "touch[es] a *who*, all over the deep surface of his/her irresidual appearance—because this, is love: a relationship that constitutes an existence as an intimate exteriority, as a singular unity always already exposed to the other" (Cavarero *Relating Narratives* 113). The reciprocity that so often emerges in Hacker's poetry places self and other within an ontological field, and within this field, subjectivity very often relates both to telling one's story and to knowing and telling the other's story.

The forty-one poems that comprise "Paragraphs from a Daybook," the last section of *Squares and Courtyards*, narrates the speaker's life through a series of flashbacks and shifts in locations between Paris and New York. However, in the telling of her own story, the speaker also tells others' stories, and in so doing, reinforces the interconnection between self and other and the ontological component of narratives. One's story seldom, if ever, remains exclusive. Throughout "Paragraphs from a Daybook," these other stories initiate and parallel the personal narrative that unfolds throughout the poems. At other times, others' stories distract the speaker from her own tale, and at still other times, the speaker turns to the stories of others in order to provide a larger context for her own. Finally, the speaker uses the stories of others in order to mitigate the pain of remembering.

The stories in "Paragraphs from a Daybook," also speak of loss, desire, death, and bodies. Although the poems do not foreground the corporeal, corporeality remains intimately bound both to narrative and desire throughout this section. Indeed, Hacker wonders

> how . . . girls complete
> a thought without a word for "clitoris"? (70)

In addition, Hacker places these bodies in geographical locations (on streets and stairs; in parks, cafés, concentration camps, and in sweatshops; in cities—Paris, London, New York, Harlem, and Kosovo), marks them racially and ethnically (white, Chinese, Jewish, German, Mexican, Tunisian, and English), and describes their failings (illnesses, aging, and dying). This attention to the specific details of the bodies, and by extension to the stories that circulate in the forty-one poems, underscores the significance of the body as the story and the storyteller.

In the first poem Hacker introduces "the bums / long-term jobless, stateless, *sans-abir*" who inhabit the market street in Paris (67). She draws attention to their "rag-swaddled legs" and takes care to tell us that the bums, both men and women, "are white" (67). Amid this homeless, shelterless, and stateless population, the speaker singles out a "tall" woman who, with her girlfriend, appears in three of the poems, and in each, Hacker provides physical details. The second woman, the girlfriend, is "a tiny skinny woman with blue eyes," who in the summer "turn[s] crinkled coffee-brown" (68). In the twenty-sixth poem in the section, the speaker notes the first woman's ruddy face. Through these bodily descriptions, the speaker reads/writes the women's stories. She acknowledges that the ruddiness of the woman is "most likely . . . due to 'alcohol'"; however, the speaker refuses to accept this explanation because she has "never seen" the women with any alcohol, not even wine (92). The speaker dismisses the popular narratives of the homeless as inadequate; instead, she narrates what she sees and what she speculates about the exhaustion caused by ". . . Wild Nights! Or unsubtle dawns" (92). This reference to Emily Dickinson's poem clearly inserts desire into the story of the two women. For Hacker, desire propels one's own narrative as wells as others' stories.

Generally, in her work, the link between desire and narrative circulates within a corporeal and sexual register. However, in some instances, desire, narrative, and bodies emerge sans overt sexuality. Instead, desire involves illness, death, and loss—the ill or dying body. The desire then initiates narratives of nostalgia, longing, sometimes hope, and sometimes regret. On a flight from Paris to New York, the speaker of poem twenty-nine in "Paragraphs from a Daybook" names desire, not the body, "as [the] locus of loss" (95). The next three lines in the poem contextualize this displacement as the speaker remembers the tangible feel of her breast cancer ("palpable mass"). The body, this body, the speaker's body, carries the story of her breast cancer, of understanding the failings of one's body, and of confronting one's mortality. The body here is the plot and the theme, and it is a story overlaid with the irony of making a "last-minute flight" (95). Thus the body no longer provokes feelings of loss because over time it has again become "whole," albeit a reconfigured wholeness. In other words, the cancer, the speaker's survival, and the mastectomy scars paradoxically make visible and blur the story of loss. Desire, however, initiates feelings of loss because desire can never be complete or completed. Desire always involves slippage—a gap of incompleteness.

However, this realization occurs amid the speaker's uselessness in the face of a friend's "corporeal distress." The story of an illness other than her own opens the space of memory for the speaker as her story emerges separate from but also connected to the stories of others. In "Paragraphs from a Daybook," as we move through the stories of the two homeless women in Paris, the Chinese schoolgirls who "draft their own / fables," and an elegy for Muriel Rukeyser, "a woman" "quixotically prolific," "a Jew," who "died too young," we also encounter retrospection and nostalgia. Veronica Mitchell reads *Squares and Courtyards* as "one long, elegiac poem," and she identifies "Paragraphs from a Daybook" as a "loosely . . . extended sonnet sequence that examines territory mined by [Hacker's] life as an activist, socialist, daughter, mother, lover, and now, a single-breasted Amazon" (41). The story that unfolds in "Paragraphs from a Daybook" is indeed the speaker's (Hacker's) history. The speaker remembers herself at three being able to read and at four unable to recognize her father because of her "flawed vision"; she recalls the 1970s in London and "the inexplicable sobriety / attendant upon sexuality" (97); her paternal grandmother, Gísela; "a midsummer memory"; and the objects of her "own history: / music carved wood, a blue ceramic tile" (106). Mitchell rightly calls *Squares and Courtyards* "a book of witness" (41). Through Hacker's commitment to testify to her story, the story of others, and the story of other times as well as to our own times, a poetics emerges that posits the body as a crucial link in understanding oneself, one's world, and oneself in relation to other human beings. "Paragraphs from a Daybook" insists that one can and must read and write these things with and onto the body.

Hacker opens *Winter Numbers* with "Against Elegies," a poem that presents a litany of the dead and dying, deaths from cancer, AIDS, and "gass[ing] in Montpeyroux" (11–12). "Against Elegies" does more, however, than memorialize particular people. The speaker tells of "pregnant women with AIDS, schoolgirls, crack whores" and of a century "in which we made death humanly obscene" (12, 15). Following a chronicle of twentieth-century horrors from Auschwitz to Soweto, Hacker positions each of us as

a survivor
who will, or won't bear witness for the dead. (14)

This bearing witness involves a testimony.[11] To bear witness means to tell what occurred, in other words, to narrate an unfolding of events. The speaker of "Against Elegies" bears witness

for [her] own
dead and dying, whom [she'd] often failed. (14)

In its entirety, the poem gives meaning to particular deaths of particular people (Natalie and Ralph), to particular people diagnosed with terminal illness (James, Catherine, Melvin, and Lidia), as well as to groups of dying and dead ("pregnant women with AIDS, schoolgirls, crack whores"; children who die because of wars begun generations ago; the victims in wars and genocides across the century and around the globe; those who die from "hunger," "murders," and "diseases").

Bearing witness infuses dying with significance; narrating a life gives that life meaning, and the telling presents a coherent life story. Indeed, Cavarero argues that "everyone looks for that unity of their own identity in the story (narrated by others or by herself), which, far from having a substantial reality, belongs only to desire" (*Relating Narratives* 41). This desire to hear one's story seems to propel much of Hacker's poetry. In poem after poem, she tells the *stories* of lovers, friends, mothers, and daughters, of falling in love, being in love, and losing love, of joyous living, confronting death, and dying. Hacker's poetry foregrounds (as does most poetry) the *necessity* for words, testimony, and narrative. Hacker, however, keeps the body plainly in view as her poems question what it means to be, and she presents us with a poetry that celebrates the body with all its attendant characteristics. Many of her poems give us a body that is both the self and not the self and a body that is both the story and the storyteller. In these roles, then, it becomes the ontological body and the epistemological one. Implicated in being and knowing, the body also possesses the power to ground, for a moment, subjectivity. Although Arendt explicitly ties being to narrative, her theory implicitly ties both to the body: "Human essence—not human nature (which does not exist) nor the sum total of qualities and shortcomings in the individual, but the essence of who someone *is*—can come into *being* only when life departs, leaving behind nothing but a story" (193, emphasis added). Throughout life, an individual remains constantly in the state of be*ing*, identity caught within a matrix of flux. At the moment of death, however, identity is no longer changeable, and ironically, the body's own instability (its constant state of decay) emerges as the thing that stabilizes identity.

With "Against Elegies," Hacker both complicates and reinforces Arendt's notions by seemingly rejecting the power of storytelling to fix meaning. She does, however, depict one's death as the moment of fixed, stable, and coherent subjectivity:

> At the end, Catherine will know what she knew,
> and James will, and Melvin,
> and I, in no one's stories, as we are. (15)

These lines make clear that for each individual both life and death have meaning and that one does not need his or her story told in order to understand that meaning. However, at the moment of death, Catherine, James, Melvin, and the speaker (Hacker) will know what they know *as they are*. Knowing and being become fixed, no longer processes, at the moment the body ceases to live. The telling that the poem demands and performs is the recounting of the process of dying, a process inseparable from the body. In "Against Elegies," Hacker once again links language, meaning, and body.

Perhaps "Scars on Paper," from *Squares and Courtyards*, most poignantly details the connections among words, body, and meaning. In this poem, Hacker again revisits her experiences with breast cancer, and, typical of Hacker, the poem expands beyond her personal fears and horror to include the fears, suffering, and death of her friends and of those whom she does not know but to whom she feels deeply connected: "the Harlem doctor, the Jewish dancer," and the dean of "the Boston seminary," each of whom died from AIDS or cancer (16). This poem focuses not only on a body marred by the scars of an amputated breast but also on a body whose every ache might be "rogue cells' new claw, or just a muscle ache" (16). Hacker's body (and that of most cancer "survivors") has the potential to extend the narrative, to add to the story of living, or surviving, or dying. The speaker asks,

> Is that brownish-black
> mole the next chapter? (16)

However, "Scars on Paper" does not reject the body because of its betrayal—through illness or through aging; rather, the poem holds the scarred and reconfigured body up to glaring scrutiny. The breasts become "an unwrapped, icon, too potent to touch" (15). Hacker's missing breast, like "an anecdotal photograph," conveys a story. This comparison again underscores the body's ability to tell a story, to narrate a life.

Conversely, words possess the ability to resurrect the dead:

> On paper, someone flowers
> and flares alive. I knew her. But she's dead. (15–16)

However briefly, words on paper bring life to a dead body, and with the same swiftness, "words take the absent friend away again" (16). Throughout her poetry, Hacker lays bare the body's processes, its desires and urges, its place within a system of meaning and signification, its power to be and tell the story of our lives, its ability to destabilize and stabilize our identity, its status as both the self and not self, and finally its mortality. Within the poetry of Marilyn Hacker, I find the body intimately intertwined with language, and so, according to this poet, "Persistently on paper, we exist" ("Scars on Paper" 15).

CHAPTER 6

INTERVIEW WITH MARILYN CHIN

MARILYN CHIN IDENTIFIES HERSELF AS A "POET OF THE BODY," and in the following conversation, she explains the importance of the literal, meta-phorical, and cultural body in her poetry. She speaks candidly about her position as a poet—specifically a Chinese American woman writing poetry and fiction. Unabashedly feminist, Chin weaves the personal into the polit-ical and makes the personal political, and this interweaving implicates the body. She notes the influence of feminist poets such as Adrienne Rich, June Jordan, and Misuye Yamada, among others; however, she also attributes her activism and her "allegorical imagination" to both her Chinese roots and her familial experiences. Although these cultural and familial contexts emerge as important aspects of Chin's poetry, they do not stand alone. As Chin makes clear, she feels a deep commitment to putting history on paper in order to address contemporary social and political issues.

The following interview evolved out of two very long conversations and several e-mail exchanges. The first interview took place on October 19, 2007, and the second on September 6, 2008. For the purposes of clarity and coherence, I have blended the two conversations and e-mail exchange into a whole.

> *Cucinella:*[*] You're a professor at San Diego State University (SDSU). How do you balance teaching and writing?
>
> *Chin:* It's very difficult. Basically, I take leave without pay. I find that when I'm teaching, I'm always giving out. I have nothing left for myself at the end of the day, so it's been a struggle. Recently, [over] the last five or six years, I've taken every other semester off. I go to an artists' colony like Yaddo, or I'll have a gig. Last semester [Spring 2007], I went to

---

[*] Editorial and grammatical changes were made to the following dialogue, but the text has remained the same for the most part.

Bucknell where I was a poet in resident. There I taught one class that was very cushy. I'm not a fast writer. I publish a book about every seven years. I'm very careful with editing the craft. It's been a struggle. This semester I'm teaching three classes, and it's still a struggle.

Cucinella: What classes are you teaching?

Chin: I'm teaching a special graduate workshop that I created called International Prose Poem and Short, Short, Short Fiction, an undergraduate poetry workshop, and American ethnic literature. I love all these classes. Normally, when I'm directing the MFA program at SDSU, I teach two courses. It's a fairly hefty load. The semester is traumatic.

Cucinella: "Traumatic" is a great word.

Chin: [*laughs*] I have a low-grade depression throughout the semester. It's like you have a beloved child in the next room, and you can hear the child crying, yearning for attention, but you have to close the door for the semester. That's a sad analogy for one's art, but I just don't write well during the semester. Right now I'm doing a little translation, which makes me feel as if I'm doing something. My best time for writing is seven to nine in the morning; I wake up early and try to read a little Chinese poetry in the original, then some poetry in English. This engagement is a way to remind myself that I am a poet. I might write a line, I might not, and then the rest of the day is occupied with other things.

Cucinella: So that's your routine when you're teaching?

Chin: I try, but it doesn't often work.

Cucinella: When the semester ends or when you take leave, can you get right to your writing or do you have to transition?

Chin: Again, I begin with a lot of reading. Feeding the muse is a good way to decompress from a heavy semester.

Cucinella: What are you drawn to right now, fictionwise?

Chin: Right now, I'm teaching and, therefore, reading for three very different courses, and my ethnic literature course is very interesting to me because I'm teaching an adolescent graphic novel by Gene Luen Yang—the students love it. Then I'm teaching a session on comedy. I bring in the work of Margaret Cho, Dave Chappelle, and Carlos Mencia. It's a lit class, but I want to test the boundaries. I look to comedians to give me the unvarnished discussion on race. In both my own poetry and in my teaching, I want to test the edges of expression: from the most heartfelt lyric poem to the most transgressive stand-up comedy. Right now, I am asking the students to write their own stand-up vignettes about race relations in California. We'll put bars on the door and eat almond cookies . . . I'll let you know what happens [*laughs*].

Cucinella: That assignment sounds very fun and very challenging. How do you stay fresh in your teaching?

Chin: I always bring in new material and new work because it's easy to get hardened, and teaching the same thing over and over would bore me. Also, teaching poetry workshops day in and day out can ruin your own ear.

I have a hard time teaching the novel. I prefer to teach short, compressed novels a la Kafka's novella *Metamorphosis*. As a poet, it's hard for me to read novels. I try to get into a new novel, and there's a saggy middle, and I just can't continue.

Cucinella: That's an interesting point, and yet, I just read an interview where you said that you wished the people would teach or comment on your long poetry. Are you moving toward writing longer poems?

Chin: Yes, I find the long poem very challenging. I usually put in three long poems per book. They work like a pyramid; they sort of ground the book. I love the long poem. I let the imagination meander a bit. I begin with a little narrative, go off on a little tangent, focus on an image, explode it, meditate on the flora and fauna in my backyard, come back to the narrative, observe my racist neighbor, get on a soapbox for a little while . . . love my mother . . . and so on. It's a lot of fun, and as a poet, I like to have a large palette—a varied palette. I can write short lyric: haiku, quatrains that sound like Chinese quatrains, very compressed and contained, and I like to write longer, more discursive poems, more meditative, so that I can open the poem up to many possibilities. I can bring in history, and I can bring in philosophy, some character building, some dialogue, some political mantra, and some satire and humor into the imagination. When I am writing short lyrics, it's hard to include material. Much of poetry is about what you don't say. That's the power and craft of the short poem. The long poem uses different esthetic muscles, different strategies.

The last poem, the title poem, in *Rhapsody in Plain Yellow* is a long meditation. It took me about five years to write. Because of its length, I can make multiple references. There are points where I mock everybody. I mock Shakespeare, Tu Fu, Kafka, Eliot, Ginsberg, and Whitman.

Cucinella: I love that you identify it as "mocking"!

Chin: [*laughs*] Borrow, steal, whatever. I like to be satirical, to "mock," and have some intertextual fun. Make fun of Whitman's beard but simultaneously pay homage to his long ecstatic line and democratic vistas.

Cucinella: I see that range that you're talking about in all of your work, but I really see it in *Rhapsody*, a little bit less narrative than in your earlier works.

Chin: Yes, I guess it's my "postmodern" book. I enjoyed interrupting conventional Western forms and ideas with fresh Eastern intervention. I cut up some old sonnets with cuticle scissors and reconstituted them like a mosaic. I infused the blues poem with Chinese American immigrant history; I made the English ballad collide with the Chinese quatrain. In *Rhapsody*, I enjoyed "performing identity" through formal and stylistic strategies, through the crafting of lines and forms as opposed to just discoursing through narrative.

Cucinella: It's a fabulous book.

Chin: Are you a poet?

Cucinella: I'm not. I write on poets and poetry, but I'm not a poet.

Chin: But your book topic, you're covering Bishop and Marilyn Hacker, and . . .

Cucinella: . . . and Millay.

Chin: Whom I love, and I think she's underloved.

Cucinella: I think that your point about Millay being underloved partly has to do with the fact that critics don't know what to do with her. Feminists want to claim her, but then there's things about her poetry that bug feminists.

Chin: [*smiling*] Because she's a little smultzy.

Cucinella: Yes!

Chin: You know, she's the writer of 10,000 sonnets—she's allowed to be smultzy.

Cucinella: Yes. I think too many people just don't know what to do with her, and then there are her propaganda poems. Yet, students love her.

Chin: Some poets just listen to a different drummer. Like Edgar Alan Poe living in the mix with the Romantics. [It's] very weird that he lived in the age of Thoreau and Emerson and high English Romanticism. But his work survives as a counterpoint to that era. Poets like Millay and Poe have the last laugh. The reading public refuses to let their legacies fizzle into oblivion.

Cucinella: I think that's why I'm including her in *Poetics of the Body*. Actually, she's the most difficult to write on, so I've kind of bracketed her for now. She's written so much, and it's not all good.

Chin: You're right. There are two kinds of poets: the Bishop kind who keeps one poem and throws out twenty and the Millay kind who gets into a groove and writes a hundred sonnets and can't dispose of one. I am a Bishop-kind poet. I studied her work intensely in my earlier years. From her, I learned the virtue of the seamless poem. The finished piece looks so effortless, but each word is highly considered and reconsidered. She had incredible patience. She was queen of precision and clarity and final polish. It's trendy now to opt for process, disjunction, and all that's fun, too. But I always go back to Bishop as the primal example. She had concentration and focus. Once you lose that focus, it is difficult to gain it back. I feel this way about this culture: it is very impatient, frenetic, and suspicious of perfection.

Cucinella: Yes, you can't find a bad poem in Bishop's work, a published poem. I can't find a bad published poem in your work either. I'm not being a supercritic. I'm just addressing my experience.

Chin: [*smiling*] Thanks, I like being in her company. Bishop and I are perfectionists. Then there's her compatriot Robert Lowell. I tried going through his collection of 1,000-plus pages, and I felt like I'd been smashed in the head with his diary in iambic pentameter. And Millay was the sonnet queen and couldn't stop at just one. I am happy to write less; and I want for each poem to mean "more." It seems to me that we don't need a zillion mediocre poems floating in the universe.

Cucinella: I find your connection to Bishop enlightening and rather serendipitous for my project!

Chin: Yes, Bishop and I are control freaks and are very penurious with our words. Then Hacker and Millay are prolific sonneteers. Perhaps, the sonnet is habit forming. I am drawn to the idea that such an ancient form could be shape-shifted over and over again . . . and that there are endless variations. And I admire a poet who believes that everything she writes is indispensable. I wish that I had that chutzpah and temerity.

It's a source of frustration for me too because I just don't let a poem go. I keep it for a long time. Right now, I have pages of poems and various drafts in a drawer, but I can't let them go because they don't feel finished, and I won't let them go until the muse figures them out. I guess different poets feel different ways about process, and it's all good.

Cucinella: You received your MFA from the University of Iowa.

Chin: I studied with Donald Justice, who had a perfect ear and who wrote a very spare line and honored perfection. "Perfection" now is a suspect word because it's not "postmodern." We talk more about randomness and process now. It was quite a challenge in the writing of *Rhapsody*. I had to wax and wane between the yin- and yang-ness of control and chaos. I was able to tap into randomness, let the muse meander and have the poems be well crafted and polished as well.

Cucinella: I agree. *Rhapsody* is very postmodern, perfected, and well crafted.

Chin: I owe a lot to Bishop. I really did look to her *Collected Poems* as a bible. I just loved her crafting, precision, her perfect ear. Then there's my teacher, Donald Justice, who was a formalist who honored perfection and virtuosity over "content." In our private conferences, he was very supportive of my phrasing and careful word choices.

I left Iowa feeling that my craft would carry my "message" through. Justice didn't really want to discuss my personal and political concerns in my poems. He was interested in how I managed the balance of my lines and how I controlled pacing. He liked to pick my brain regarding Chinese poetry. His attention meant a lot to me. Now, I know he was right. He couldn't really comment on *what* I was writing about . . . hey, I wanted to be a revolutionary and that was totally foreign to him. He was dead right to encourage me to perfect my craft. Now, I can wear my refinement like an armor.

Then, I learned from my early years as a classical Chinese scholar, about compression, how to pare down a poem to its essentials. A poem is like an ideograph packed with meaning. Somehow, I was poised to write that "perfect" poem. But, at this postmodern moment, it's not hip to talk about "perfection" right now, is it? [*laughs*]

Cucinella: But we can because you are!

Chin: The Chinese five-character line is a fragment, but it could also be a complete idea, a piece of brilliant wisdom, a compelling landscape expressed in a montage of images. A Chinese character could be a complete thought itself—just one word could demand long contemplation. In my mock series "Chinese Quatrains," I wanted the quatrains to have the power and density of the original Chinese quatrains. I wanted to pay homage to the old Poundian idea of letting the concrete image speak for itself but, of course, always with a defiant Chin edge: "Plucked of arms and legs, a throbbing red pepperpod" goes against Basho's insistence that one must not be destructive with one's imagery. That's not Buddhist nice.

Let's say that I have been respectfully disrespectful. I can't make a commentary on the pain of living if my dragonfly is too beautiful. I've been working with hybridizing East-West sensibility for a number of years now. In *Rhapsody*, I feel that I made a breakthrough—using fragmentation without disrupting the integrity of the poem, letting contradictory elements fly against each other. There was a lot of intertextual fun. It was a fun book because I let that imagination roam.

Cucinella: You can see the playfulness there, yet it doesn't lose its intensity.

Chin: Lyric intensity comes with lived experience. Lately, people are bashing autobiographical poems and "identity poems." The last poem in *Rhapsody* is about the death of my boyfriend. He was killed in a horrific Singapore Airline crash. I finished a draft of that poem about a year before he died. I showed it to him, and he said, "Oh, thanks, I don't get it. Whatever. Thanks honey." After he died, I just put his name beneath the title, and both the poem and the book completed themselves. The muse was clairvoyant and knew something catastrophic was going to happen. The poem read like a substantial elegy; it closed the book physically and symbolically to an era.

Cucinella: You brought up the idea that people bash autobiographical poems. It seems to me that a poem can be both autobiographical and not at the same time.

Chin: It's a constructed self. Also, I still believe in writing identity anthems and Chinese American anthems. One of the poems that people love to anthologize is "How I Got That Name."

Cucinella: It's a great poem.

Chin: When I read it out loud, people respond. I'm a short Chinese American woman, and how many short Chinese American women get a chance to speak? When I speak, I have to have a few poems that are truly about the people and that are part lyric, part anthem, part rallying cry. I see myself as an activist poet. I often begin my readings with "How I Got That Name" and "Blues on Yellow." Both are "autobiographical," and yet both are "universal anthems." Often during a reading, I go from personal to wide angle to poems about the people and then to more personal poems. As I write, I think about the personal as representing something larger than myself. It is important for me to be "on message." I believe that my best work is a conflation of vivid lyric and political and social critique.

Cucinella: I generally teach students who are not English majors, who do not read poetry, yet they respond to your poetry. For these students to read and understand a poem can be a political act. Your poetry can tell us about being Chinese, being female, which is important. Here in San Diego, a lot of my students *are* immigrants, so the poem "How I Got That Name" speaks to them. These students need to hear that voice. This poem is a great poem on all the levels that you just mentioned.

Chin: It's also a monologue, so when I reading it out loud, I am truly addressing and interacting with the audience in the classic dramatic sense and in the Brechtian sense that one must engage with the audience to change their lives. I am very proud to be included in the new Sandra Gilbert and Susan Gubar *Norton Anthology of Women's Literature*. They included "How I Got That Name" and several poems from the new book, "The Half Is Almost Gone," which is also a personal anthem; and the "The True Story of the Mortar and Pestle," which segues to the prose poems I've been writing lately, prose poems—short, short fiction.

Cucinella: That move is exciting. What does this genre give you different from the forms in which you usually work?

Chin: I like developing characters. In my book of tales, *Revenge of the Mooncake Vixen*, which will come out in 2009, the major characters are a pair of rambunctious, chaotic twins who are always defying their cleaver-wielding grandmother. One gay, one straight. One is libidinous, the other a total control freak—a great allegory for the multiple schisms of a bicultural identity. I also fashioned many of these pieces after Chinese revenge tales, which satisfies the neoclassicist in me. Some of these tales are also revisionist feminist revenge tales. They're quite fun, political, and extreme. I also played with some of the famous Zen tales with a bitchy matriarch at the center in place of that cliché Zen patriarch. [*laughs*] There is something for everyone in these tales.

Cucinella: It's that palette that you spoke about earlier.

Chin: Yes. Which poems of mine do you teach?

Cucinella: "How I Got That Name," "The Colonial Language Is English," "Hospital Interlude," and "Hospital in Oregon" The students love . . .

Chin: Oh yes, the repetition in "Hospital Interlude."

Cucinella: We read it broken up and as a full line.

Chin: Yes, the form and content work beautifully together in "Hospital Interlude." It's about me trying to find my mother's room in this huge labyrinth of a hospital on "pill hill" in Portland, Oregon. I had rented a little red car; and I drove around, around in search of the hospital parking lot. It's a carefully orchestrated piece about a daughter's inability to process the horrific loss of her mother. The repetition is a dance of despair. Here is a personal story that opens up to universal mourning. It was very challenging to write. It took forever for me to get it right. It doesn't seem that way. It seems to flow effortlessly.

Cucinella: Yes, it seems breezy.

Chin: It's the same thing with Bishop, how her lines read with ease, but she took forever to finish a poem.

Cucinella: I read that she worked twenty years on "The Moose."

Chin: That's well worth it. It's an important poem in the treasury.

Cucinella: You're participating in the 2007 MLA panel "The State of Poetry in Asian American Literature." You mention that you're the only poet on the panel. How do you feel when you're included on a panel such as that one? Do you look at the selections of your anthologized poems? Are you pleased with those?

Chin: First of all, as a poet and someone who is writing in somewhat of a marginalized genre, hey, include me in whatever. I'm pleased when scholars like you take interest, and I'm pleased when you teach my poems in class. I want to be included. You can put me in a formalist anthology, an Asian American anthology, in a children's anthology, in a "womanist" anthology, in the various Norton teaching anthologies. I want to be included. It's very important for my survival. To be read is very, very important.

About the Asian American panel: Many Asian American scholars come to me and say, "Oh, I love your work, but I'm sorry, I don't get poetry, I can't write about it. It's too difficult." There are hundreds of monographs on Maxine Hong Kingston, Amy Tan, and Jhumpa Lahiri but very few on Asian American poetry. I think that there are quite a few good Asian American poets writing today. I hate going to chilly Chicago around Christmas, but I feel like I need to speak about this because I think it is important to change the direction of Asian American scholarship. I hope that scholars can move on from their fear and loathing of poetry. I know that it's a treacherous task: the scholar who works on me must have a deep knowledge about the forms in several cultures, not to mention historical and literary allusions. There's so much intertextual stuff to deal with. Furthermore, things are complicated by the problematic category "Asian American" in the first place. I am interested in hearing about what has happened to "the coalition" in its ever-changing condition. Nonetheless, it's wonderful when someone like you has the courage to take on a Chinese American poet.

Cucinella: I didn't really know your work, but when I edited a book on contemporary American women poets, I started digging and digging, reading contemporary poetry anthologies, and talking to poetry scholars. I compiled a list of poets to include in the book, and you were on it. The scholar who said she would write your entry ended up not being able to do so. So I did. I went out and bought your books and read all about your work. It was like a gift. Reading your work and writing about it has been a real pleasure and intellectually very challenging. You've taken me into areas where I would have never gone.

I'm also struck with the fact, as you acknowledged earlier, that you consider yourself an activist poet. What about that feminist slogan "The personal is political"? Don't you consistently make the personal political?

Chin: Yes, all the time. It doesn't matter if I'm writing a love poem. By the end [of the poem], the lover turns into the imperialist pig (my ex-boyfriends got bashed on many levels; the vector quickly goes from lover to imperialist) [*laughs*]. I can feel him morphing into the enemy archetype, and I just let the poem do it. Personal relationships are often about power struggle. So my love poems are fraught. I believe that I have an allegorical imagination that goes back to my Chinese folk roots.

When I write about my mother being oppressed by my father—it's personal witness—but personal witness has huge implications about patriarchy, feudalism, sexism, and unequal power and how those problems deepen with immigration and American racism. I feel that my mother was destroyed by my father and that my father's self-hatred and hatred of us were formed by the historical forces of both countries. Everybody is culpable. A poem like "A Portrait of the Self as Nation" is about a personal love affair, and it is also an antiwar poem about the Gulf War. Both personal love story and the history of a nation are inextricably bound.

"Personal and political" definitely came from second-wave feminism, but that feminism is an important part of my upbringing. I honor the activist work of Adrienne Rich and her generation of feminist poets: June Jordan, who was really strident, taught me how to me strong, and I really miss her; Muriel Rukeyser; Audre Lorde; Denise Levertov (also one of my teachers); Gwen Brooks; Margaret Walker; radical women of color such as Gloria Anzaldúa and Cherríe Moraga; and early Asian American activist poets such as Nellie Wong and Misuye Yamada. These women poets took on the issues while I was in graduate school perfecting my lines. I was lucky to have these important role models.

Cucinella: What do you think about feminism today? What does the "new" feminism look like?

Chin: [*smiling*] I've been looking at my students. I wrote this series of haikus, and the last line is "Don't touch him, bitch, we're engaged and besides he's wearing my nipple ring." I got that line from one of my students sitting there talking on her cell phone, talking jazz like that, garbage like that. She's very self-assured and strident, and she's not politically correct, and she has boy-toys and "friends with benefits"; she maxes out her credit cards; she might be a vegetarian, but that's only because she has this sentimental love for her dog. She's multifaceted. I watch my students, and I see that they're able to negotiate a lot because there are so many of us who worked hard, who marched the streets before them. Actually, I came a little after the turbulent 1960s, and I was born in 1955, but still, Vietnam was in our consciousness, and I felt that I was in the trenches every day.

Cucinella: Is it a less political feminism that we might be seeing in some ways?

Chin: The thing is many young women don't like the "F word." They call feminism the "F word."

Cucinella: Yes, many young women don't want to be called feminists.

Chin: What often gets me is that they're blatantly materialist, and they're totally unapologetic about it. So there goes the Marxist/class discourse of feminism.

Cucinella: Yes, they're very entrenched in the capitalist-consumer society.

Chin: The postmodern movement says, "That's great! Embrace it!" Embrace all that stuff; embrace stuff! This phenomenon is very interesting to me, given my early studies in Marxism. But I think feminism is going in a good direction. I don't know what to do about my female students except to be amused by them.

Cucinella: You enjoy them, which is important.

Chin: The feminist in me is always indignant. I think it all comes from how my mother was treated by my father, by her in-laws, by the oppressive Chinese family structure. I can never erase these experiences or the memories of them. So my feminism is deep. Feminists are idealists: we're dreaming and working toward a better, more just world. Some people say that we live in a postfeminist, postracial moment. They think that institutional racism is now a blip in the history books. They say the identity poem is over; then they say the lyric is dead; then they say feminism is passé. Well, "they" say a lot of things.

I believe that there is a lot of denial in this society. Otherwise, the horrors of Katrina wouldn't have happened. The invisible underclass suddenly became visible. I believe that it is important to be true to the muse and be committed to the issues that drove us to write in the first place. I believe that we need to put history on paper. And when teaching young women, we need to remind them about the long journey that came before them.

Cucinella: I wonder if some young women mistake personal choices as freedom. Yes, earlier feminism proclaimed "the personal is political," but we can't drop out the political aspect of feminism. I agree with you regarding the direction of feminism. I see a lot of assertiveness in young women and a lot of claiming life on their terms. These moves are very different from women's experiences when I grew up. Feminism came along and pretty much gave us permission to be assertive and encouraged us to claim life on our terms. Perhaps, now these attitudes are more taken for granted.

Chin: I believe that "feminism" is a lifelong task. I have been traveling a lot, and my feminist concerns are global. Each time I hear that a brown girl is stoned or is burned for her dowry or is forced into slavery to feed her father's heroine habit, I feel enraged. All these issues demand my attention. The bodies of the poor floating in the aftermath of Katrina must also get my attention. The work of an activist feminist poet is never finished.

Cucinella: I'd like to talk with you regarding the sense of place in your poetry. How does sense of place work for you? How does moving from Hong Kong or traveling between Hong Kong and the United States play into your poetry? I certainly get a real sense of place in many of your poems.

Chin: Right. Place works on many levels for me. When I'm working with landscape, for instance, in a poem called "Tonight when the Stars Are Shimmering," I try to use the Tang dynasty flora and fauna as stock Chinese imagery to represent that classed society in a Tang dynasty love poem. Then I also infuse it with Southern California landscape, verbena and hibiscus, all the stuff in my backyard. I do this so that the poem has the layering of the past and present through imagery, through flora and fauna. It's like excavating into many layers of fossilization to get to the present. I've been working on this East-West hybrid land-scape for a while. The poems are about displacement, and yet I feel per-fectly placed in ancientness (or what John Gery calls "Chineseness") as it is filtered through Californianess. My body is scarred and nourished by both histories.

I go away a lot. It's really important for me. I'm really a nomad. I don't feel that San Diego is my home.

Cucinella: You've expressed that sentiment in other interviews. Can you elaborate?

Chin: I don't think San Diego is my home although I have been teach-ing here for over fifteen years. I don't feel Hong Kong is my home, or Portland, Oregon, where I was raised. When I'm in Hong Kong, I defi-nitely don't fit in: I'm too loud, and my Cantonese is not good enough. Though, I do feel strongly that I'm a West Coast, Californian poet. I am also a Pacific Rimmer, a transnational Asian poet. I travel to various parts of Asia every year.

This semester [fall 2008], I am going to teach in Beijing. In Hong Kong, I speak a broken Cantonese, Toisan, English argot. I get by. In Beijing, I will speak a very bad Mandarin. It is strange to live in these "mother" countries and be confined to a limited verbal vocabulary. I often feel infantilized—especially when my eighty-year-old grand-mother had to bargain at the street market for me and then, afterward, buy me sweet bean cakes at the night market. It is both humbling and wonderful. And it is also important to have a chance to defend my Americaness once in a while. I can only know my privilege when I am juxtaposed against those with less.

Cucinella: Obviously, this displacement implicates the body. It is the thing displaced or the thing that is uncomfortable in its various locations. Can you speak about the body in your poetry?

Chin: You know that I love those French feminists—Cixous, who said, "Write with our bodily juices." My work is sensual, and I am "a poet of the body." I write out of "feelings" (goodness, this word would make the cognoscenti gag) and out of womanly bodily juices, heart, womb, clitoris—the Chinese would call it "heart and liver." I also like Kristeva's notion that we are always trying to return to the womb. I have yearned to return to my mother's womb for love and for safety, only to receive rejection, because she was depressed, because she couldn't negotiate for a happy life in the new nation.

"Mother China" will always reject me; she no longer recognizes me as one of her own. "Father America" continues to erect his perennial walls and exclusion acts. My own father was a bigamist and left us for a white woman (a metaphor for assimilation and ultimate rejection of his past). I was born in colonial Hong Kong, which meant that my passport was meaningless. I was neither Chinese nor British. I was raised by my grandmother who spoke a subdialect of Cantonese, and in Hong Kong we were seen as interlopers from the country. We were poor peasants, and the fact that we survived through the turbulent history of modern China was because of a few strong-willed matriarchs who kept us running. We were shunned everywhere we went—perhaps all this explains my "outsider" sensibility.

My feelings of exile are real. I don't feel that I have roots in San Diego or Hong Kong. At one time, I considered San Francisco my home, but she seems distant to me now. Perhaps, I am happiest in this perennial condition of dislocation and exile, and I shall be eternally restless in this rootless, borderless, transnational body.

Chin: The body is important in many of my poems. I am really a love poet. I would love to write a long sexy poem, all about body fluids and juices—and some pseudopornography. I'd like to write about an older woman–younger man relationship. That idea is still verboten in our puritanical culture and in the polite poetry world, a territory unexamined. The body would be terribly important in that poem. I look at someone like Bishop, and I don't see a lot of body in her poems. However, it's not totally absent either.

Cucinella: I'm really intrigued because I do think that you'll write that long poem about the older woman loving the younger man relationship.

Chin: I went through this period in which I was indulgent, so I have to write about it, and, of course, I have to make some big political statement about it, right? [*laughs*] With my middle-aged, allegorical, libidinous, vulvic mind, the middle-aged American woman accrues a lot of history, wisdom, and power, but with that power, the culture expects her to give up her youthfulness and sexual self. I would like to play with these assumptions a bit.

Cucinella: You will! I agree with you about Bishop and the body. The body in her poetry is often a very coded one.

Chin: There seems to be a lot of self-hatred in Bishop. Her identification with a moose and other ungainly creatures is interesting.

Cucinella: "Pink Dog" is a poem that comes to mind, and "O Breath," poems like that. One of the reasons that I picked the poems that I did from your work is because of the images that emerge in poems like "The Last Woman with Lotus Feet." In this poem, I see the traumas of being Chinese and living the Chinese immigrant experience in the United States implicating the body: it's marked; it carries these traumas. I find multiple moments like that in your poetry. Hacker very blatantly addresses body; it's just all over the place. I find your use of the body not coded like Bishop's, and you address it more subtly than does Hacker. I'm thinking of the Diana Toy poems, which I find heartbreaking.

Chin: My grandmother had a friend with bound feet, one of the last victims of that horrific 1,000-year-old cultural practice. We visited her a few times in Hong Kong. I was only six, and I remember crying after seeing her. The history of injustice is openly marked on her body.

As for Diana Toy, I worked as a rehabilitation specialist at this psychiatric facility in California, and Diana Toy weighed about 250 pounds when they put her in the facility. She had syphilis. Diana said that she was in pain, and nobody would believe her. She said that she was raped, but a lot of patients had sexual ideation problems, so nobody listened. So I complained to the psychiatrist. Then they finally gave her a checkup, and indeed she had syphilis; they finally gave her drugs for it. It was such a depressing job. There were stories about that place that are so horrific that writing about them would sound sensational. Yes, the body is very much in the work.

Cucinella: It wastes away; she doesn't eat.

Chin: Her weight would yo-yo up and down. Most of this happened because of the side effects of the psych drugs. They would give a patient a drug, and the patient would blow up because of the body's rejecting the medication. Some patients looked bloated, and some would lose their appetite and stop eating. Some would lose fifty pounds in a month. Some would tremble. Some would be comatose. I learned a lot from that dreary experience. Their physical pain mirrored their inner pain.

My mother stopped eating in the last year of her life—she wanted to die. That was her last protest. She expressed her anger with self-immolation and self-denial. Food is really a serious topic in American culture. Greed knows no satiation. Abundance is not salvation. With women, self-image, bulimia, and anorexia, the media is relentless in its disapproval of us. In Asian cultures, food is always associated with feasting and celebration and, on the flip side, famine and poverty. In Chinese history, we have gone through so many droughts, devastations, locusts, and so forth, that the vacillation between feasting and starving is traumatic: feasting and having nothing; having a rich spring especially in Southern China where everything is in blossom; where vegetables are in abundance with tiers and tiers of green rice paddies. Then two years of drought or locust would wipe everything out. It would be difficult for us to fathom that millions could die in a famine caused by natural disasters and man-made disasters . . .

Cucinella: So excess and lack?

Chin: China is an ancient country; the physical memories of starvation and oppression are deeply etched into the flesh. The Chinese American food trope is not just decoration. Food and celebration is always associated with its spiritual shadow: suffering, starvation, deprivation, and loss. I really believe that China needed a revolution to get rid of feudalism, and there's no other way about it. I resent the idea that there is a one-size-fits-all brand of democracy to fit every circumstance.

Cucinella: That dynamic does emerge in many of your poems. What fascinates you about writing poetry?

Chin: I just think that there is so much work for me to do as someone coming from two rich cultural histories. I want to play with more Asian forms and with hybridity. Recently, I was reading up on the American transcendentalists, comparing their "zen" landscapes to those of Wang Wei and Tao Qian. I want to write that downright lusty poem of the body. I want to finish a smart translation of Tu Fu's antiwar poems. He is so brilliant and passionate in the original—and I don't think that he has come across very well in translation. I am researching revolutionary female icons. I want to write poems that address important, pressing American issues. I am working on a piece about Katrina. [*pauses*] We must not forget the American underclass.

There's so much to do, so many ideas keep me awake at night. I'm very excited about the genre. I try to keep focused and turn myself off from that decorous poe-biz world, where conformity trumps excellence. I want to keep my "originality," which is, of course, another suspect word these days. I want to keep my oppositional, sassy voice. I am over fifty. Alas, there is so little time, and so much poetry to write!

Cucinella: I also want to ask you about teaching your poetry. How would you like your poetry taught? This question is very self-indulgent on my part. I mentioned that I teach mostly lower division, general education courses. How do you want me to teach your poems? How does one introduce students to your work? What's the ideal for you?

Chin: What you're doing is great. Teaching is very personal, isn't it?

Cucinella: Yes, but as a poet, as the person who creates these poems, what do you envision? What kind of reception do you want? Or does it not matter?

Chin: [*laughs*] I just want love.

Cucinella: OK, we can do that. That's great. We can do that.

Chin: One way to teach my poems is through the images. I believe that my poems are image driven and highly symbolic. One student who read "The Floral Apron" sent me an essay on the image "six tiny squid / lined up so perfectly on the block." She began by saying that it was a gross image but went on an inspired tangent and related the squid to "Abu Grab and the images of torture." She was dead right. As political poet, I often will use imagery to argue my views. Another student responded to the poem by sending me a floral apron she made herself.

Another student wrote an essay about "blue" and "yellow," trying to unravel why I used these particular colors. This is a rich discussion, of course. Yellow is the emperor's color, but it is also a way to categorize Chinese, Chinese Americans, and Asian Americans, in general, in derogatory language. "The Yellow Peril" harks back to Chinese American history and to the language of discrimination. "Blues," of course, pays homage to the great African American tradition, but I add to it with some drops of "yellow blood."

One student sent me a JPEG of a mortar and pestle to respond to the tale "The True Story of Mortar and Pestle." She discussed the process of "grinding" down something to powder as an obvious metaphor of oppression and went on to discuss the "womanist" food tropes in my work. I love that my images generate these responses.

As an activist poet, I believe that it's my responsibility to write a poetry that is accessible on some level. Why write a poetry that nobody but a few elitists could understand? The Tang dynasty poet Bo Juyi used to read his poems to his illiterate maid first, and if she didn't understand a line, he would rework it until it became clear to her.

Once again, I go back to my early training. Chinese poets honor a clear surface. They don't like "muddy waters." Bishop's clarity is stunning. We see the moose and the fish as large and as clearly as possible on the first read. Don Justice had said that clarity takes a disciplined mind and that obscurity is often just "sloppiness" indicating that the poet's not working hard enough.

On the other hand, I also want to make the poem as rich and as playful as possible so that a student or reader will have a good exploration of it. A good poem should be layered with plenty of intertexual fun. This is where I turn to my longer poems. I had a good laugh when I wrote, "To Maui, to Maui, to Maui," mocking Macbeth's famous speech, "Tomorrow, tomorrow, tomorrow." I bury lots of goodies in the title poem "Rhapsody." Sometimes, I bring out the pyrotechnics, not to make the poem unnecessarily difficult, but to entertain myself. The poet, herself, must love the process to be able to make it fun and interesting for the reader. But, then, it would be a shame if nobody gets it but a handful of elitist poets.

Cucinella: That perspective seems to align with your earlier comments about a poetry of activism, not that every poem has to totally work on that level. However, if you have something you want to say and people don't understand it or are afraid of it, how do you make your point? Anything you want to add? Anything that we haven't talked about, something important for scholars, critics, and students to know about you?

Chin: I know how lucky I am to be living purposefully and writing poetry in the new century. I have crossed the age of fifty. Most dark-skinned women in the world won't make it to this decade, and millions who do make it to fifty are victimized and oppressed by unjust wars, prejudice, poverty, and by the idiocy of corrupt governments and intransigent patriarchies. The fact that femicide and genocide still exists in the twenty-first century is shameful. For these reasons and others, I must continue the work of an activist poet. I must not take my freedom for granted. I was lucky that my grandmothers had the courage and foresight to escape starvation in the turbulent 1940s. (How they delivered all of us to the land of plenty was a miracle . . . wasn't it?) I am lucky to have had a chance to nourish my art and to have some voice and comfort in this world.

[*laughs*] I am excited about the next fifty years (yes, I am determined to live past 100). I feel very inspired, and I believe that I am now writing the best work of my life. I want to write beautiful poems and simultaneously rattle some cages. All activists are idealists, right? Despite everything, you and I believe that we are working toward creating a better world.

Conclusion

Contemporary concerns with the body reverberate within a long tradition, and this scrutiny crosses the boundaries of scientific inquiry, historical documentation, and humanistic theorization. In addition, several critical modes of thought, study, and discourse foreground the body's importance in relation to gender, sexuality, and race. Feminism; New Historicism; and gay, lesbian, and queer theories; along with post-colonialism and race theory, all raise and answer questions regarding the body's construction by and function within often competing systems of power. Most contemporary scholars seem to take the body-power connection for granted, and explicitly or not, when one raises questions about the body, one raises questions about power. Certainly, Foucault's influence tinges our acknowledgment that "bodies matter" just as feminism has convinced us that the "personal is political." Because we do generally concede the forgoing (power, bodies, and personal or political), we may lose sight of the significance regarding how bodies, power, the personal, and the political intersect.[1] Therefore, I end this study of Edna St. Vincent Millay's, Elizabeth Bishop's, Marilyn Chin's, and Marilyn Hacker's poetics of the body with a look at how female poets past and present find ways to negotiate the complexities of representing the female body within this intersection.

Early in her career, Millay saw, and participated in, changes in the political and social landscapes of early twentieth-century America. Bohemianism, radicalism, urbanization, and industrialism, along with the emergence of the "New Woman," influenced gender and domestic ideologies. In some cases, women literally reshaped their bodies—binding breasts and bobbing hair as the body became the visible marker of shifts in attitudes about women and their sexuality. As expectations for and by women altered, fields of power also shifted, and as many women experimented with new freedoms (sexual and other), anxieties regarding how to contain women's sexual and creative expressions arose. Millay, then, offered the poetic body as one that defied confinement by displaying the excesses of the female body; however, as I have argued, Millay's poetics of the body relies on her representations of its uninterpretability. This poetic body often challenges existing power or disciplining structures because one cannot offer a definitive reading of its compliance or defiance within these structures. Millay presents effective resistance as that which invites confusion: Does this body openly defy conventional gender "rules?" Has this body internalized these rules? Does this body comply, or does it parody expected gender behaviors? This inability to interpret the intentions and actions of the body disrupts the disciplining aspects of power—what exactly then needs disciplining?

The body in Elizabeth Bishop's poetry also circulates within systems of power as it eludes attempts to cast it as a fixed, static object. Bishop's poetics of the body foregrounds the liminal space between what is and what appears to be, and from this position, the body often exposes and challenges gender ideologies. Bishop wrote against the backdrop of World War II and cold war rhetorics and Freudian-influenced domesticity, as well as within the intersections of several social movements: civil rights and early second-wave feminism. The former exposed assumptions about differences predicated on the body (skin color), while the latter shifted our understanding of sexuality, gender, and gender relationships. As a visual marker of both race and gender, the body signifies a potential disruption to dominant ideologies regarding race, gender, and sexuality. Most fields of power rely on clearly defined and visibly marked oppositions (white or black, male or female, heterosexual or homosexual, us or them); therefore, to engage in a poetics that places the body between terms and concepts is to upset one of the fundamental aspects of power. While I do not suggest that Bishop wrote a poetry of protest, I do see her poetic bodies as revealing the politics of power and as offering a body politics that implies resistance. Attending to the body in the poetry written by women keeps in view the various ideologies and strategies that seek to define "woman" and to contain most aspects of femininity.

Both Marilyn Chin and Marilyn Hacker bring to their poetry a clear understanding of feminist and gender politics, and both overtly challenge hegemonic discourses and ideologies. The body, in their poetry, emerges as one mode of unraveling the complications of negotiating interlocking systems of power and oppression. Despite ideological similarities, Chin and Hacker do not "treat" or represent the body in exactly the same way. Hacker celebrates the body as she positions it as both the narrative and the storyteller, and she presents a body clearly marked by desire. Chin's poetic body also tells stories as it serves as the site of convergence—a place where familial, cultural, and generational histories collide. Hacker offers a desired and desiring body, and she reconfigures the subject-object model of sexual desire that generally structures female sexuality to one of subject-subject. Sexual desire in Hacker's poetry depends on reciprocating desires that reconstitute female desire as active. Although Chin does not generally address female desire in her poetics of the body, she does, like Hacker, challenge assumptions regarding the body by making clear that politics of inclusion and exclusion in white America depend on identifying and defining the foreign other— even when that other is *an American.* This identification depends on how the body looks and acts.

In the introduction to their work on the body in early America, Janet Moore Lindman and Michele Lise Tarter indicate the effects of cultural and physical displacement and of encounters between peoples with distinct physical differences: "Many bodies and many interpretations of bodies were coming together in the transitional world of cultural contact, conquest, and adaptation in early America. Inhabitants of the 'New World' ascribed cultural meanings to corporeal variations based on race, gender, ethnicity, and status that eventually developed into concrete social categories" (5). The relocation of the body with its visual markers of difference generates various and reconfigured understandings of it. These possibilities of interpretation of the body disturb what one knows about his or her own body and, by extension, what one knows about the generalized body. For example, in one location or in one cultural context, the body may signify privilege and position whereas that same body moved to a different location may signify otherness and marginalization, points that Chin makes clear in her concern with the immigrant body, displacement, and assimilation. The femaleness of the body adds another dimension to one caught up in a "transitional world of cultural contact, conquest, and adaptation." The work of all the women in this study spans cultural transitions.

None of the poets in this study presents the body as ahistorical, and yet, women's struggle to represent and understand the body occurred in earlier historical periods. Before pointing out the implications of my analysis for the study of other contemporary women poets, I take a brief "backward look" at the work of two earlier female poets and their poetics of the body: Anne Bradstreet and Emily Dickinson.

As an eighteen-year-old bride, Bradstreet carried a body literally relocated and displaced into the "New World." This relocated and displaced body circulates in much of her poetry and prose. Sixty years after her first glimpse of America, Bradstreet wrote, "I fovnd a new world and manners, *at which my heart rofe*" (*Works in Prose and Verse* 5, emphasis added). Thus Bradstreet recollects and records her physical reaction to the land where she would grow to womanhood; conceive, bear, and raise her children;

bury her mother and father as well as several grandchildren; and write her poetry.

Bradstreet writes from a position of both power and subordination. Although an immigrant like Chin, Bradstreet entered America as a colonizer, a white woman affiliated with males holding significant political influence. Rather than marginalizing her, Bradstreet's status as immigrant positions her as conqueror of the "vast and unpeopled countries of America, which are frutfull, and fitt for habitation; being dvoyd of all civill inhabitants; wher ther are only salvage, and brutish men, which range up and downe, litle otherwise then the wild beasts of the same" (Bradford 96–97). Her poetry, then, emerges from within this legitimizing discourse of the Puritan sense of mission—the mandate to establish a City on a Hill. From this vantage, the immigrant body signifies privilege, and the bodies of the indigenous peoples become the excluded others. Simultaneously, however, Bradstreet also writes within religious and medical discourses that render the female body as that of the "daughter of Eve" and "as weak and deficient" respectively (Lindman and Tarter 5). Finally, Bradstreet also wrote at a time when "emphases on women's bodily difference from men was linked to a renewed ideology of domesticity that celebrated women's material and maternal state" (Lindman and Tarter 5). When we examine how Bradstreet used the body as metaphor as well as representations of the body itself, we can discern clear patterns of how she struggled to celebrate her "material and maternal state" within interlocking patriarchal systems: religion, medicine, and family.

The body emerges as a staple in Bradstreet's work, and it both exposes and reinforces the dominant patriarchal and colonial ideologies. In "The Four Elements," she personifies fire, air, earth, and water; and "Of the Four Humours in Man's Condition," as the title indicates, deals with the humors of the body. In these poems, the body provides a familiar ordering metaphor for understanding the natural and political worlds. In "A Dialogue between Old England and New," Bradstreet embodies Old England as mother and New England as daughter. These uses of the body are straightforward, invoking prevailing poetic conventions and cultural understandings or universal truths about the body, as the formality of these poems keeps the body in check, and we do, indeed, find the body decorous and well behaved, offering certainty, coherence, and stability in a world desperate for these things.

However, in her more personal poetry (the poetry most commonly anthologized and discussed), Bradstreet uses the body to present the trauma of physical relocation, of separations between husband and wife, of childbirth and illness. These poems often reflect on the weakness and mortality of the body, yet in doing so, they keep the body in view and often render it the subject of the poem. This body, however, does not signify the stability and coherence that it does in Bradstreet's more public poetry. In these personal and occasional poems, the poet reconfigures the body as the site of emotional and spiritual pain rather than only as the location of physical pain, and the body makes spiritual doubt visible. This use of the body suggests that it is a crucial component in resolving these doubts as the poetic body often emerges as the battleground for struggles between the spiritual and material worlds. For example, in "The Flesh and the Spirit," the body (flesh), the spokeswoman for the lived, material world, argues that the value of earthly things lies in their substance or materiality. Spirit counters flesh's claim by evoking the Platonic notions of the body thus casting flesh as the deceiver:

> How oft thy slave, hast thou me made,
> When I believed what thou hast said. (*Works* 216)

In this poem, Bradstreet makes clear that spirit must overcome the flesh:

> My greatest honour it shall be
> When I am victor over thee. (216).

However, in poems such as "A Letter to her Husband," "To My Dear and Loving Husband," and "As Weary Pilgrim," Bradstreet seldom presents the body as the thing to be conquered, denied, or transcended. Instead, she offers the body as a *necessary* element in religious experiences, in understanding one's place within both material and spiritual worlds, and in claiming subjectivity.

Bradstreet wrote within a complicated matrix of ideologies—Puritanism, patriarchy, domesticity—all of which influenced her poetry, and most of which she challenges at some point in her work. She confronts the difficulty of writing poetry *as a woman*, and much of what confines her creative efforts (childbirth, illness, housekeeping) generate from or are imposed upon the female body, and her poetry presents constant negotiations with that body. Indeed, the poets in this study, along with most contemporary women poets, also write a poetics of the body that must negotiate impositions similar to those imposed on Bradstreet. And, like Bradstreet, rather than viewing poetry as a way to escape bodily confinement, they invite the body into their poetry, using it as a means of expressing their creativity and intellectuality. Through the trope of the maternal body in "The Author to her Book," Bradstreet legitimizes her "illegitimate" poetry by seemingly disavowing her creation. She casts her poetry as an "ill-formed offspring," an incomplete body not yet ready to stand on its own, yet through the maternal, the poet claims this "brat" despite its "defects." Bradstreet literally embodies the creative process and the product of this process, an embodiment that marks the link between poet and poetry as a physical one. More importantly, the *female* body legitimizes creative production, a legitimization that contemporary women poets reinforce in their very act of writing and in the various representations of the body that we find in their poetry.

Emily Dickinson's poetry also evidences an awareness of the physical body while simultaneously realizing the limitations of the female body on her acceptance as poet. However, Dickinson does not jettison the body; instead, she places it in a reciprocal relationship with the intellect or spirit, and she recognizes the importance of the body in the creative process. Dickinson, like Bradstreet, acknowledges a physical aspect to poetry. In her often-quoted definition of poetry, she uses language that privileges the body and its reactions: "If I read a book [and] it makes my whole body so cold not fire can even warm me I know *that* is poetry. If I feel physically as if the top of my head were taken off, I know *that* is poetry. Is there any other way?" (*Selected Poems* 20–21). Dickinson knows poetry through her body, and in many of her poems, the body functions as a metaphoric register of understanding. Her definition of poetry implies that knowledge includes excess (extreme coldness) and violence.

Throughout her poetry, Dickinson returns, again and again, to extreme coldness as a prerequisite for understanding and for meaning thus positing the body as a crucial element in both. In poem no. 986 ("A Narrow Fellow in the Grass"), the bone-chilling experience of "zero degree" moves the poem away from a boyhood encounter with a snake to a terrifying awareness of the destructive and alienating potential of male-dominated language:

> But never met this Fellow
> Attended or alone
> Without a tighter breathing
> And Zero at the Bone. (460)

This poem, then, locates a recognition, a knowing, in coldness *felt* in the body. This link between the body and knowledge positions both as threats to moderation, decorum, and stability, a threat that remains constant throughout Dickinson's work, sometimes emerging as veiled and slant and, at other times, wild and bold.

In Dickinson's poetry, the body and its attendant sensations ground and legitimize meaning, and it serves as the site where the personal and the political converge. The paradox of the American promise shaped the political climate in which Dickinson lived and wrote, a promise to maintain a stable and democratic nationhood while simultaneously expanding national boundaries. As the political rhetoric at the midpoint of the nineteenth century focused more and more on issues of expansion (which also involved accommodating non-Anglo immigrants), questions regarding that "peculiar institution" (i.e., slavery), troubled the debates on how this nation would and could grow. Extension of the nation entailed not only reconfiguring geographical boundaries, but it also meant redefining, or at least rethinking, citizenship. In a very literal physical sense, inclusion of bodies that looked different from those of Anglo-Americans mandated this reappraisal of the terms of American citizenship. The anxieties that this reexamination generated also evidence ontological fears, and the attempts either to eliminate or to retain slavery dealt with ontological questions: Who was or was not a citizen? Who was or was not property? In addition, these ontological questions clearly indicate anxieties regarding the body and the rights of ownership over specific bodies, bodies literally pawns in the politics of power.

Dickinson wrote most of her poems during this period, a period of civil war whose causes included an "unsettled and unsettling population."[2] Linking the disputes over mass immigration, national expansion, states' rights, and slavery to fundamental understandings of being reveals that Dickinson's poetics often manifests a political influence. The politics—the concerns of the government as well as the power relations that shaped the social and cultural institutions of the mid to late 1800s—generate an ontological poetics that clearly implicates the body. Dickinson utilizes the body, or various bodies, to further examine and complicate the political: relationships among national, gendered, and sexualized bodies. Attention to how poets directly represent or rely on metaphors of the body exposes networks of power relationships and how these relationships shift.

As Elaine Scarry's work demonstrates, the body cannot sever its tie to political, cultural, or social structures. Indeed, the body becomes the nexus between political and personal identity, as well as between juridical and personal subjectivity. Scarry links the political to a "learned culture in the body," and the body serves as the ground for this learned cultural politeness or the politics of concession (109).[3] Dickinson's poetry demonstrates an understanding of cultural politeness and the politics of concession,[4] and it recognizes the politeness that American culture imposed on women: an etiquette that allowed women to voice only the moral and republican truths authorized within the political and public discourse of men. Dickinson's speakers do, on one level, concede to a culture of politeness. On another level, they offer this concession only as an effective rhetorical strategy, a concession and strategy that adheres to the body in poem after poem. The speaker in poem no. 1129 directs,

> Tell all the Truth but tell it slant
> Success in Circuit lies. (506)

Truth will be told through the biased experiences and perceptions of a teller (subject). In addition, Dickinson's use of metaphors of vision implicates the body and its functions in the processes of intellectual, creative, or moral enlightenment. Thus, within the rhetoric of this poem, "all Truth" demands a "Circuit" through a body—a teller—and understanding filters through the perceptions of the body, specifically through distorted perceptions. Truth in the abstract blinds:

> The Truth must dazzle gradually
> Or every man be blind. (506)

Truth presented free from the material or experiential—in other words, truth that transcends the body—reveals nothing. Dickinson certainly does not reduce knowledge or truth to the body alone; rather, she posits the body as a crucial component in epistemological and ontological processes.

When we attend to tropes and poetic representations of the body, we can better understand the matrices of power and politics that affect our sense of being, our understanding of the world, and our relationship to both. As countless scholarly works have demonstrated, female writers and poets must confront their femaleness, with all its attendant gender expectations, in order to write. Generally, creative or intellectual production is not an aspect of femininity (although women are expected to *pro*create). Therefore, recognizing how women negotiate their femaleness, femininity, and sexuality by evoking tropes of the body and theorizing about representations of the body reveals the place of the female body in relation to creativity and intellectuality as well as to dominant ideologies and hegemonic discourses. Women writers and poets do not present a universal or essentialized body, nor do they view the body in the same way. Questions such as the following open spaces of inquiry regarding domination, discipline, and resistance: Does this poet present blatant images of the body along with its attendant sexualities and desires? Does she celebrate the body? Does the body emerge as defiant and rebellious? Is this poetic body demure and compliant? Does the poet costume or adorn the poetic body thus suggesting masquerade, mimicry, or drag? Where does this poet position the body itself? Does she locate it as space clearly marked feminine, or does the body blur the lines between gender distinctions? Do we see a disavowal of or ambiguity about the body? Looking at the body in the poetry of women also provides insight into the historical and material conditions that influenced women's relationships to and images of their own bodies and into the ways in which these attitudes influence contemporary notions regarding the body.

Either consciously or unconsciously, women seem to have a sense of their bodies' position within systems of power. While many women leave the relationship between power and body unexamined, there have always been women who possess, what Gerda Lerner calls, a "feminist consciousness." These women examine the relationship between the body and gender roles and restrictions, and through this scrutiny, they reveal and question power structures and naturalizing discourses about womanhood. Slowly, the questions and arguments of these women disseminate throughout society, often changing how individual women view and treat their bodies. At this moment, then, the personal becomes political as a change in personal perspectives very often spurs political and social changes.

In a bit of digression here, I turn to a volume containing vintage photographs from the 1850s to 1920s, *Women in Pants: Manly Maidens, Cowgirls, and Other Renegades* by Catherine Smith and Cynthia Greig: "By wearing pants, a woman outwardly associated herself with the authority exclusively held by men. In daring to be photographed while wearing trousers, these iconoclasts broke the delicate and fragile mold in which the ideal female image had been made and re-created themselves as autonomous and self-made women" (17). It seems significant to me that these women so clearly understood that they had to present their bodies differently in order to reconfigure authority and power. These "iconoclasts" did not, however, locate autonomy in the female body itself; rather, they located it in a female body dressed like a man. These early feminists recognized that "bodies matter"; that patriarchal hegemony restrained, punished, and disciplined the female body; and that patriarchy depended on a clear (and visible) separation between masculinity and femininity. In addition, these mid-nineteenth-century reformers realized the insidiousness and danger of "fashion" for women: "In 1865 Marie Jones noted that while a man's dress is 'allowed to fit his body, a woman's body is compelled to fit her dress'" (Smith and Greig 19). This awareness of the mandate that women manipulate their bodies to "fit" essential and essentializing images of beauty and femininity and Smith and Greig's argument that through the presentation of the body and its coverings women can claim autonomy and authority brings me back to this present study. Poets such as Sharon Olds, Ana Castillo, Gwendolyn Brooks, Nikki Giovanni, and Sonia Sanchez, to name a few, all engage in a poetics of the body, and through their poetry, they present spaces where women need not dress as men to claim legitimacy, autonomy, and power.[5] However, we cannot situate this poetics into a one-size-fits-all framework. Many similarities do exist among contemporary women poets regarding their representations and use of the body in their poetry, and each of these women, like the women in pants, understands the cultural significance of the female body itself and the difficulty and consequences of presenting that body. Each poet asks questions regarding how to display, hide, or disguise the body, and the various representations and multiple bodies that emerge in their work remind us of the complicated and contested place of the body within our cultural perceptions of embodiment. As I have argued, the body in and of itself is not disruptive (although one can use the body to disrupt and disturb the status quo); therefore, a poet's use of the body is not necessarily resistive or rebellious (however, it may be, despite intentions to the contrary). However, *any* attention to the body underscores its location within several dichotomous relationships—mind-body, spirit-flesh, intellectual-emotional, rational-irrational—the body's relationship to power and authority, and its position as subject and object. Attending to how the body functions within the aesthetic and cultural production of women reveals politics of power, attitudes toward gender and sexuality, hierarchies based on race or class, and perceptions regarding intellectuality, rationality, and emotionality. Specifically, a poetics of the *female* body provides a glimmer of how that body might look, how it might act, and what it might signify free from the constraining and disciplining gaze and discourses of patriarchy heterosexualism and hegemonic whiteness.

NOTES

CHAPTER 2

1. In her chapter on Millay in *Masks Outrageous and Austere*, Cheryl Walker examines Millay's self-presentation and self-commodification, and Walker argues that while at times liberating the poet's fascination with her body, its physical presentation and poetic representations, unconsciously recuperates "oppressive patriarchal attitudes" (136). In her study, Walker presents a meticulous and convincing analysis of Millay's place within and plays with the intersections of patriarchy, capitalism, and consumerism.

2. Not surprisingly, Millay does not acknowledge her whiteness because whiteness *is* the unacknowledged norm. However, the body that Millay describes here, as well as her poetic bodies, is white. Thus, Millay participates in what Renée Curry labels "a complicated positionality of white women writers [and] their near-blindness to aspects of their whiteness" (*White Women* 7). Throughout this chapter, I do at times qualify the femininity that Millay accepts and challenges as white femininity.

3. Indeed, Gilbert identifies a "bleakness" in many of Millay's poems that celebrate "female survival" (303). However, Gilbert uses the term "femme fatale" to connote independence and defiance. She argues that Millay's canny use of verse and form exposes the fiction of "woman" while simultaneously giving the poetry a "special power [that comes] from [Millay's] brilliance" in crafting the exposure (310).

4. Walker asserts that "this poem makes an implicit connection between a candle and a female body. For many, Millay's own diminutive figure was part of the poem's evocative potential" (*Masks* 137).

5. If this doubly burning candle evokes the old warning, "Don't play with fire," the danger remains.

6. In "The Female Body as Icon: Edna Millay Wears a Plaid Dress" and in *Masks*, Walker argues that despite her manipulation of her image, Millay could not remain immune to the effects of a system that commodifies and objectives the female body.

7. Here I refer to drag without the element of camp that emerges when both the performer and the audience read irony and parody in the "doing." Rather, I use drag to mean that Millay does more than imitate or put on femininity. I suggest that she claims some phallic power in identifying with male poets or traditions and does so from a blatantly feminine position.

8. This masquerading aspect of the sonnet makes it an important form when discussing a poetics of the body. Masquerade obviously implicates the body, and Millay uses this poetic form to represent the body's changeability. Just as she "plays" with the subject of the sonnet, she also "plays" with cultural understandings of the female body.

9. I agree with Walker's assessment here, and I extend her point to argue that because the body remains enmeshed within disciplining regimes and that our inability to definitively read it opens a space for and in which to recognize resistance.

10. Selene, the moon goddess famous for her numerous love affairs, evokes passion, romance, and obsession. Falling in love with the sleeping Endymion, Selene visits him, kisses him, and sleeps by his side thus seducing Endymion in his dreams. When Endymion awakes Selene, of course, has fled, and wishing to hold forever the dream, he asks Zeus for eternal sleep. Thus, Selene can eternally pay her nocturnal visits to Endymion.

11. According to Peppe, "[Millay] suggests that because men, regardless of their intentions, have a resistance to intimacy and relationships, they are simply not emotionally or psychologically equipped to answer the needs of the women who fall in love with them" (62).

12. Specifically, the poem references Cressid, Elaine, and Isolt, all of whom enchant and or deceive their lovers.

13. Debra Fried identifies eros as prison as a recurring image in Millay's sonnets (237).

14. Millay devotes the entirety of Sonnet 46 to the speaker's awareness of the doomed nature of the affair further undercutting the sense of agency that the speaker claims in ending the affair.

15. Walker makes this point when she identifies the speaker as defenseless. Here I mean to extend Walker's argument. Walker argues that the speaker has no real choice because Millay depends so heavily on the value of her body within the patriarchal economy. This dependence supersedes the mind's ability to temper the pain of the "lover's dismissal of her body" (158). Although I agree in the lack of choice that exists, I believe that it exists if we identify an element of fatalism and not entirely because of Millay's reliance on the body.

CHAPTER 3

1. Although I do not qualify the body in this chapter as white, the poetic body that Bishop presents in the poems that I discuss is white.

2. The substitutions or supplements that comprise Derrida's field of play depend on the presence of "the sign which replaces the center, which supplements it, taking the center's place in its absence—this sign is added, occurs as a surplus, as a *supplement*" (289).

3. I wish to thank Renée Curry for her insightful observation about the "hand of the poet." Curry also provides a critical look at Bishop's alcoholism and its

relation to her poetry in "A Thirst for Reverie: Alcohol, Despair, and Dream Space in Elizabeth Bishop's Poetry."

4. Sedgwick cautions that "sex, gender, sexuality [possess] usage relations and analytical relations [that] are almost irremediably slippery" (27). She further details the difference between the three terms. Drawing from both Freud and Foucault, Sedgwick suggests that "the distinctively sexual nature of human sexuality has to do precisely with its excess over or potential difference from the bare choreographies of procreation, 'sexuality' might be the very opposite of what we originally referred to as (chromosomal-based) sex; it could occupy, instead, even more than 'gender,' the polar position of the relational, the social/symbolic, the constructed, the variable, the representational" (29). Sexuality then loses its connection to sex as procreation and allows for "unnatural" sexual object-choices, and according to Sedgwick, "The essentialism of sexual object-choice is far less easy to maintain, far more visibly incoherent, more visibly stressed and challenged at every point in the culture than an essentialism of gender" (34). In her paradigm sexuality becomes, "with its far greater potential for rearrangement, ambiguity, and representational doubleness, . . . the apter deconstructive object" (34).

5. This "knowing" poetry through the body echoes Emily Dickinson's explanation of how she knows poetry: "If I read a book [and] it makes my whole body so cold not fire can ever warm me I know *that* is poetry. If I feel physically as if the top of my head were taken off, I know *that* is poetry. These are the only way I know it. Is there any other way?" (*Selected Poems and Letters* 20–21). Bishop also seems to make this link between body and poetry.

6. Kathryn Kent reminds us that "Bishop identified as a 'lesbian,' a named sexual subjectivity with a history and subculture, of which she was clearly aware and in which she participated to a greater and lesser degree during her lifetime" (182).

7. Written during her stay at Yaddo in 1950, "O Breath" appeared in Bishop's *North & South—A Cold Spring*, published, in 1955. As Steven Axelrod rightly points out, Bishop wrote this poem along with several others that deal with lesbian desire at "the height of Cold War homophobia" (62). In *Elizabeth Bishop's World War II–Cold War View*, Camille Roman offers an in-depth analysis of Bishop's poetry during this time. Roman makes clear that within the cold war climate, Bishop's lesbianism was "unacceptable and therefore quasi-(in)visible, signaling a high-risk position" (14). The historical context in which Bishop wrote "O Breath" contributed to the need for concealment or camouflage; however, I argue that Bishop's desire to both reveal and conceal lesbian sexuality and desire in her poetry parallels her insistence on presenting conceptual possibilities rather than either-or dichotomies. Axelrod elucidates Bishop's strategy of "trouble[ing] and disable[ing] special dichotomies" in "Heterotropic Desire in Elizabeth Bishop's 'Pink Dog.'"

8. Millier asserts that ultimately the speaker of "O Breath" sees in her lover's chest "evidence of a fatal and final difference, a fundamental incompatibility" (232).

9. Gender, according to Grosz, "is not an ideological superstructure added to a biological base" (*Volatile Bodies* 58), and Butler argues that "gender ought not to be conceived merely as the cultural inscription of meaning on a given sex (a juridical conception); gender must also designate the very apparatus of production whereby the sexes themselves are established" (*Gender Trouble* 7).

10. Kent points out that in the poem, Bishop acknowledges the possibilities of cross-dressing while simultaneously depicting its dangers. In her reading of "Exchanging Hats," Kent sees cross-dressing as upholding and undermining various norms (206).

11. Butler argues "that the substantive effect of gender is performatively produced and compelled by the regulatory practices of gender coherence . . . [G]ender proves to be performative—that is, constituting the identity it is purported to be" (*Gender Trouble* 24–25). According the Butler, no core sexual identity exists; rather, the performance of femininity or masculinity functions to create an illusion of a coherent sexual identity.

12. Addressing specifically the line "he thinks what might a meter matter," Kent writes, "In its almost tongue-twisting alliteration and assonance, [this line] mimics the implied chaos that might accompany drastic gender transvestism" (203).

13. Tyler synthesizes various perspectives (feminist, gay, lesbian) on drag, and she situates her own arguments within a psychoanalytical framework. Her discussions on "the phallic woman" and "dragging in differences" provide critical insights into the psychic consequences of drag and or transvestism. She also points out, what I believe crucial in understanding Bishop's use of cross-dressing in "Exchanging Hats," that "the pleasure of tranvestism . . . is exhibitionistic as well as voyeuristic" (95).

14. Axelrod offers an insightful analysis of the contradictory aspect of Bishop's use of the carnival in "Pink Dog." Axelrod maintains that while "the poem elaborates the Bakhtinian schema whereby carnivals invert normal cultural codes and suspend hierarchic difference, becoming sites of freedom, good humor and renewal," "Pink Dog" simultaneously includes the more sinister qualities of the carnival (66).

15. "Pink Dog" extends the voyeuristic and exhibitionist representations that emerge in "Exchanging Hats."

16. Costello offers the most clear-cut statement regarding Bishop's use of the grotesque and her relation to it: "Bishop turns to carnivalesque images of the misfit who resists the social and cultural norms through which nature is disciplined and controlled . . . Bishop takes on the stance of someone living within the fragile norms of the dominant culture, but susceptible to the challenge of the misfit, who embodies the expelled elements of the speaker's life" (*Elizabeth Bishop* 80).

17. In his work on the carnivalesque and the grotesque, Bakhtin argues that "carnival laughter is the laughter of all the people . . . [and] it is universal in scope" (11). Bakhtin also identifies "the grotesque body [as] cosmic and universal" (318).

18. According to Butler, "The abject designates . . . precisely those 'unlivable' and uninhabitable zones of social life which are nevertheless densely populated by those who do not enjoy the status of the subject, but whose living under the sign of the 'unlivable' is required to circumscribe the domain of the subject" (*Bodies* 3).

19. According to Kristeva, the abjection "does not respect borders, positions, rules . . . [It is] the in-between, the ambiguous, the composite" (4).

20. The substitutions or supplements that this field of play affords depend on the presence of "the sign which replaces the center, which supplements it, taking the center's place in its absence—this sign is added, occurs as a surplus, as a *supplement*" (Derrida 289).

21. Axelrod points out that "the fact that the *másquara* in this instance hides not a human face, but, impossibly and whimsically, a canine one implies that being is figurative all the way through" (76).

22. Butler explains the threat that the exposed female body poses: "The [Symbolic] requires that castration is the 'already having happened' for women . . . whereas castration signifies as what is always almost happening for men, as anxiety and the fear of losing the phallus, where the loss that is feared is structurally emblematized by the feminine and, hence is a fear of becoming feminine, becoming abjected as the feminine" (*Bodies* 205).

23. This exclusion occurs through the merger of the superego with the ego. This superego, according to Kristeva, requires the abjection in order to solidify its own existence: "To each ego its object, to each superego its abject" (2). The abjection both safeguards and annihilates, and its banishment consolidates the I, but its acknowledgment destroys the I.

24. Axelrod, in his discussion of "Pink Dog," not only contextualizes Bishop's inclusion of the Brazilian dispossessed but also draws a connection to today's dispossessed peoples (66–68).

CHAPTER 4

1. In the introduction to *Asian American Poetry: The Next Generation*, Victoria Chang provides a concise overview of a Chinese American poetic tradition. Chang places Chin in the tradition of "first generation" Asian American poets because Chin, like the other first generation poets, often used their poetry to expose "their inferior treatment by mainstream culture" (xv–xvi). Chang identifies this poetry as "protest literature." See also John Gery's article "'Mocking My Own Ripeness': Authenticity, Heritage, and Self-Erasure in the Poetry of Marilyn Chin" in *Literature Interpretation Theory*. Gery identifies the social, theoretical, and literary contexts within which Chin writes. Gery does not directly associate Chin with the social milieu of Maxine Hong Kingston or Mitsuye Yamada, but he does argue that "their accounts of their own racial and gender consciousness" influence and help explain Chin's social milieu (26). More importantly, Gery details the fraught position of Asian American writers and poets such as Kingston and Yamada in relation both to

racism and sexism, in general, and, specifically, to racism within early feminism. The necessity for women of color to choose between social activisms (challenging racism *or* sexism) causes, according to Gery, "a conflict not only in terms of one's social commitment but also, more subtly, on one's very own identity" (27). This critic finds "this *internal* tension" in Chin's poetic voice. Theoretically, Gery aligns much of Chin's poetry with Trinh T. Minh-ha's work on authenticity and identity in the work of any "Third World" woman writer (27–31). Finally, Gery locates Chin within a poetic context of both traditional Chinese and American poetry.

2. Renée Curry writes in *White Women Writing White: H. D., Elizabeth Bishop, Sylvia Plath, and Whiteness* that "white women who write do so as white women, from within ideological, social, economical, political, and psychological frameworks of whiteness; yet simultaneously they reveal limited, if any, conceptual relationship to the conditions of whiteness or to the effects that whiteness has on the written product" (1).

3. Erika Lee argues that the Chinese Exclusion Act provided the legal, rhetorical, and theoretical framework for the inclusion or exclusion of all immigrant groups in the twentieth century. Lee also opines that this act "was instrumental in the formation of the nation itself and in articulating a definition of American national identity and belonging. Americans learned to define American-ness, by excluding, controlling, and containing foreign-ness" (41). By extension, then, this exclusion, control, and containment applies in very real ways to the body of the immigrant, and Chin offers poetic representation of effects of this policy as well as the body's resistance to it.

4. Although at times I seem to use the terms *Asian American* and *Chinese American* interchangeably, for the most part, however, Asian American refers to points regarding *generalized* experiences of immigrants from China, Japan, and Southeast Asia. Chin herself writes about a shared cultural confusion and displacement among various Asian immigrants. She also clearly identifies a specific Chinese American experience through her use of Chinese myths, legends, histories, names, symbols, vegetation, and images.

5. Here I am thinking about Cynthia Wong Sau-ling's contention that Asian Americans must swallow or internalize their own inferiority and disavow their Asian identity.

6. In *Aching for Beauty: Footbinding in China*, Wang writes, "The pain of footbinding, so intense that it is beyond words, forces the little girl to relearn language, a language more preverbal, transmitted from mother to daughter and shared among women" (9). She also argues that through foot binding, Chinese women appropriated both power and language from men "through imitation, simulation, and inversion." The culture of foot-bound women turned both into "their own—female language, female writing, and female culture" (226). In her study, Wang does, however, reiterate the link between violence and beauty, and she stresses that the politics of foot binding places the female body as the site of cultural, religious, and political struggle. Thus, in "The Last Woman with Lotus Feet," the image of the woman with the

lotus feet (along with the title) carries with it the history and acknowledgment of the fraught position of the female body in Chinese history and, by extension, Chinese American history.

7. In a 2007 article, Susie Lan Cassel looks at foot binding in several novels written by Chinese Americans, and she takes first-world feminism to task for its inability to tell the whole story about foot binding. This lack raises crucial questions about our historical and cultural understanding of this practice. Cassel asserts that the activist agenda "ironically objectifies, homogenizes, and ahistoricizes the Chinese subaltern woman in the name of anti-racism and anti-sexism" (32). Chin, I believe, in "The Last Woman with Lotus Feet," while suggesting that women do often suffer in the name of beauty, neither condemns nor celebrates foot binding. Instead, the lotus feet reinforce the notion of the body as palimpsest, making the historical legible.

8. Heidegger identifies the present as the site of inauthenticity: the place of the "anonymous one" or reduced subject, and he locates *Dasein*—being there or an individual's mode of being-in-the-world, which involves relatedness—within a temporal register possessing three distinct features: factuality that aligns with the past because an individual is brought into situations that already exist; existentiality that suggests the future because it reveals an individual as a project and possibility, and fallenness that signifies the present because it involves "on handness," the preoccupation with the things at hand. For Heidegger, this merging of factuality, existentiality, and fallenness must occur in order for *Dasein* to exist authentically. In other words, being means movement: arriving from the past, moving into the future, and choosing in the present *to become*, or realizing the possibilities residing in the past and waiting in the future. *Dasein* then involves a unified or authentic self (307–41).

9. The ellipses contain the following images: "bamboo shoots," a "red wheelbarrow," and reference to the soap opera *Santa Barbara*. Gery points out that this section "mixes Chinese symbols . . . with highly allusive American phrasing . . . in a bitterly satiric depiction of Chinese American stereotypes" (36).

CHAPTER 5

1. Suzanne Juhasz argues, "For all the degrees of separation implicit in the language act, there is another way to think about language's relationship to touch . . . : as a way to counter loss of human separation. Language, too, possesses the ability to connect to and arouse the body" (25).

2. Alicia Ostriker, in her review of Hacker's eleventh volume of poems, *Desesperanto*, draws attention to Hacker's formalism as well as her "impulses to excess": "Hacker has always been the kind of formalist for whom traditional form is challenge and play, yes, but also the necessary container and shaper of her impulses to excess—excess desire, pleasure, fear, anger, grief, excess attention to the minute abundances and shatterings of our world" (x).

3. This separation works on the Cartesian model, a model that persists today despite postmodern theorizing of the body.

4. The ghazal emerged in Arabia around the seventh century and became prominent in the thirteenth and fourteenth centuries in the works of poets such as Rumi and Hafiz. Comprised of five to fifteen structurally and thematically autonomous couplets, the ghazal depends on a scheme established in the first couplet. This scheme is made up of rhyme followed by a refrain (traditionally the last word of the couplet). Following this initial scheme, the subsequent couplets repeat the refrain in their second line. We often find the poet's "signature" in the final couplet, and as is the case in Hacker's "Ghazal," the closing couplet frequently includes the poet's name or a deviation of its meaning.

5. Etty Hillesum, a Dutch Jew who died at Auschwitz in 1943, began a diary in 1941. She left over six hundred pages detailing her struggle to find voice as both a woman and a Jew. She also worked as a representative of the Jewish Counsel, and in this capacity, she came into contact with Jews as they left for Auschwitz. In a volunteer capacity, Hillesum counseled and comforted those facing deportation. Eventually, she was also detained at Westerbork, a holding camp before final deportation to Auschwitz.

6. In her study on whiteness, Ruth Frankenberg notes, "Ashkenazi Jews have frequently been viewed by non-Jews as racial Others, and continue to be viewed as some, notably the neo-Nazi movement" (216).

7. In "'Present, Infinitesimal, Infinite': The Political Vision and 'Femin' Poetics of Marilyn Hacker," Mary Biggs asserts that "the ordinary comfortable and flawed things of life are the things that illuminate, that must be brought to alien spaces and cherished. Women have to know this" (15). Most critics comment on Hacker's use of everyday things and occurrences in her poetry.

8. Cavarero locates this narratable self "in the spontaneous auto-narration of memory" (*Relating Narratives* 33). Importantly, narratable refers to the process of narration, the possibility and recognition that all selves can be narrated. However, for Cavarero, this narration is not equivalent to the interpellation of the subject, and she insists that the narratable self depends on the presence of an other. This other, however, need not and usually is not in opposition to the narratable self. For Cavarero, the other necessary to recognize or to narrate the self's story is often a lover or friend.

9. In *Questions of Possibility*, David Caplan, identifies *Love, Death, and the Changing of the Seasons* as among "some of the most distinguished and widely admired poems in this form" (62–63).

10. Cavarero debunks the myth that "the language of the body does not need to involve the language of storytelling [and] that the first is most perfect when the second is totally absent" (*Relating Narratives* 114–15).

11. Addressing the poems in *Winter Numbers*, Biggs writes eloquently regarding Hacker's personal voice and its connection the world at large: "The poems in this book throb with personal pain, but even more with the pain of the wide world: of warfare and historical and current atrocities, and of the vast, omnipresent human misery caused by poverty and innumerable categories of injustice" (8).

CONCLUSION

1. Janet Moore Lindman and Michele Lise Tarter summarize generally accepted views regarding these issues: "Political power serves as a primary means to regulate bodies; whoever governs, controls, punishes, or owns other's bodies wields terrifying authority over the dependent, the captive, the convictive, and the enslaved. Thus, the cultural meanings projected onto bodies reflect a process of mapping: a political cartography that is demarcated by categories of difference, including race, gender status, ethnicity, religion, and sexuality" (6).

2. The dilemma of building a nation, and a national identity, when a large part of the population remained physically and bodily enslaved, permeated the political, social, and religious institutions of mid-nineteenth-century America. As Toni Morrison reminds us, these same concerns also influenced the American literary imagination: "The very manner by which American literature distinguishes itself as a coherent entity exists because of this unsettled and unsettling population" (6).

3. Scarry evokes Pierre Bourdieu's explanation regarding the term "polite." In other words, she defines a cultural and political politeness that manifests through physical or bodily performance: "The words 'polis' and 'polite' are etymologically related, and 'the concessions of politeness always contain political concessions'" (109).

4. This same observation applies to Millay, whose poetry often demonstrates her comprehension of the politics of politeness and concession.

5. In his review of Sharon Olds's most recent poetry collection, *One Secret Thing*, Mark Doty writes that Olds possesses "a remarkable feel for how it is to be a body" (222). Certainly, when we look at the work of Sharon Olds, we cannot deny the body, and we may be tempted to reduce her poetics to the body. However, to do so may deflect us from asking the questions that will lead us to a greater understanding of the social and political implications of the body.

WORKS CITED

Althusser, Louis. *Lenin and Philosophy and Other Essays*. New York: Monthly Review Press, 1971. Print.

Arendt, Hannah. *The Human Condition*. 1958. 2nd ed. Chicago: U of Chicago P, 1998. Print.

Axelrod, Steven Gould. "Heterotropic Desire in Elizabeth Bishop's 'Pink Dog.'" *Arizona Quarterly* 60.3 (2004): 61–81. Print.

Bakhtin, Mikhail. *Rabelais and his World*. Trans. Helene Iswolsky. Bloomington: Indiana UP, 1984. Print.

Barfoot, C. C. "Edna St. Vincent Millay's Sonnets: Putting 'Chaos into Fourteen Lines.'" *Uneasy Alliance: Twentieth-Century American Literature, Culture and Biography*. Ed. Hans Bak. Amsterdam: Rodopi, 2004. 81–100. Print.

Bedient, Calvin. Interview with Marilyn Chin. *The Writer's Chronicle* 31.3 (1998): 5–15. Print.

Biggs, Mary. "'Present, Infinitesimal, Infinite': The Political Vision and 'Femin' Poetics of Marilyn Hacker." *Frontiers* 27.1 (2006): 1–20. Print.

Bishop, Elizabeth. *The Complete Poems: 1927–1979*. New York: Farrar, Straus and Giroux, 1991. Print.

Bookman. "The Literary Spotlight: Edna St. Vincent Millay." Thesing 107–14. Print.

Boone, Joseph Allen. *Libidinal Currents: Sexuality and the Shaping of Modernism*. Chicago: U of Chicago P, 1998. Print.

Bordo, Susan. *Unbearable Weight: Feminism, Western Culture, and the Body*. Berkeley: U of California P, 1993. Print.

Bradford, William. *History of Plimoth Plantation*. *The Puritans: A Sourcebook of Their Writings*. Ed. Perry Miller and Thomas H. Johnson. Mineola: Dover, 2001. 91–117. Print.

Bradstreet, Anne. *The Works of Anne Bradstreet*. Ed. Jeannine Hensley. Cambridge: Belknap Press of Harvard UP, 1967. Print.

———. *The Works of Anne Bradstreet in Prose and Verse*. 1867. Ed. John Harvard Ellis. Whitefish: Kessinger Publishing, 2006. Print.

Butler, Judith. *Bodies that Matter: On the Discursive Limits of "Sex."* New York: Routledge, 1993. Print.

———. *Gender Trouble: Feminism and the Subversion Identity*. New York: Routledge, 1990. Print.

———. *The Psychic Life of Power: Theories in Subjection*. Stanford: Stanford UP, 1997. Print.

Caplan, David. *Questions of Possibility*. New York: Oxford, 2005. Print.

Cassel, Susie Lan. "'. . . The Binding Altered Not Only My Feet but My Whole Character': Footbinding and First-World Feminism in Chinese American Literature." *Journal of Asian American Studies* 10.1 (2007): 31–58. Print.

Cavarero, Adriana. *Horrorism: Naming Contemporary Violence.* Trans. William McCuaig. New York: Columbia UP, 2009. Print.

———. *Relating Narratives: Storytelling and Selfhood.* 1997. Trans. Paul K. Kottman. New York: Routledge, 2000. Print.

———. *Stately Bodies: Literature, Philosophy, and the Question of Gender.* 1995. Trans. Robert De Lucca and Deanna Shemek. Ann Arbor: U of Michigan P, 2002. Print.

Chang, Victoria. *Asian American Poetry: The Next Generation.* Urbana: U of Illinois P, 2004. Print.

Cheng, Anne Anlin. *The Melancholy of Race: Psychoanalysis, Assimilation, and Hidden Grief.* Oxford: Oxford UP, 2001. Print.

Chin, Marilyn. *Dwarf Bamboo.* Greenfield Center, NY: Greenfield Review Press, 1987. Print.

———. *The Phoenix Gone, The Terrace Empty.* Minneapolis: Milkweed Editions, 1994. Print.

———. *Rhapsody in Plain Yellow.* New York: Norton, 2002. Print.

Ciardi, John. "Edna St. Vincent Millay: A Figure of Passionate Living." Thesing 157–62. Print.

Clark, Suzanne. "Uncanny Millay." Freedman 3–26. Print.

Colwell, Anne. *Inscrutable Houses: Metaphors of the Body: in the Poems of Elizabeth Bishop.* Tuscaloosa: U of Alabama P, 1997. Print.

Conboy, Katie, Nadia Medina, and Sarah Stanbury, eds. *Writing on the Body: Female Embodiment and Feminist Theory.* New York: Columbia UP, 1997. Print.

Costello, Bonnie. "Attractive Mortality." *Elizabeth Bishop: The Geography of Gender.* Ed. Marilyn Lombardi. Charlottesville: UP of Virginia, 1993. 126–52. Print.

———. *Elizabeth Bishop: Questions of Mastery.* Cambridge: Harvard UP, 1991. Print.

Curry, Renée R. "Marilyn Hacker." *Contemporary American Women Poets: An A–Z Guide.* Ed. Catherine Cucinella. Westport: Greenwood, 2002. 159–62. Print.

———. "A Thirst for Reverie: Alcohol, Despair, and Dream Space in Elizabeth Bishop's Poetry." *Literature and Medicine* 18.1 (1999): 100–113. Print.

———. *White Women Writing White: H. D., Elizabeth Bishop, Sylvia Plath, and Whiteness.* Westport: Greenwood, 2000. Print.

Davidson, Cathy N., and Linda Wagner-Martin, eds. *Oxford Companion to Women's Writing in the United States.* New York: Oxford Press, 1995. Print.

Debord, Guy. *The Society of the Spectacle.* Trans. Donald Nicholson-Smith. New York: Zone Books, 1995. Print.

Derrida, Jacques. *Writing and Difference.* Trans. Alan Bass. Chicago: U of Chicago P, 1978. Print.

Dickinson, Emily. *The Complete Poems of Emily Dickinson.* Ed. Thomas H. Johnson. Boston: Little, Brown, 1978. Print.

———. *Selected Poems and Letters of Emily Dickinson.* Ed. Robert N. Linscott. New York: Doubleday, 1959. Print.

Doty, Mark. "Secrets of the Flesh: Tender, Unsparing Poems on the Art of Forgiving." Rev. of *One Secret Thing*, by Sharon Olds. *Oprah* Oct. 2008: 222. Print.

Elise, Dianne. "Woman and Desire: Why Women May *Not* Want to Want." *Studies in Gender and Sexuality* 1.2 (2000): 124–45. Print.

Epstein, Daniel Mark. *What Lips My Lips Have Kissed: The Loves and Love Poems of Edna St. Vincent Millay*. New York: Henry Holt, 2001. Print.

Frankenberg, Ruth. *White Women, Race Matters: The Social Construction of Whiteness*. Minneapolis: U of Minnesota P, 1993. Print.

Foucault, Michel. *Discipline and Punish: The Birth of the Prison*. Trans. Alan Sheridan. New York: Vintage Books, 1979. Print.

———. *The History of Sexuality: An Introduction*. Vol. 1. Trans. Robert Hurley. New York: Vintage Books, 1990. Print.

Freedman, Diane P. *Millay at 100: A Critical Appraisal*. Carbondale: Southern Illinois UP, 1995. Print.

Fried, Debra. "Andromeda Unbound: Gender and Genre in Millay's Sonnets." Thesing. 229-47. Print.

Finch, Annie. "Marilyn Hacker: An Interview on Form by Annie Finch." *American Poetry Review* 25.3 (1996): 23–27. Print.

Furr, Derek. "Listening to Millay." *Journal of Modern Literature* 29.2 (2006): 94–110. Print.

Fuss, Diana. *Essentially Speaking: Feminism, Nature & Difference*. New York: Routledge, 1989. Print.

Gatens, Moira. "Corporeal Representation in/and the Body Politic." Conboy, Medina, and Stanbury 80–89. Print.

Gery, John. "'Mocking My Own Ripeness': Authenticity, Heritage, and Self-Erasure in the Poetry of Marilyn Chin." *Literature Interpretation Theory* 12.1 (2001): 25–45. Print.

Gilbert, Sandra M. "Female Female Impersonator: Millay and the Theater of Personality." Thesing 293–312. Print.

Grosz, Elizabeth. *Space, Time and Perversion: Essays on the Politics of Bodies*. New York: Routledge, 1995.

———. *Volatile Bodies: Toward a Corporeal Feminism*. Bloomington: Indiana, UP, 1994. Print.

Hacker, Marilyn. *Desesperanto: Poems 1999–2002*. New York: Norton, 2003. Print.

———. *Love, Death, and the Changing of the Seasons*. 1986. New York: Norton, 1995. Print.

———. *Selected Poems: 1965–1990*. New York: Norton, 1994. Print.

———. *Squares and Courtyards*. New York: Norton, 2000. Print.

———. *Winter Numbers*. New York: Norton, 1994. Print.

Hall, Christine Iijima. "Asian Eyes: Body Image and Eating Disorders of Asian and Asian American Women." *Eating Disorders: The Journal of Treatment and Prevention* 3.1 (1995): 8–19. Print.

Hammond, Karla. "An Interview with Marilyn Hacker." *Frontiers* 5.3 (1980): 22–27. Print.

Han, Béatrice. *Foucault's Critical Project: Between the Transcendental and the Historical.* Trans. Edward Pile. Stanford: Stanford UP, 2002. Print.

Harpham, Geoffrey Galt. *Language Alone: The Critical Fetish of Modernity.* New York: Routledge, 2002. Print.

Heidegger, Martin. *Being and Time: A Translation of Sein and Zeit.* Trans. Joan Stambaugh. New York: State U of New York P, 1996. Print.

Heller, Tamar, and Patricia Moran, eds. *Scenes of the Apple: Food and the Female Body in Nineteenth-and Twentieth-Century Women's Writing.* Albany: State U of New York P, 2003. Print.

Hesse-Biber, Sharlene Nagy. *The Cult of Thinness.* 2nd ed. New York: Oxford UP, 2007. Print.

Honicker, Nancy. "Marilyn Hacker's *Love, Death, and the Changing of the Seasons*: Writing/Living within Formal Constraints." *Freedom and Form: Essays in Contemporary American Poetry.* Ed. Esther Giger and Agnieszka Salska. Lódź: Wydawnictwo Uniwesytetu Lódzkiego, 1998. 94–103. Print.

Hubbard, Stacy Carson. "Love's 'Little Day': Time and the Sexual Body in Millay's Sonnets." Freedman 100–116. Print.

Juhasz, Suzanne. *A Desire for Women: Relational Psychoanalysis, Writing, and Relationships between Women.* New Brunswick: Rutgers UP, 2003. Print.

Kawano, Kelley. "Conversation with Wang Ping." *Random House.* Web. 9 July 2006.

Kennedy, X. J. "Edna St. Vincent Millay's Doubly Burning Candles." *New Criterion* 20.1 (2001): 96–101. Print.

Kent, Kathryn. *Making Girls into Women: American Women's Writing and the Rise of Lesbian Identity.* Durham: Duke UP, 2003. Print.

Kincheloe, Joe L., and Shirley R. Steinberg. "Addressing the Crisis of Whiteness: Reconfiguring White Identity in a Pedagogy of Whiteness." Kincheloe, Steinberg, Rodriquez, and Chennault 3–29. Print.

Kincheloe, Joe L., Shirley R. Steinberg, Nelson M. Rodriquez, and Ronald E. Chennault, eds. *White Reign: Deploying Whiteness in America.* New York: St. Martin's, 1998. Print.

Kövecses, Zoltán. *Metaphor: A Practical Introduction.* Oxford: Oxford UP, 2002.

Kristeva, Julia. *Powers of Horror: An Essay on Abjection.* Trans. Leon S. Roudiez. New York: Columbia UP, 1982. Print.

Kumin, Maxine. "Gymnastics: The Villanelle." *An Exaltation of Forms: Contemporary Poets Celebrate the Diversity of Their Art.* Ed. Annie Finch and Kathrine Varnes. Ann Arbor: U of Michigan P, 2005. 314–21. Print.

Lacan, Jacques. *Écrits: A Selection.* Trans. Alan Sheridan. New York: Norton, 1977. Print.

Lee, Erika. "The Chinese Exclusion Example: Race, Immigration, and American Gatekeeping, 1882–1924." *Journal of American Ethnic History* (2002): 36–62. Print.

Lerner, Gerda. *The Creation of Feminist Consciousness: From the Middle Ages to Eighteen-seventy.* New York: Oxford UP, 1993. Print.

Lindman, Janet Moore, and Michele Lise Tarter, eds. *A Centre of Wonder: The Body in Early America.* Ithaca: Cornell UP, 2001. Print.

Lombardi, Marilyn May. *The Body and the Song: Elizabeth Bishop's Poetics*. Carbondale: Southern Illinois UP, 1995. Print.

Lowe, Lisa. "The International within the National: American Studies and Asia American Critique." *Cultural Critique* (1998): 29–47. Print.

Mairs, Nancy. "Carnal Acts." Conboy, Medina, and Stanbury 296–305. Print.

McCabe, Susan. *Elizabeth Bishop: Her Poetics of Loss*. University Park: Pennsylvania State UP, 1994. Print.

McElroy, Bernard. *Fiction of the Modern Grotesque*. New York: St. Martin's, 1989. Print.

"Memory." *Webster's New Universal Unabridged Dictionary*. 1989. Print.

Millay, Edna St. Vincent. *Collected Poems*. New York: Harper & Row, 1956. Print.

———. *Letters of Edna St. Vincent Millay*. Ed. Allan Ross Macdougall. New York: Harper, 1952. Print.

Milford, Nancy. *Savage Beauty: The Life of Edna St. Vincent Millay*. New York: Random House, 2002. Print.

Millier, Brett C. *Elizabeth Bishop: Life and the Memory of It*. Berkeley: U of California P, 1993. Print.

Mitchell, Veronica. "Private Spaces Made Public." Rev. of *Squares and Courtyards*, by Marilyn Hacker. *The Gay & Lesbian Review Worldwide* 8.4 (2001): 41. Print.

Morrison, Toni. *Playing in the Dark: Whiteness and the Literary Imagination*. Cambridge: Harvard UP, 1992.

Moyers, Bill. *The Language of Life: A Festival of Poets*. New York: Doubleday, 1995. 67–80. Print.

Ngai, Mae M. "Legacies of Exclusion: Illegal Chinese Immigration during the Cold War Years." *Journal of American Ethnic History* 18.1 (1998): 3–35. Print.

Oktenberg, Adrian. "Our Living Treasure" Rev. of *Desesperanto: Poems 1999—2002*, by Marilyn Hacker. *The Women's Review of Books* 21.10–11 (2004): 6–7. Print.

Oliveira, Carmen L. "Elizabeth Bishop and the Brazilian Genius." *The Art of Elizabeth Bishop Conference*. Ouro Prêto, Brazil. 21 May 1999.

Ostriker, Alicia. "The Art of Excess." Rev. of *Desesperanto: Poems 1999-2002* by Marilyn Hacker. *American Book Review* 25.3 (2004): N. pag. Print.

"Palimpsest." *Webster's New Universal Unabridged Dictionary*. 1989. Print.

Park, Eunice. "Starving in Silence." *AsianWeek*, 2006. Web. 29 Jan. 2007.

Peffer, George Anthony. *If They Don't Bring Their Women Here: Chinese Female Immigration before Exclusion*. Urbana: U of Illinois P, 1999. Print.

Peppe, Holly. "Rewriting the Myth of the Woman in Love." Freedman 52–65. Print.

"Performative." *Webster's New Universal Unabridged Dictionary*. 1989. Print.

Ping, Wang. *Aching for Beauty: Footbinding in China*. Minneapolis: U of Minneapolis P, 2001. Print.

Ricoeur, Paul. "Narrative Time." *On Narrative*. Ed. W. J. T. Mitchell. Chicago: U of Chicago P, 1980. 165–86. Print.

Roman, Camille. *Elizabeth Bishop's World War II–Cold War View*. New York: Palgrave, 2001. Print.

Sau-ling, Cynthia Wong. *Reading Asian American Literature: From Necessity to Extravagance*. Princeton: Princeton UP, 1993. Print.

Scarry, Elaine. *The Body in Pain: The Making and Unmaking of the World.* New York: Oxford: UP, 1985. Print.

Sedgwick, Eve Kosofsky. *Between Men: English Literature and Male Homosocial Desire.* New York: Columbia UP, 1985. Print.

Slowik, Mary. "Beyond Lot's Wife: The Immigration Poems of Marilyn Chin, Garret Hong, Li-Young Lee, and David Mura." *MELUS* 25.4–3 (2000): 221–42. Print.

Smith, Catherine, and Cynthia Greig. *Women in Pants: Manly Maidens, Cowgirls, and Other Renegades.* New York: Harry N. Abrams, 2003. Print.

Smith, Ernest. "'How the Speaking Pen Has Been Impeded': The Rhetoric of Love and Selfhood in Millay and Rich." Freedman 43–51. Print.

Spivak, Gayatri Chakrovorty. *The Post-Colonial Critic: Interviews, Strategies, Dialogues.* Ed. Sarah Harasym. New York: Routledge, 1990. Print.

Stallybrass, Peter, and Allon White. *The Politics and Poetics of Transgression.* Ithaca: Cornell UP, 1986. Print.

Stanbrough, Jane. "Edna St. Vincent Millay and the Language of Vulnerability." Thesing. 213–28. Print.

Thesing, William B. *Critical Essays on Edna St. Vincent Millay.* New York: G. K. Hall, 1993. Print.

Tyler, Carole-Anne. *Female Impersonation.* New York: Routledge, 2003. Print.

Walcott, Delores D., Hellen D. Pratt, and Dilip R. Patel. "Adolescent and Eating Disorders: Gender, Racial, Ethnic, Sociocultural, and Socioeconomic Issues." *Journal of Adolescent Research* 18.3 (2003): 223–43. Print.

Walker, Cheryl. "The Female Body as Icon: Edna Millay Wears a Plaid Dress." Freedman 85–99. Print.

———. *Masks Outrageous and Austere: Culture, Psyche, and Persona in Modern Women Poets.* Bloomington: Indiana UP, 1991. Print.

Weis, Gail. "The Body as Narrative Horizon." *Thinking the Limits of the Body.* Ed. Jeffery Cohen and Gail Weis. New York: State U of New York P, 2003. 25–35. Print.

Wiltenburg, Robert. "Millay and the English Renaissance Lyric." Thesing 287–92. Print.

Worra, Bryan Thao, "An Interview with Marilyn Chin." *Asian American Press. Voices from the Gap,* 2006. Web. 28 Jan. 2007.

INDEX